LINDA SANCHEZ was born and educated in England. After studying modern languages at Brasenose College, Oxford and living and working for a short spell in Paris, she moved to Spain and eventually settled in Cadiz Province, where she lived for over twelve years. She has two children and also works as a language teacher and professional translator and interpreter.

Acknowledgements

Firstly, I would like to thank the many people who have answered my innumerable questions, particularly the staff of the tourist information offices of El Puerto de Santa Maria, Jerez, Cadiz, Arcos de la Frontera and Conil. Thanks also to the Patronato Provincial de Turismo in Cadiz for their collaboration in providing the films for the map of the province.

Thanks also go to Roger Lascelles, Bryn Thomas and Yvonne Messenger for their help, patience and encouragement. Also to my father for 'introducing' me to them. Special thanks to my mother Hazel for accompanying me on many trips which involved a lot of climbing up and down hills to see 'a load of old stones'.

Finally, thank you to all those who have contributed photographs.

Note from the author

The information contained in this book is as up-to-date as possible at the time of going to print. The province of Cadiz is in a stage of growth as far as the tourist sector is concerned and things have a habit of changing fast. Prices, particularly, tend to go up a lot faster than any of us would like. The prices quoted in this book are offered as a guideline but readers should not be surprised if they have changed. The author hopes that the information and advice offered here will be of help and, if you would like to comment on any significant changes that should be included in the next edition, you are invited to write to the author c/o the publisher (address on title page).

Front cover: *Expensive boats and luxury living in Puerto Sherry, the only marina of its kind on this stretch of the Costa de la Luz; definitely for up-market messing about in boats. (Courtesy of Puerto Sherry press department)*

Lascelles City Guides

CADIZ PROVINCE
WITH GIBRALTAR

Linda Sanchez

Roger Lascelles, Cartographic and Travel Publisher
47 York Road, Brentford, (Middx) TW8 0QP. Tel: 081 847 0935 Fax: 081 568 3886

Publication Data

Title	Cadiz Province with Gibraltar
Printing	Kelso Graphics, Kelso, Scotland
Photographs	By the author unless specified
ISBN	0 903909 99 5
Maps	John Gill, Chessington, Surrey
Edition	First January 1993
Publisher	Roger Lascelles
	47 York Road, Brentford, Middlesex, TW8 0QP
Copyright	Linda Sanchez

Distribution

Africa:	South Africa	Faradawn, Box 17161, Hillbrow 2038
Americas:	Canada	International Travel Maps & Books, P.O. Box 2290, Vancouver BC V6B 3W5.
	U.S.A.	Available through major booksellers with good foreign travel sections
Asia:	India	English Book Store, 17-L Connaught Circus, P.O. Box 328, New Delhi 110 001
Australasia:	Australia	Rex Publications, 15 Huntingdon Street, Crows Nest, N.S.W.
Europe:	Belgium	Brussels – Peuples et Continents
	Germany	Available through major booksellers with good foreign travel sections
	GB/Ireland	Available through all booksellers with good foreign travel sections.
	Italy	Libreria dell'Automobile, Milano
	Netherlands	Nilsson & Lamm BV, Weesp
	Denmark	Copenhagen – Arnold Busck, G.E.C. Gad, Boghallen
	Finland	Helsinki – Akateeminen Kirjakauppa
	Norway	Oslo – Arne Gimnes/J.G. Tanum
	Sweden	Stockholm/Esselte, Akademi Bokhandel, Fritzes, Hedengrens. Gothenburg/Gumperts, Esselte. Lund/Gleerupska
	Switzerland	Basel/Bider: Berne/Atlas; Geneve/Artou; Lausanne/Artou: Zurich/Travel Bookshop

Contents

Part I: Preparation and information:

Part II: The Route Guide

Appendices

Index

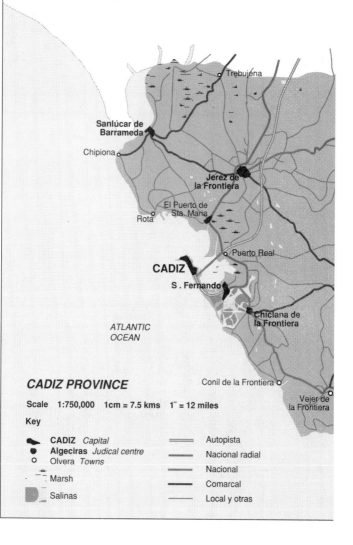

HUELVA
PROVINCE

Trebujéna

Sanlúcar de
Barrameda

Chipiona

Jerez de
la Frontiera

El Puerto de
Sta. María

Rota

Puerto Real

CADIZ

S . Fernando

Chiclana de
la Frontiera

ATLANTIC
OCEAN

Conil de la Frontiera

Vejer de
la Frontiera

CADIZ PROVINCE

Scale 1:750,000 1cm = 7.5 kms 1″ = 12 miles

Key

CADIZ *Capital*

Algeciras *Judical centre*

○ Olvera *Towns*

Marsh

Salinas

Autopista

Nacional radial

Nacional

Comarcal

Local y otras

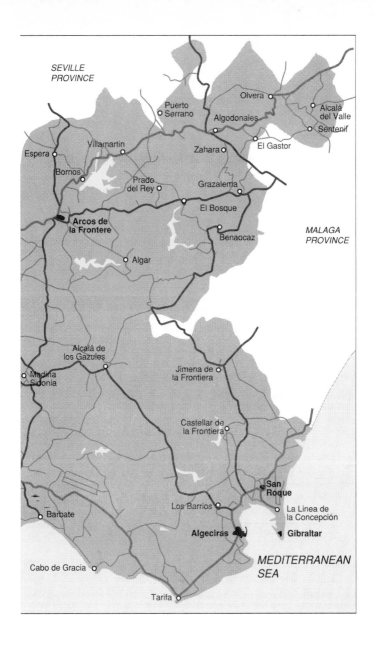

ONE

Introducing the Province of Cadiz

Province of contrasts

On January 1st 1986, Spain became a fully fledged member of the EEC. The changes that have taken place in this country since the death of Franco in 1975 have been tremendous and whilst there may still be a lot of ground to cover, Spain is eager to compete, eager to make up for lost time and anxious to erase that clinging image of a rather backward nation with little more to offer than beaches and bullfights.

Much has been written about Spain since the nineteenth century Romantic writers began to discover its charms but most of what was written until very recently belongs to another time. This is no longer the same world so hauntingly evoked by Hemingway, Michener, Laurie Lee and other writers. There is much of that Spain that is, one hopes, abiding but there is also much that is irretrievably lost. Even Spain's more recent image as a holiday-makers' paradise offering instant fun in the sun is in for a face-lift. Spain is expecting to play a prominent role in the future. The Olympic Games in Barcelona and the World Fair in Seville mark 1992, in many people's minds, as the year of Spain's coming of age. One of the slogans to be seen on posters announcing this fair read: 1992, The Discovery of Spain.

This book is written for those who would like to take part in this discovery, starting in Andalusia; for those willing to explore beyond the neon boundaries of the package tour; those who are prepared to sample the different flavours of somebody else's culture on its own terms.

The south-western province of Cadiz is one of eight that make up this region called Andalusia whose 87,268 square kilometres cover more or less the whole southern part of Spain. Cadiz is a concentrated example of that well worn phrase that for years has described Spain

There is nothing quite like a fresh coat of whitewash for covering up the cracks. Houses that might otherwise look poor and drab dazzle the eye as they reflect that brilliant Andalusian sun back at you.

as a 'land of contrasts'. The province has some 260km of gorgeous blue and gold coastline including some of the country's most unspoilt beaches. Its Atlantic coast is part of the Costa de la Luz which it shares with the neighbouring province of Huelva. The average 3200 hours of brilliant sunshine enjoyed annually along this coast have given it this name which means Coast of Light.

Further inland you can explore the Costa de la Cal, the Whitewash Coast, a name aptly phrased to describe the sierra region with its picturesque mountain villages where you can quietly enjoy a breath of cool, fresh air amongst flower filled patios and silent, whitewashed walls. Cadiz has so much to offer, with the old and the new side by side: it is filled with colour, with legend and tradition, with contradiction, beauty and contrast.

This book will help you find your way down many different roads. You can explore the narrow, bustling streets of the capital city, Cadiz, which claims to be the most ancient city in the Western World. You can enjoy the exciting, outgoing atmosphere of El Puerto de Santa Maria, a town that is poised to become one of Spain's more important, modern tourist resorts. Some roads lead to remote villages where tall, fair-haired people are still unashamedly stared at, and other roads lead to modern tourist installations with luxury hotels and residential complexes. You can choose between long and lonely beaches with white-gold sands and cool, transparent waters or the fun and excitement of a modern aqua-park. You can watch the proud and tragic fighting bulls grazing peacefully in their pastures or those renowned Andalusian horses in the beauty and discipline of equestrian ballet. You can taste the local wines in the cool of cathedral-like *bodegas* and sample a whole host of gastronomic delights. You can visit museums and art galleries, castles and Roman ruins. Whatever sort of holiday you are looking for, you should be able to find it somewhere in this far corner of Spain.

Some facts and figures

Cadiz, whose economy depends more on agriculture and fishing than it does on industry, is the southernmost province of Spain; indeed the little town of Tarifa sits on the southernmost tip of the continent of Europe, 14km from the coast of North Africa. It is the smallest of the eight Andalusian provinces but one of the most densely populated with a total population of just over one million. The largest towns are: Jerez de la Frontera, followed by Cadiz (the capital) and then

Algeciras, La Linea, El Puerto de Santa Maria, San Fernando and Sanlucar de Barrameda. In 1981 Andalusia voted in favour of its first Statute of Autonomy, or self-government, and in 1982 elections were held for the first Andalusian parliament. The elections were won by the Spanish Socialist party, PSOE, who, at the time of writing, are still in power.

Climate

The southerly position of the province of Cadiz offers the visitor a very warm climate with long, hot summers and short, mild winters. Average temperatures are as follows:

    January, February and March: 14°C.
    April and May: 17°C.
    June, July and August: 22°C.
    October and November: 18°C.
    December: 15°C.

The coastal areas have the mildest climate all round and within this category the Bay of Cadiz area has a more favourable microclimate than the Bay of Algeciras. The inland agricultural area registers both the highest and lowest extremes of temperatures and Jerez, without the cooling sea-breezes, can experience summer highs of 40°C. The mountain areas can have equally hot, sometimes stifling, summers though winters are colder, especially in the north-eastern corner of the province. Temperatures rarely fall below zero however. Rain tends to come throughout the winter months, though the pattern and the amount can vary a great deal from year to year. It usually falls in the form of short, torrential showers that clear up quickly but sometimes this can go on for several days at a time. The mountain village of Grazalema, somewhat surprisingly, records the highest annual rainfall in the whole of Spain, owing to its position and altitude, but even here the summers are invariably long and hot. Grazalema is also one of the few places that is likely to have a snowfall once or twice during the winter. Indeed, snow is so unusual in the province that when it does fall, people flock to Grazalema from the coast to see it.

The winter months are generally very mild and there are plenty of those lovely, bright, crisp days celebrating the winter under a dazzling blue sky. However, although the winters are far milder here than in most of the rest of Europe, visitors are often taken by surprise because the cold can be quite damp and because the houses are not built to be warm. Houses here are quite naturally designed to be as cool as possible in the summer. They have no central heating, floors are usually bare stone or tiles and walls are not insulated so that, for a few days out of the year, it can actually be colder inside one's house than it is outside.

Under the table

It is common in winter in an Andalusian home to see the family crowded around a table with their legs tucked under the heavy, floor-length tablecloths. If you come in as a guest you will be invited to take a seat and the cloth will be lifted for you to tuck your legs under too. This may seem a rather peculiar habit until you discover that underneath these tables there are little round electric heaters that generate a very welcome warmth in otherwise unheated houses. In more rural areas some people still use the more traditional method of placing a pan of glowing embers under the table.

There is nearly always some sort of wind blowing along the Atlantic coast though the only one that is unpleasant and uncomfortable is a wind called the Levante. It is a strong, hot and dry wind that comes in from the Sahara and blows dust into every imaginable nook and cranny. It makes going to the beach unbearable, (except perhaps in the morning when the wind tends to die down) but it does have its positive side. It is possibly one of the main reasons why this Atlantic coastline, with infinitely more beautiful beaches than the neighbouring Mediterranean ones, was not included in the tremendous tourist boom that transformed the Costa del Sol into an artificial holiday package, gift-wrapped in white concrete. The Levante also makes an important contribution to the the local sherry industry since it helps keep the grapes dry on the vines and prevent mould. This wind rarely lasts for more than three days at a stretch and there are plenty of beautiful inland areas to explore whilst waiting for it to die down. So, if you do happen to get caught by a day of Levante, grab a bottle of *fino* and head for the hills!

The rocky heights around Grazalema afford some magnificent views of this inner, lesser known part of Andalusia.

A glance at the landscape

Owing to the warm climate and (droughts permitting) an adequate amount of rain, a great diversity of plants are to be found within the province: some 900 indigenous varieties and about 200 imported varieties that now live wild in the area. Although the colours of the countryside in the summer tend to be made up more of browns, greys and yellows, in spring-time the fields are still fantastically green and the country lanes are bordered by a profusion of brightly coloured wild flowers which attract an abundance of butterflies. You will soon get used to the sight of cork-oak trees for the cork forests of Cadiz produce 24 per cent of all Spanish cork. Bushy headed pine trees and the tall, pale trunks of eucalyptus trees are also a familiar sight here.

The changing colours of the seasons in the province of Cadiz are strikingly different to those of England and other, more northern regions. By the end of the summer, the landscape is often dramatically harsh and barren. The heat seems to ooze from the very pores of the ash-coloured earth; gnarled old olive trees cling grimly to steep, rocky slopes; newly-denuded cork trees blush a rusty red like wrinkled old men caught with their trousers down; armies of sunflowers march across rolling hills until the sun dries up their golden smiles; ripe cotton plants stand upon brittle stems, shaking their ancient, white heads.

The coast from Tarifa to Cape Trafalgar is particularly wild and beautiful – an ideal haunt for nature lovers. Inland there is plenty of game, from rabbits, quail and partridges to deer and wild boar, and hunting is very popular. Roe deer abound in the Sierra areas and also in the countryside around Jerez. They live amongst the cork forests and the gall oaks and they are difficult to observe because of their understandably unsociable nature and the thickness of the undergrowth. For this reason the roe deer is known as the *'duende del bosque'* or spirit of the forest.

Blind and hairy

Although the local wildlife is varied and abundant it is, quite naturally, elusive to the average human eye. If you take to the mountains and the country lanes and footpaths you may be able to see mountain goats, wild pigs, deer, mongoose or genets as well as all kinds of lizards and the odd snake or two. No doubt the most elusive of all the sierra creatures is the legendary *alicante* which some of the mountain folk claim to have seen. It is said to be a long snake-like creature which is both hairy and blind! There is an old local saying that goes: if the viper could run and the *alicante* could see, none would dare go to the mountains!

All the carnivorous species typical of the Mediterranean woodland may be found here in the forests of Cadiz with the exception of the wolf, which disappeared at the beginning of this century. The Egyptian mongoose, only European representative of the mongoose family, has one of its most numerous and stable populations in these mountains. Within the province there are also wildcats, genets, stone martens, otters, badgers, mountain goats and more, but most are very difficult to observe, especially from a car!

One particularly curious creature to be found in the western part of the province is the endearing but endangered chameleon, whose only other European relatives are to be found in lesser quantities on the coast of Malaga and in Isla Cristina (Huelva).

Bird watchers should find this province fascinating, not only for the rich variety of sedentary species but also because it lies in the path of one of the two main routes for migrating birds in Europe. Ornithologists from all over Europe, and indeed the world, come to

The interior patio with its tiled walls and marble floor, often open to the sky and always filled with plants and flowers, is an unmistakable feature in traditional Andalusian town houses. (Photo by Catherine Cavanaugh)

observe the unforgettable spectacle of these migrating birds crossing the Straits of Gibraltar.

There is indeed much about this part of Spain that will prove unforgettable. Part One of this book is designed to provide you with all the practical information you may need to know before you get here as well as the kind of background information you will need once you arrive. Part Two is a Route Guide giving detailed information on the different towns and areas of interest within the province including lists of accommodation and places to eat.

TWO

Planning your trip

Where to stay

Choosing a base from which to explore the area is an important first step in planning a holiday. Your choice of such a base in the province of Cadiz will depend on exactly what kind of holiday you are looking for and whether or not you have a particular sport or hobby that you wish to pursue whilst on holiday, such as wind-surfing, horse-riding, bird-watching (or wine tasting!).

The coast

If your main reason for coming to this part of Spain is to be within easy reach of the beach, there are several towns to choose from. At first sight **Cadiz**, the capital, might seem the best choice and indeed a great many Spanish tourists spend their summers here each year but, apart from being much more of a city in terms of traffic, noise and general activity, it is also stuck out on an island joined to the mainland only by a thin strip of land and a bridge. Getting to the old part of the town involves a long drive down a busy avenue lined with tall blocks of flats which can be rather tedious if you enjoy making frequent day trips to other towns in the area.

The coastal resort par exellence is without doubt **El Puerto de Santa Maria**, first and foremost thanks to its position. It has good communications by road and rail with Seville, and Jerez airport is only 25km away. The road from Gibraltar via Medina Sidonia is very good and the trip takes only about two hours. The journey by car from Malaga is possible in about three hours, if traffic is good, via the N340 coastal road and the C440 through Los Barrios and Medina Sidonia.

Puerto's climate is another of its great attractions. Being on the coast, the summer temperatures are never as stifling as they can be in Jerez, for instance, whilst the winters are milder and drier than they are in the mountain villages. On the inner shore of the Bay of Cadiz, the town is more sheltered from the wind than many of the other coastal towns and its waters are warmer than those of the open Atlantic. And yet Cadiz, Jerez, the mountain villages and the beautiful white-gold beaches between Tarifa and Conil are all within easy reach. Day trips can be made quite comfortably from here to any part of the province and also beyond the boundaries to places such as Seville, the Doñana Nature Reserve, Ronda, Gibraltar, Ceuta or Tangiers. The overall facilities offered in terms of accommodation, entertainment and refreshment are probably the best on this coast. There are several ambitious projects in the pipeline to add to the facilities and attractions already available in Puerto, such as an archeological park and an Undersea World which, if accomplished, will add much to the area without changing the face of the town itself. Owing to its popularity and the fact that there is at present only one small bridge crossing the Guadalete river towards Cadiz, the town does have some acute traffic and parking problems, especially in the summer months.

Sanlucar de Barrameda, Chipiona and **Rota** are three more important and popular coastal resorts on a rather more modest scale than Puerto de Santa Maria but with easy access to some very good beaches. Each of these towns has at least one very attractive hotel and various other types of accommodation but in Chipiona most places close down during the winter months. On the southern Atlantic stretch of coast you can find the most beautiful stretches of beach in the province, without doubt some of the most unspoilt coast in Spain, although parts of it are starting to be encroached upon by residential developments. Chiclana's **La Barrosa** beach area is fast becoming an important tourist resort with the building of a huge complex called Novo Sancti Petri which includes several four-star hotels and a 27-hole golf course designed by Severiano Ballesteros. When finished this is going to be an attractive and luxurious holiday centre right on the edge of a very beautiful beach. (See Chapter Nine for more details, also the Golf section in Chapter Four).

Farther down the coast is the attractive little town of **Conil** which would make a good base for exploring the wilder, more unspoilt part of the coast, and if you really want to get away from it all on a beautiful stretch of beach but without giving up your luxuries, then the four-star hotel at **Atlanterra**, south of Barbate, might be your best choice. (There is also some more economical accommodation in the same village.) For windsurf enthusiasts **Tarifa** is definitely the place to be; there are several hotels and camp sites along the coast between the town itself and Punta Paloma. This stretch of coast between Tarifa and Conil would also be a good choice if you are particularly keen on scuba-diving and sea fishing.

On the Mediterranean coast the **Sotogrande Estate** is already very much a British enclave, just 15 minutes drive from Gibraltar. Peaceful and luxurious, its facilities include a four-star hotel set between two championship golf courses.

For nature lovers

On the threshold of two continents, between the Atlantic and the Mediterranean, the province of Cadiz posesses a wide variety of habitats with a tremendous natural wealth in terms of flora and fauna, including some endangered species that are now protected within a total of five national park areas.

The Parque Natural de la Sierra de Grazalema covers an area of 33,200 hectares and was declared a Biosphere Reserve by the UNESCO in 1977. Its most important feature is made up by the forests of Spanish firs *(abies pinsapo)*, unique in this part of Western Europe. The park also has one of Europe's greatest concentrations of tawny vultures. This park includes the towns of Grazalema, Zahara, El Gastor, El Bosque, Ubrique, Benaocaz and Villaluenga within its boundaries.

The largest of these nature reserves is the Parque Natural de los Alcornocales which covers 160,000 hectares and includes one of the largest cork oak forests in the world. Amongst its rock formations you may be able to find the beautiful yellow flowers of a carnivorous plant that is exclusive to the area. Alcalá de los Gazules, Medina, Algar, Jimena, Castellar and Los Barrios are the towns included within the park area.

The Parque Natural del Entorno de Doñana covers an area of 3,400 hectares and includes the pine forest of La Algaida and the marshlands of Bonanza between Sanlucar and Trebujena. This is really an extension of the Doñana Reserve across the river Guadalquivir and in this area there may be a few surviving Imperial Eagles and Iberian Lynx as well as the smaller chameleon, all three of which are endangered species.

There is a park within the municipal district of Barbate with a large area of pine forests and practically inaccessible cliffs and the fifth park is the Parque Natural de la Bahia de Cadiz with a wide variety of habitats including marshland and salt evaporation pools which provide important resting areas for migrating birds. This park covers an area of 10,000 hectares in the municipal districts of Cadiz, El Puerto de Santa Maria, Puerto Real, San Fernando and Chiclana.

You might be considering **Gibraltar** as a base for your holiday but although you may well enjoy spending a few days there I would advise against it as a base for a longer stay, particularly if your intention is to explore the province of Cadiz. Having a car in Gibraltar is something of a liability – there simply is not room and getting back and forth across the border by car is a tedious and time consuming business that involves a lot of sitting in queues. One solution is to leave your car in La Linea.

Inland

If frequent trips to the beach are not first on your list of priorities then **Jerez de la Frontera** would make a very good holiday base, except perhaps in July and August when the heat might be too much for those not used to it. In recent years a lot has been done in Jerez to restore some of the town's former beauty and there is a lot to do and see there. There are also some very attractive hotels and communications with Seville, Gibraltar and the rest of the province are good.

Farther inland the stunning hilltop town of **Arcos de la Frontera** is another possibility. It stands at the entrance, as it were, to the sierra region and although the town itself is small and its facilities more limited, it has one of the beautiful state-run Paradors as well as other attractive accommodation. Close by is the Arcos lake with a small tourist complex by its shores.

The sierra

If you are looking for quiet villages, beautiful mountain scenery and a healthy fresh air kind of holiday, there are two small sierra towns that would make a good base for spending all or part of a holiday. **Grazalema** is the more picturesque but **El Bosque** has a milder climate. Both are small but both have good accommodation available.

You may decide to divide your holiday between two or more parts of the province or, if travelling out of season, you may just decide to go where the fancy takes you and there are certainly plenty of attractive places to stay the night all over the province. Remember that high season includes not only July and August but also Holy Week, Carnival, Feria and other more local fiestas in the different towns and villages. (See Chapter Six for details.)

Types of accommodation

The category rating of accommodation in Spain is as follows: H stands for Hotel, Hs for Hostal, M for Motel, and P for Pensión or Guesthouse. You will see these letters plus their star rating (white letters on a square blue background) at the entrance to the different establishments. The letter R usually indicates that the establishment does not provide restaurant services although it may provide breakfast as well as the services of a cafeteria. Breakfast is not included in the price of a room in any of these categories. Theoretically, these categories have been combined to simplify them into just two groups: one to five-star hotels and one and two-star guesthouses, but in practice you will still see the aforementioned symbols as well as the letters CH which also stand for Guesthouse or Boardinghouse. You may even see the letter F which stands for Fonda, the lowest category of old style boarding houses but these are definitely dying out. The difference between a guesthouse and a hostal can be quite significant. On the whole, guesthouses are in older buildings in the older quarter of a town, some of them having been open as such since the end of the last century. A pensión like this offers no kind of luxury and one usually shares a bathroom with other guests. Hostals tend to be in more modern buildings and most rooms have their own bathroom. A hostal is simple but can be a perfectly comfortable and pleasant place to stay.

One other symbol you may see is AT in gold letters on a square red background with a key rating as opposed to a star rating. These are touristic apartments for self-catering holidays providing bed linen and usually a once a week cleaning service.

Possibly the best known kind of hotels in Spain are the Paradors, a chain of state-run hotels that claim to be unique in the world for their originality and value. Many of them are breathtakingly beautiful, often in restored castles or other historical buildings and they specialise in good service at reasonable prices.

Where information on hotels is given in Part Two or elsewhere, the letters DR stand for double room. VAT is not included in the prices mentioned.

Booking

It is perfectly possible to make your own reservations in hotels, hostals and even guesthouses by writing to the addresses given in Part Two (adding the name of the town and then the province). The hotels should have someone who speaks English if you wish to telephone but the hostals are unlikely to. Hotels do not always require a deposit but hostals usually expect a deposit covering at least the first night's stay. You can equally well book a room in one of the many beautiful Paradors along the routes down through Spain to Cadiz as well as in other Spanish hotels through agencies such as Keytel International, 402 Edgware Road, London W2 1ED, Tel: 071 402 8182, or Hotels of Spain, 315-6 London House, 26/40 Kensington High Street, London W8 4PF. Tel:071 938 3792.

Rented accommodation

Apart from the aforementioned types of accommodation there are a great number of flats, houses and villas available to rent privately or through estate agencies. Private rentals have to be arranged on the spot and obviously offer no guarantees if anything goes wrong so unless you are dealing through people you know and trust it is wiser to go through an agency. There are a number of agencies that deal with renting holiday apartments, mostly in the coastal resorts. One can write to such an agency asking for details of accommodation available, stating your own requirements and then make a booking by sending a deposit (usually 30 per cent by international money order or whatever means they suggest). In this connection it is worth mentioning that the word villa, which British people tend to associate with houses in this part of Spain, does not have that meaning in Spanish. Detached houses with their own garden are called chalets. The word bungalow is used here to refer to one in a row of small, terraced, two-storey houses, usually designed specifically as tourist accommodation. In the last few years a lot of *casas unifamiliares* or *casas adosadas* have been built. These are two-storey, terraced, town houses with a small garden or patio.

It is difficult to recommend a few estate agencies from amongst the many that there are within the province. The following is a list of some you could write to for information:
• Agencia Inmobiliaria Lares: Arboleda Perdida 2. El Puerto de Santa Maria. Tel: 872018.
• Aginsur: Avenida Eduardo y Felipe Osborne, Vistahermosa. Tel: 852111. Also, Avenida de la Paz, Valdelagrana. Tel:863767. Both in El Puerto de Santa Maria.
• Perfil Sur: Avenida de la Libertad, 22. El Puerto de Santa Maria. Tel: 874200.
• Urvasa: Avenida de la Paz, Valdelagrana. El Puerto de Santa Maria. Tel: 861140
• Residencial Bahia: Paseo Marítimo Playa de Valdelagrana. El

Puerto de Santa Maria. Tel: 863721.
- Inmobiliaria Apis: Columela 33. Cadiz. Tel: 211981.
- Agencia Inmobiliaria Frontera: Virgen 5. Conil. Tel: 441201.
- Los Castillejos: La Fuente 27. Chiclana. Tel: 401405.
- Las Mogarizas: Alameda del Rio 7, Chiclana. Tel: 400611.
- Agencia Inmobiliaria Beltrami: Plaza de los Cisnes 4, bajo derecho. Sanlucar de Barrameda. Tel: 366401.
- Agencia Inmobiliaria Puerto Lucero: Ramon y Cajal 2. Sanlucar de Barrameda. Tel: 365250.
- Comercial Inmobiliaria Ibañez S.L: Fernando Magallanes 15. Sanlucar de Barrameda. Tel: 364309.
- Estudio 21: Batalla del Salado 33, Tarifa. Postal address: Apartado 133, 11380 Tarifa. Tel: 684147. Fax: 643558. Dealing with rentals in and around Tarifa, also in the area of Zahara de los Atunes, Caños de Meca etc.
- Soto Estates: Paseo del Mar, Puerto Sotogrande. Tel: 615351/615352.
- Fincasol Developments S.A: km 135 CN340, Sotogrande. Tel: 794511. Fax: 794561. They also have an office in England dealing with rentals in the Sotogrande area: Fincasol Ltd, 4 Bridge Street, Salisbury, Wiltshire SP1 2LX. Tel: 0722 411644. Fax: 0722 411909 Telex: 477517 FISO G

Camp sites

All official camp sites in Spain, whether first, second or third class, have the basic facilities of showers, wash basins and toilets, electrical points and the sale of camping gas, although you sometimes have to pay extra for hot showers. Due notice is given of the proximity of camp sites by means of road signs showing the outline of a tent with the name of the site in question and the distance in kilometres.

In the route guide in Part Two, to give an idea of relative prices, two will be given for each site; a) the price per day for a car, caravan, two adults and two children, and b) the price per day for a car, two adults and a small tent.

When to go

August is the month in which a large majority of Spaniards take their annual holidays and flee from the heat of cities like Madrid and Seville to the country or to seaside resorts. August is nearly always the hottest month of the year, often too hot for many paleskins. July is the second busiest and usually the second hottest month. From mid July to the end of August a town like Puerto de Santa Maria becomes overwhelmingly crowded with Spanish holiday-makers who spend most of the day on the beach and most of the night in bars, restaurants and discotheques. The atmosphere is exciting, festive, effervescent; but because so many of these visitors bring their cars with them, traffic becomes a tremendous problem and parking a nightmare. If you can plan your holiday to avoid the month of August you will avoid these problems of overcrowding with the added advantage that your holiday can work out cheaper. Also, if you are planning to drive down to the province or do quite a bit of exploring, either walking, cycling or by car, you should realise that the heat in mid summer is just too much. The best time to explore most of the routes described in Part Two is in the spring when the countryside is still green and the weather can be hot but not stifling. Having said that, if your main reason for coming is to spend a lot of time on the beach and you opt for one of the more luxurious and fairly self-contained hotels in Novo Sancti Petri or Zahara de los Atunes for instance, then the guaranteed intense heat of July and August may well be just up your street.

September is one of the best months to visit the coastal resorts as the weather is usually still marvellous but the crowds have gone home and the atmosphere is more mellow and less hectic. Spanish children go back to school around the middle of September and a lot of people just stop going to the beach no matter how good the weather may still be. The traffic moves more fluidly and it is easier to find a seat and get served in the more popular bars and restaurants. September is still considered high season however as far as most hotels are concerned. October is often another lovely month and although the weather can never be guaranteed, in recent years the summers have been late coming and late leaving so that by the end of October the local people are all dying for the sky to cloud over and a few drops of autumn rain to fall.

If you want to get away from the cold and wet of northern winters, January and February often have marvellous weather though again it cannot be guaranteed. Even if it does rain, temperatures are usually very mild, particularly in the Bay of Cadiz area. If you do come in the winter months then the town of Jerez de la Frontera would be one good place to stay as there is more to do and see there if the weather is bad and it is easy to get to Seville where you could enjoy shopping and sightseeing even in bad weather. November tends to be one of the wettest months of the year.

You may decide to come at a particular time of year to coincide with one of the local festivities such as Carnival or Feria. If you come for the former, you might like to think about bringing some sort of fancy dress (children and adults), as this is one of the few events in which you can participate fully along with the local people. Local shops sell an amazing variety of wigs, masks and other costume accessories and a little imagination can go a long way. On the whole, Carnival is a very enjoyable, family affair, especially in the smaller towns, and hundreds of adults dress up to go out in the evenings. You will probably enjoy the Feria too but you will not be able to participate to the same extent unless you happen to know how to dance *sevillanas*.

What to take

Clothes
Although the winters are relatively very mild in the coastal areas, the chill of winter in houses built to stay cool in the summer makes it worthwhile to bring some warm clothes with you if you are planning a visit any time between October and April, especially if you are planning on spending time in the sierra region. If you are staying in a rented house or flat during the winter months, remember that there is unlikely to be any central heating, so bring plenty of warm sleepwear, slippers and so on. However, you will also need to bring some short sleeved shirts or blouses even in January and February, when the midday sun can be really quite hot. It is worth packing a swimsuit just in case, even if you are coming well out of season.

Accessories
If you are planning on spending time on the southern Atlantic beaches between Conil and Tarifa, it would be a good idea to bring one of those curiously British contraptions, a windbreak. It could be necessary at times to give you a little shelter from the wind so that you can make the most of the brilliant sunshine.

For reasons mentioned in a previous paragraph you might find a hot water bottle welcome, especially for children, if staying in rented accommodation during the winter months.

Money
The safest way to take money abroad is in travellers' cheques which can be cashed at any bank and also in the larger hotels. If lost or stolen they can be replaced with relatively little inconvenience.

Eurocheques are another useful means of carrying your money. They are used together with a Eurocheque card and can be cashed in any bank that displays the red and blue EC sign. At the time of writing the limit for each cheque here in Spain is 25,000 pesetas, although there is no limit to the number of transactions you can make in one day. You should take your passport with you to the bank whenever you are going to cash these cheques or traveller's cheques.

The major credit cards such as Visa, Diners' Club or American Express can be used in many shops and restaurants and also to draw money from a bank. Remember to keep a separate record of your credit card number and the number you would need to ring should your card be lost or stolen.

You will also need to have some pesetas with you for immediate expenses on arrival. There are banks at the airports in Seville, Malaga and Gibraltar but there are no 24 hour exchange facilities, so if you arrive in the afternoon or evening you may not be able to change your money until the following day. It is wise to order these pesetas from your bank at least two weeks before you are due to leave. In Gibraltar you can of course use sterling.

Documentation

Passport and visas

Any foreigner can travel to Spain with an ordinary passport and stay in the country as a tourist for up to 90 days. Visitors from the United States can stay for up to 180 days. After this period of time you should either leave the country or apply for a residence permit. In theory it is no longer necessary for EEC citizens to apply for a visa in order to take up residency in Spain although in practice some local police departments may still require it. If you come from an EEC country and you wish to stay in Spain for longer than three months, check with your nearest British Consulate or ask at the local police station. If you are not an EEC citizen and you wish to stay in Spain for longer than the 90 or 180 days you are allowed as a tourist, you will need to apply for a residence visa from the Spanish Consulate in your own country before leaving.

Medical

Now that Spain is in the EEC, other Community members can receive treatment on its Social Security system but in most holiday resorts only a limited service is available. The process of getting reduced cost medical treatment may prove difficult in practice so that you may want to take out insurance against medical and hospital expenses. To get treatment under the Spanish Social Security system you will need to have obtained an E111 form from the Department of Health and Social Security (Overseas Branch), Newcastle upon Tyne NE98 1YX, England. DHSS offices issue two free leaflets; 'Medical Costs Abroad' and 'How to get treatment in other EEC countries'

All dental treatment is private. An emergency filling can cost anything from 4000–8000 pesetas.

You may think it a good idea to bring a small first aid kit with you made up of familiar products including insect repellant (especially if you are camping), calamine cream or lotion, pain killers, travel sickness pills, oral rehydration salts and anti-diarrhoea tablets. These latter should only be used if you have to travel whilst feeling unwell. Otherwise it is best to let the body get rid of any toxins for 24 hours. At the same time it is important to take oral rehydration salts to replace fluids and chemicals that are lost through vomiting and diarrhoea. This is particularly important in the case of young children.

Driving permit
If you are going to be driving in Spain you should apply for an International Driving Permit from the post office about two weeks before leaving. It can also be obtained from one of the motoring organisations for a few pounds plus a passport photograph – you do not have to take a test for it. You will also need a Green Card if driving your own car. Check well in advance with your driving association for details of the documentation you will need for your car.

Budgeting for the holiday

Transport
The question of car hire is discussed in Chapter Four and, as the section explains, it usually works out cheaper to book and pay for your rented car before you leave. Local prices can vary considerably and different companies have different offers available but to give an example: a small car such as a Renault 5, Opel Corsa or Fiat Uno with unlimited mileage can cost between 4500 and 6500 pesetas per day (plus 12% VAT), depending on the total number of days you want it for. These are national rental prices. Sometimes you can get

better local prices (see Chapter Four for more details). You can hire a car directly from the car rental office or through a travel agency.

The minimum charge for a taxi is 240 pesetas and within the town limits the price is shown on the meter, including VAT. Outside the town limits the charge is 45 pesetas per kilometre. (It works out at 90 pesetas per km if you have to pay the return journey, e.g. a taxi from Seville to El Puerto de Santa Maria). Between 6.00pm and 10.00am and also on Sundays and holidays, the price goes up to 60 pesetas per kilometre. You may also be charged 60 pesetas per suitcase.

There are basically two grades of petrol, Normal and Super as well as Diesel. At the time of writing prices are the same at all petrol stations and are as follows: Super, 95 pesetas per litre; Normal, 91 pesetas per litre; Diesel, 72 pesetas per litre and Unleaded petrol, 93 pesetas per litre. Petrol is cheaper in Gibraltar.

Although there are few towns within the province that you can reach by rail, train fares are fairly economical. For instance, a single from Cadiz to Malaga costs 1900 pesetas; a single from Cadiz to Seville, 900 pesetas; a single from Algeciras or La Linea to Castellar or Jimena costs less than 300 pesetas. Children under four travel free of charge and five to eleven-year-olds pay just over half price. Prices usually go up each year at the beginning of the summer.

Bus and coach fares are equally reasonable. Within a town you pay a standard fare of 40 pesetas whatever distance you travel. Some examples of single fares between towns are as follows: a ticket from Jerez to Ronda costs 1005 pesetas; from Jerez to Arcos, 225 pesetas; from Cadiz to El Bosque, 695 pesetas; from Cadiz to Malaga, 1940 pesetas and from Cadiz to Seville, 965 pesetas. Children under four years travel free but over fours pay full fare.

Accommodation

The range of prices available is of course very great, depending on the category of the accommodation, the time of year and so on. The following is a rough guide to what you can expect to pay per night for a double room (see Part Two for more exact details):

Pension or Hostal: 2000–5000 pesetas

3 star Hotel: 6000–10,000 pesetas

4 star Hotel: 11,000–18,000 pesetas

5 star Hotel: 15,000–22,000 pesetas

Camp sites: From 1300–2000 pesetas a day depending on number of people, size of tents and so on.

You will need to take into account the addition of VAT (known as IVA in Spanish) on to the hotel prices quoted in this book. This is 12

All you really need for a flamenco tableau is a couple of chairs. The music pours from the heartstrings of the singer and the agile fingers of the guitarist. Here in one corner of a private home, a simple tableau waits to be brought to life.

per cent for a five star hotel and 6 per cent for other categories including camp sites. All prices quoted in this book are those available at the time of writing and are subject to alteration.

Rented accommodation

Here the range of prices is tremendous and depends on many factors, particularly the area and the time of year. Rentals in resorts like El Puerto de Santa Maria are very high in season, especially in the month of August, so when writing to an agency you may want to specify the price you are thinking of paying and ask what is available at the particular time of year you want to come.

Food

Spain is no longer the cheap tourist paradise that it used to be. In the more popular tourist resorts you can expect prices to be similar to those at home. It is however still perfectly possible to find good, cheap food if you avoid the very fashionable areas and look for more down to earth bars and *ventas* and try to eat where local families do. In a restaurant, order only what you want and what you are prepared to pay for. Do not let yourself get talked into ordering a lot of extras such as platefuls of ham or prawns whilst waiting for the main dishes if you are trying to keep an eye on your budget. The following will give you some idea of how to budget for food when planning your trip.

A simple breakfast of coffee and toast in a bar can cost about 150 pesetas. A lunch of three tapas and a couple of beers can work out at around 800 pesetas. Dinner in a *venta* or a modest sort of restaurant can cost in the region of 2000 pesetas per person (including dessert and a drink). So, eating modestly one can do very well on about 3000 pesetas a day. This can of course be less if one of your daily meals consists of sandwiches and fresh fruit. It can also work out cheaper if you are self-catering and cooking meals for several people at a time. On the other hand, if you eat one of your daily meals in one of the better restaurants it can cost from about 3000 pesetas per person, depending on what you choose. A feast of oysters and lobster tails could make a slightly bigger dent in your budget!

THREE

How to get there

Planning your holiday, choosing your route, how you will travel and where you are going to stay are all part of the holiday itself; that is what gloomy British winters are all about. As far as getting to Cadiz is concerned there are many possibilities and it would be a good idea to consult a reputable travel agent to help with some of the details, although with the information contained in this book you can do much of the planning yourself.

By plane

Strange as it may seem, flying will for most people be the most economical means of getting to the province of Cadiz. Quoting air fares, however, is a tricky business because there are so many variables and prices are constantly being revised. If you want or need to have everything planned well in advance then the sooner you book your flight the better. On the other hand, if you are not restricted to specific dates and can leave at short notice, it is possible to get some fairly cheap flights by keeping an eye on the newspapers and ringing around the charter companies who often offer cut-price fares when they have seats left over. However this tends to happen at peak holiday times when it will be more difficult to find accommodation at short notice.

In travelling by plane to the province of Cadiz, there are four airports to consider: Jerez, Seville, Gibraltar and Malaga.

Flying to Jerez
Flying into Jerez's La Parra airport is the most convenient in that it brings you right into the heart of the province. Until recently, this meant taking an international flight to Madrid and then boarding a domestic flight to Jerez, which made it rather more expensive than flying direct to any of the other airports. The flight time to Madrid is

about one and a half hours with another hour from Madrid to Jerez, plus the time between flights. There is now a more direct service on GB Airways from Gatwick to Jerez twice a week on Tuesdays and Fridays. The plane does stop off in Valencia however and you may have a wait of around forty minutes while passengers are dropped off or picked up. You do not usually have to get off the plane. The complete trip therefore takes some three hours and twenty minutes and the off peak price can vary between £146 and £162 return.

The airport is small but not primitive. The plane brings you almost right up to the terminal building and collecting your luggage and going through passport control and customs are very simple procedures. When you check your luggage in at Heathrow, be sure to have it sent all the way through to Jerez so that you do not have to worry about collecting it and taking it through customs in Madrid if you are flying by that route. At the time of writing, trolleys are kept outside the terminal building and you need to insert a 100 peseta coin in a slot in order to be able to use the trolley. You get your coin back when you return the trolley but visitors coming from London are unlikely to have such a coin in their pockets. The airport has a restaurant bar in the main waiting lounge and three car-hire agencies: Avis, Hertz and Atesa. There is no bank or any kind of currency exchange facility at the airport. Immediately outside the airport is the taxi rank. There are no buses running to or from Jerez airport.

Having said all this, a large new terminal building is under construction at the time of writing so there will soon be a lot more room for both arrivals and departures and hopefully the trolley system will be simpler.

Flying to Seville

Direct flights are available from Heathrow to San Pablo, Seville's airport, every day. The flight takes only two hours and ten minutes and, once in Seville, you have a short and simple trip down to the province of Cadiz by road or rail. Flying by this route gives you the opportunity of spending a day or two in the city of Seville on the way out or back as a sort of added extra to your holiday in Cadiz but at the time of writing there are few, if any, charter flights available to this airport. An off-peak return ticket can cost between £124 and £140.

San Pablo is 12km out of the city on the main N1V road from Madrid. It is an international airport with direct flights coming in from London, Paris and Frankfurt. It has a brand new terminal building which is a little clinical with its very modern fixtures and artificial lighting but certainly a great improvement on the old one.

The arrivals section is downstairs and here you will find four car hire agencies (Atesa, Europcar, Hertz and Avis), a small cafeteria, a bank (open from 9.00am to 2.00pm on weekdays and from 9.00am to 12.00 noon on Saturdays), a tourist information desk (open from 8.30am to 2.30pm on weekdays and from 9.00am to 1.00pm on Saturdays), an Iberia baggage information desk and other information desks including hotel booking facilities and so on. Trolleys are old-fashioned looking blue ones and are rather scarce. There does not seem to be a specific place to get one from, just grab one when you see one!

The high ceilinged departure lounge is on the first floor and has a cafeteria, a restaurant, a shop selling newspapers and magazines, an information desk and Iberia ticket sales counters. There is a British Airways desk where you can also buy GB Airways tickets. The taxi rank is immediately outside the airport building.

Buses from the airport into Seville leave at frequent intervals: on the hour between 7.00am and 9.00am and then every half hour until 10.00pm. A last bus leaves at 11.00pm. These buses will take you into the centre of Seville and can stop at the new Santa Justa railway station, which is where regular trains to Cadiz leave from, but you must tell the driver you want to get off at the station or he will not stop there. On the way back, buses leave Santa Justa for the airport at frequent intervals but you have to signal to the bus to stop when you see the 'Sevilla Aeropuerto' sign on the front. These buses will also stop at the camp site, Camping Sevilla, which is close to the airport.

If you are renting a car and heading straight from Seville to Cadiz, you drive out of the airport following signs to Cadiz by the N1V or the E5 which are one and the same thing until you get right out of Seville and then the dual carriageway becomes a two lane motorway, the E5. (You can turn off to the right and take the N1V road if you prefer.) This two-lane motorway with tolls is usually virtually empty of traffic because it is considered too expensive for regular use. The first toll point is at Lebrija where you pay 770 pesetas and the second is between Jerez and El Puerto de Santa María where you have to pay another 315 pesetas. If you are heading for El Puerto de Santa Maria it is just as easy to come off the motorway at the first exit for Jerez (exit 4) and then join the N1V road to Cadiz, as it is to come off at the Puerto de Santa Maria exit (6) and backtrack to Puerto on the same N1V road. By coming off at Jerez you avoid the second toll point. The motorway has recently been resurfaced and, being so empty, makes for fast and comfortable driving. The N1V, however, is also quite a good road and the journey by this route may only take about half an hour longer if traffic is not too heavy: approximately one hour by motorway, one and a half to two hours by the N1V.

Note: when you leave the airport, it is very easy to find the road to Cadiz but on the way back, the airport is rather poorly signposted. You must follow signs to Cordoba and ignore some small signs that say Poligono aeropuerto. The airport is easily visible from the main N1V road.

Flying to Gibraltar

Many people might be equally attracted by the idea of flying into Gib in order to spend a couple of days there as part of their holiday. Flights are direct from Gatwick airport every day by GB Airways or Dan Air. The flight takes approximately two hours and forty-five minutes and you can sometimes get charter flights as well as cheaper stand-by single tickets both ways if you are prepared to take the risk. An off-peak return ticket can cost £150 whilst in the peak season the price can go up to £215. Once in Gibraltar, the province of Cadiz is just one step over the border but if you are going to use Puerto de Santa Maria or Jerez as a base for your holiday, flying into Gibraltar is less convenient than Seville unless you are going to hire a car on arrival.

As you might expect, Gibraltar airport is very small. The landing strip runs crosswise to the rock very close to the border on the only bit of flat land available and is built out into the sea. The main road to the border crosses the landing strip, which is used by the Royal Airforce. The airport has recently undergone fairly extensive remodelling and improvements.

If you have hired a car and are heading for Puerto de Santa Maria or Jerez, the best route to take from Gibraltar is the C440 via Los Barrios and Medina Sidonia. (For El Puerto de Santa María turn left about 8km after passing Medina Sidonia and go through Puerto Real). It is on the whole a good road, usually with little traffic. The journey takes approximately two hours by this route and avoids Algeciras and the twisting hill road to Tarifa entirely. You will almost certainly have to queue to cross over the border by car from Gibraltar into Spain, especially in the summer. On the way back to Gibraltar be careful to get back onto the C440 road to Medina Sidonia rather than following signs to Algeciras if going through Puerto Real. To do this you need to go over a bridge that crosses the railway line but there are no signs to Medina Sidonia.

If you are not hiring a car you can cross over the border into La Linea to catch a bus. The airport is just a three minute walk from the border. There are only two buses direct to Cadiz every day. If you miss these there are regular services to Algeciras and connections from there to Cadiz. There is a taxi rank just over the border in La Linea as taxis cannot cross over from Gibraltar into Spain or vice versa.

There is a railway line running between Algeciras and Bobadilla (in the province of Malaga), with stops in Los Barrios, San Roque, La Linea, La Almoraima, Castellar and Jimena within the province of Cadiz, carrying on to Bobadilla via Ronda. (See Part Two for hotels in Gibraltar.)

Flying to Malaga

This is another airport you might consider. Whilst the price of regular scheduled flights varies little between Seville, Jerez, Gibraltar and Malaga, most of the cheaper charter flights come into Malaga and there are flights from many British airports: Luton, Birmingham, Manchester, Heathrow and so on. Prices for a regular return ticket range between £119 off peak and £183 in peak season. The drive from Malaga to Cadiz takes between three and four hours and by the coastal route this could be longer in the summer because the N340 road from Malaga along the Costa del Sol becomes one of the busiest roads in the whole of Spain during the peak holiday season. Charter flights are more likely to be delayed than regular ones, and if you needed to spend the night in Malaga on the way out or back, remember that in the peak season you would need to book well in advance.

Malaga airport is 8km out of the town on the main N340 coastal road between Malaga and Torremolinos. Its new Pablo Ruiz Picasso international terminal is impressive, to say the least. The Arrivals area on the ground floor has a cafeteria, a bank (open from 9.00am to 2.00pm and from 3.20pm to 9.00pm), a tourist information desk (open from 9.00am to 9.00pm), several car hire agencies including all the major ones and an airport information desk. The taxi rank is immediately outside the terminal building and buses leave for Malaga every twenty minutes between 7.00am and 9.00pm. There are also trains which leave at twenty minute intervals going either to Malaga or to Fuengirola and Torremolinos.

The international departure lounge on the first floor is big enough to hold a football pitch. It has a high ceiling and a clean, shiny floor and at either end of this amazing expanse there are many international airline offices. There is also an airport information desk and an Iberia ticket sales desk. Once you go through passport control you will find cafeterias, a restaurant, shops (including the duty free shop) and a supermarket.

If you have hired a car and wish to head straight for the province of Cadiz you drive out of the airport and turn right along the N340 towards Marbella and Algeciras. This is the main road along the Costa del Sol and takes you through all the well-known names: Torremolinos, Benalmadena, Fuengirola, Marbella and so on. You can carry right on along the coast as far as the C440 road, turning off to the right between San Roque and Algeciras, which takes you to Puerto de Santa Maria or Jerez via Los Barrios and Medina Sidonia as described previously. Alternatively, you can take the mountainous route through the beautiful town of Ronda with its famous gorge and ancient bull ring. For this route, turn right off the N340 soon after Marbella, following signposts to Ronda along the C339. Ronda indeed would be a good place to spend the night if it is getting late and you do not want to hurry along mountain roads. The Reina Victoria is a four-star hotel whose gardens overlook the Ronda gorge (address: Jerez 25. Tel: 871240). The following day you would carry on along the C339 to Algodonales, where you turn left along the N342, which takes you through Villamartin and Arcos de la Frontera to Jerez, Puerto de Santa Maria and Cadiz.

Another possibility is to head north from Malaga on the N331 to Antequera and then west on the N342 through Arcos to Jerez. This route would be especially good if you are heading for the sierra region of Cadiz, and it takes you through some of the lovely white villages. Some stretches of the road are a little twisty and although the distance is less in kilometres, this route may be slower than the other two. Distances: Malaga–Jerez = 248 km (via Los Barrios), 226 km (via Ronda), 223 km (via Antequera).

There are direct coaches from Malaga bus station to Cadiz three times a day. There are also regular buses from the same bus station to Algeciras with connections from there to Cadiz.

It is possible to go from Malaga to Cadiz by train, though it is a rather roundabout route involving a change of trains in Utrera. The Malaga – Utrera stretch takes you through some impressive scenery.

You may prefer to spend a night in Malaga rather than travelling late in the evening but you should take into account the time of year if you have not booked accommodation, remembering that Malaga gets extremely crowded in the high season. There are of course a great many hotels, hostals and so on to choose from.

Driving through Spain

The only car-ferry service from Great Britain to Spain is the Brittany Ferries service from Plymouth to Santander. If you are thinking of coming down to Cadiz by car, perhaps with a caravan, this ferry service would make the journey a lot easier by cutting out driving through France but it does not necessarily make it any cheaper.

The crossing to Santander takes 24 hours in which time you can sleep and relax, ready for the drive down through Spain. Air conditioned two-and four-berth cabins are available. You can eat, drink, dance, watch a film and shop in the duty free shop while on board. There is also a games room and a children's room. The ships are fully stabilised but you might want to think twice about that rather long stretch across the Bay of Biscay if your sea legs are a bit wobbly. The longer drive down through France might be preferable if you are prone to sea sickness.

The ferry service runs all year round from Milbay docks in Plymouth. Once you are in Santander it is then at least a two-day drive down to Cadiz.

When you look at a road map of Spain you will see that there are basically two routes to choose from between Santander and Cadiz.

Motor route 1

You can drive straight down to Madrid via Burgos and then on to Seville and Cadiz via Cordoba or via Merida. That is, take the N623 to Burgos, the N1 to Madrid (393km) and then either the N1V to Cordoba, Seville and Cadiz (663km) or the NV to Merida, N630 to Seville, and then the N1V road or the E5 motorway to Cadiz (some 720km). The total distance 1,056km or 1,113km. Both are good routes and worth considering. The route via Cordoba is now a toll-free motorway all the way from Madrid to Seville (the last few stretches of it should be open by 1992) and you can cover the journey to Cadiz in six or seven hours.

If you choose to go via Cordoba you could circle Madrid on the M30 ring road looking out for the N1V exit to Andalucia and spend the night in Aranjuez, famous for its Royal Palace and gardens as well as for its strawberries. If you are making good time and would like to spend the night in one of Spain's famous Paradors, there is one at Manzanares, 175km from Madrid.

Although slightly longer, the route via Merida is a pleasant road to drive on and there are some long stretches of motorway under construction at the time of writing. Getting through Seville can be a bit more tedious on this route although this situation should also improve. For this route, circle Madrid on the M30 ring road looking out for the NV exit to Extremadura. You could spend the night in the very beautiful Parador Virrey Toledo at Oropesa, 149km from Madrid. This, like many of these state run hotels, is in a restored castle which is visible from the main NV road.

Motor route 2

If you wish to avoid Madrid altogether (which is quite a good idea considering the terrible state of traffic in and around Madrid and the possibility of holdups), you can take the route from Santander that goes through Palencia and Valladolid and spend the night in Salamanca, a beautiful old city whose university dates back to the thirteenth century, the oldest university in Spain. That is, take the N611 to Palencia, then the N620 to Salamanca. The total distance is 363km.

Salamanca has a modern Parador situated on a small rise on the left bank of the river Tormes with an impressive view of the city. If you leave Santander by about 10.00am, you should be in Salamanca by early afternoon, which would give you time to take a stroll around the centre of this fascinating city, have a drink or two and a *pincho* (a little snack like the Andalusian tapa) in the Plaza Mayor before going down one of the three stairways that lead you down to the Plaza del Mercado, where there are several restaurants you could dine at.

The following day you would take the N630 from Salamanca to Seville via Caceres and either the N1V or the motorway to Cadiz (distance 599km).

Alternative scenic route

Those travelling down to Cadiz by car who have plenty of time to spare might consider driving west from Bilbao or Santander along the Cantabrian coast to La Coruña and then south through Portugal to the Algarve via Lisbon and finally east again through Huelva to Seville and south to Cadiz. This would take at least four days but it could be a very beautiful drive.

Driving through France

If you decide to drive down through France there are a number of channel crossings to choose from and their suitability will depend partly on where you live. Brittany Ferries, for instance, have three crossings which are worth considering. The average day crossing time on the Portsmouth to St Malo route is nine hours. The Plymouth to Roscoff route adds some 130km on to the drive through France but the average day crossing time is only six hours. The third crossing is the Portsmouth to Caen route which Brittany Ferries call 'the Calais, Cherbourg, Le Havre, Dieppe by-pass'. The average day crossing time is five hours and forty five minutes and it brings you to within 12km of the Autoroute to the south.

From your port of arrival in France you will head south for Bordeaux and you can carry on along the motorway across the border into Spain as far west as Bilbao and then south to Burgos. From Burgos you can carry on down to Madrid or take the Valladolid, Salamanca, Caceres route as described in the preceding section.

As far as staying the night in France is concerned, a good thing to do would be to get the book *Logis de France* from a good bookshop or from the French Tourist Office in London. This lists hundreds of places to stay, from small country inns to four-star hotels. Another useful book is the *French Entrée*, the Townsend Thoresen guide to the French channel ports and their environs, by Patricia Fenn. This lists hotels in an area of approximately 100 miles around the main channel ports. The Michelin *Camping and Caravanning France* guide is another helpful book that grades the camp sites all over France.

If you prefer a more picturesque route through the northern part of Spain you could come off the motorway at Bayonne in the South of France, cross the Pyrenees through Roncesvalles and head for Pamplona. From Pamplona follow the N121 which turns briefly into the C101 before joining the N122 to Soria. From Soria you would head south on the N111 which joins up with the main N11 Zaragoza to Madrid road.

Canary Islands ferry

Another ferry service worth mentioning is the Trasmediterranea car ferry between the Canary Islands and Cadiz. This would be ideal for British or other residents in the Canary Islands who would like to start getting to know mainland Spain. What better place to start than the province of Cadiz? There is one ferry a week during the winter months and from June to early October there are crossings every two days. You can board the ship at Santa Cruz de Tenerife or Las Palmas de Gran Canaria and the crossing takes nearly 48 hours. Described as floating hotels, the 'Manuel Soto' and the 'J.J.Sister' are both 10,200 ton ships capable of carrying 750 passengers and 250 vehicles. However, if you do not want to bring a car over and are not interested in the pleasure side of the cruise, it is actually quite a bit cheaper to fly to the mainland.

By yacht

There is one way of getting to Cadiz completely by sea and that is, of course, if you have your own boat. Chapter Four gives details of yacht facilities and clubs.

By train

The first step in travelling to Cadiz by train is to get to Paris. There are several routes to choose from and you can cross the channel by ferry or by Hoverspeed hovercraft. You will get into either Paris Nord or Paris St Lazare, connections to Spain leave from Paris Austerlitz. There is a large selection of trains with sleeping cars and couchettes that make the overnight journey to Spain. A daily service leaving Paris at 8.00pm, for instance, gets you into Madrid at 8.55am the next day, without any change of train at the border. In Madrid you usually have to change from Chamartin station to Atocha station for trains to the south. There is, however, a direct train from Paris Austerlitz to Algeciras, leaving Paris at 10.15pm and arriving at Algeciras two days later, but do remember that there are no trains from Algeciras to Cadiz, Puerto de Santa Maria or Jerez. Intercity European timetables tend to give the route to Algeciras rather than to Cadiz. The route from Madrid to Cadiz is different, so be specific when booking. The price of a return ticket (between £200 and £215) really does not compensate for the time consumed or the discomfort of spending so long on a train. You can fly to Spain for less and if you were thinking it would be a good way to see the countryside from a train, remember that much of the journey is done at night.

If you arrive in Santander on the ferry without a car, you can catch a night train to Madrid Chamartin and get a connection within about three hours from Madrid Atocha to Cadiz. Travelling by train in Spain is cheaper on what are called blue days (*dias azules*). These are in fact the majority of days in the year, except for many Sundays, public holidays and peak holiday dates. Spain's faster, air-conditioned train is called the Talgo. A supplement is payable on this train and reservation is advisable. An ordinary second class return fare from London to Cadiz is approximately £160.

Recently inaugurated, Spain's first high speed train known as AVE (the letters stand for Alta Velocidad but they make up a word which means 'bird') runs between Madrid and Seville several times a day. The journey takes just under three hours which is certainly a great improvement on what used to be an all day or all night journey.

By coach

Eurolines is the collective name of a group of coach companies with members all over Europe. Eurolines have a service from London Victoria to Algeciras which leaves every Friday and also on Mondays from April to October. The journey takes some 40 hours and you should check whether the coaches are the modern luxury kind with air-conditioning, toilets, bar services and so on. If not then they will stop every four hours or so for refreshment and a bit of leg stretching and you should remember to have French and Spanish currency with you for these stops. On this service you are allowed two medium sized suitcases plus hand luggage free. The return fare for adults over 26 is little less than the price of an air fare. There is a reduced rate for 13–26 year-olds.

There are also daily services from London Victoria to Barcelona where you can get connections to Algeciras. The London to Barcelona stretch takes about 25 hours and the second leg of the journey takes another 24 hours or so.

If you are determined to go by coach you might also consider the Eurolines service called London Bus run by the Spanish operator SSS Express from London to Santiago de Compostela or to Santander. Both these services are by modern, comfortable coaches with air-conditioning and video, and both stop in Bilbao en route. The one to Santiago leaves Victoria station every Tuesday morning from April to September, arriving in Bilbao some 24 hours later. There are two coaches daily leaving from Bilbao and going via Madrid, Cordoba and Malaga to Algeciras. Autocares Apime SA have another service that also leaves Bilbao in the afternoon and goes via Madrid and Seville, stopping in Jerez, Puerto de Santa Maria and Cadiz (the following morning). Both these services leave Bilbao from the Plaza del Ayuntamiento.

Remember to take into account the fact that you will be spending money on food and drink en route. The Spanish Tourist Information Office in London should be a helpful source for up-to-date information on coach and train times and fares in Spain (if you can manage to get through to them!).

Cycling

If you were considering a cycling holiday in Cadiz, the best way to get yourself and your bicycle there would be to fly to Seville, Jerez or Gibraltar. Bicycles go free on a plane as they are counted as hand luggage, though they are obviously stowed in the hold with all the suitcases. Another alternative would be to take your bicycle across to Santander on the ferry (at minimum extra charge) and then travel down to Cadiz by train. You should check very carefully whether or not your bicycle can travel on the train you wish to catch. Not all trains have a guard's van and, if not, it would be much wiser to wait with your bicycle for another train rather than leaving it to be sent on behind you. It could take a lot longer than you expect to catch up with you!

Hitch-hiking and cost sharing

Hitch-hiking is legal in Spain. Girls have no problem in getting a lift. Whether or not they have problems after that depends very much on their own attitudes. Couples and young men by themselves can have some very long waits. A young Spaniard in military uniform will usually get preference since most drivers are sympathetic towards those doing their military service. How you are dressed and where you stand are very basic keys. Girls hitch-hiking alone should have their rucksack or other luggage visible and try to look the part of a tourist in order not to be confused with young Spanish prostitutes (usually drug addicts) who in some areas stand by the roadside 'hitch-hiking' to attract their customers.

There are organisations all over Europe that deal in what could be called organised hitch-hiking or hitch-hiking by telephone. The idea is that if somebody is planning to drive long distances and would like to take passengers to share the journey and share costs, he or she can get in touch with these offices and offer places. Similarly, if a person has no transport and would like to travel in someone else's car they can get in touch with the same offices. Two such offices in Great Britain are:

Lift Off P.O.Box 1000. London SE17 2VA. Tel: 081 654 3210.
Interstop 56 Howard Street, Glasgow G14BB. Tel: 041 654123.

In Spain the nearest offices to the province of Cadiz are:
Iberstop Maria 11, 29013 Malaga. Tel: 254584.
Compartecoche SA Amparo 22, 2D, Seville (100m from La Encarnacion). Tel: 4214895.

For instance, a passenger travelling from Malaga to London would contribute a maximum of 9500 pesetas to the driver's costs (not including ferry). A passenger travelling from Malaga to Berlin can expect to pay 11,800 pesetas; 10,000 pesetas to Amsterdam and 7600 pesetas to Paris. These same organisations may well have information about cheaper bus fares, cheaper flights and so on, especially in the summer.

Useful addresses

The Spanish National Tourist Office 57/58 St James Street, London SW1. Tel: 071 499 0901.
French Government Tourist Office 178 Piccadilly, London W1V 0AL. Tel: 071 491 7622. 24 hour recorded information service Tel: 4996911.
Iberia Airline Office 130 Regent Street, London W1. Telex 25308. Reservations Tel: 071 437 5622. InfoIberia Tel: 4379822. (Iberia also has offices in Birmingham, Bristol and Manchester).
GB Airways Head Office: Iain Stewart Centre, Beehive Ring Road, Gatwick Airport South, West Sussex, RH6 0PB. Tel: 0293 664239. Fax: 0293 664218.
Dan Air Services Ltd. (for flights to Gibraltar) Newman House, Victoria Road, Horley, Surrey, RH6 7QG. Tel: 0293 820700. Reservations: 0345 100200.
Brittany Ferries Milbay Docks, Plymouth PL1 3EW. Tel: 221321.
P&O European Ferries Head reservations office, Channel House, Channel View Road, Dover, Kent CT17 9TJ. Tel: 0304 203388. Note: P&O has plans to open a new Portsmouth to Bilbao service although, at the time of writing, there is no definite date for its commencement.
Trasmediterranean Shipping Company Muelle Santa Catalina, Las Palmas de Gran Canaria. Tel: 260070; Marina 59, Santa Cruz de Tenerife. Tel: 287850; Avenida Ramon de Carranza 26, Cadiz. Tel:284350; UK Agents, Melia Travel, Tel: 071 409 1884.

Coaches

National Express (Eurolines) Enquiry Centre: London Tel: 071 730 0202.

SSS International (for London Bus) 138 Eversholt Street, London NW1. Tel: 071 388 1732.

Viajes Rico Cadiz. Tel: 214494.

Julia SA (Europa Bus Eurolines) Algeciras Tel: 651000/ 666806. Bilbao Tel: 4453004.

Autocares Apime SA Malaga. Tel: 314186.

Bacoma SA Barcelona. Tel: 2313801.

Trains

British Rail reservations to the continental ports and enquiries for all European rail services can be made by telephone from 8.00am to 7.00pm every day. Tel: 071 834 2345 (automatic call queueing).

Renfe (Spanish railway telephonic information) Tel: Cadiz 254301; Seville 4414111; Madrid 7333000 or 7332200; Bilbao 4238634; Santander 210288.

FOUR

General information for visitors

Archaeology

For anyone with a particular interest in archaeology, the province has a number of interesting sites, in various stages of excavation, that may be visited. They are as follows:

• In Puerto de Santa Maria: **Torre de Doña Blanca** (on the road to El Portal), town and necropolis being excavated. Dates from 8BC to 3BC, Phoenician colonisation. This is one of the most interesting sites in the province and there is an important project in the pipeline to convert the site into an archaeological park and centre of Phoenician studies. Among other features there will be a study area with rooms to house students attending summer schools.
• Near Guadarranque (Algeciras): Roman town of **Carteia** (see Part Two Chapter 11).
• Near Tarifa (off N340 some 15km north of Tarifa): Roman town of **Baelo Claudio**, being excavated and reconstructed. Founded in 171BC, this is considered to be one of the most complete and best preserved Roman sites in Spain. Open to visitors except Mondays. (See also Part Two, Chapter 9).
• Near Ubrique: Iberian-Phoenician-Roman remains of **Ocurris** near Castillo de Fatima, Ubrique. This town was first excavated in the eighteenth century and many objects and the remains of many buildings were found, most of which are no longer there. The ruins are on a hilltop known as Salto de la Mora overlooking Ubrique on private land. You can try asking for permission to visit the ruins at the Cortijo de Santa Lucia on the road to Benaocaz. On the way up to the hilltop is a reconstructed columbarium where the ashes of the cremated were kept in niches. Further up there is a flat area where remains indicate that a foundry may have been situated. Further still in another flat area are the remains of buildings and cisterns that were filled by canalisation from a main cistern on the top of the hill which maintains a good level of water all the year round.

Vejer is the only part of Cadiz province with windmills. Short and squat, without their sails, though apparently still in working order, they stand high above Cape Trafalgar on a hill that is also popular with hang-gliders and parascenders.

• Near Espera are the Roman ruins of **Carissa Aurelia**.
• Near Prado del Rey: At a place called Cabeza de Hortales, Iberian Roman town of **Iptuci**. An inscription in Latin found at this site was embedded in the base of the church tower in Prado del Rey. The town was razed to the ground in 1133 and although plenty of coins and other objects have been found here in the past, there is little to see here except overgrown rocks. Fairly recently an important find was made here: a peace treaty engraved on bronze drawn up between Iptuci and another town in the province of Cordoba. This piece may be seen in the archaeological museum in Cadiz.
• Near Benalup, in the area of Medina Sidonia there is a small cave known as **El Tajo de las Figuras**, with cave paintings.

These are by no means the only sites within the province but they are probably the most interesting ones and the only ones possible to visit.

The two main archaeological museums of the province are those of Cadiz (Plaza de la Mina, 11004 Cadiz Tel: 212281. Open 9.00am to 1.30pm and 5.30pm to 7.30pm on weekdays, closed Saturday afternoons and Sundays) and Puerto de Santa Maria (Pagador 1, El Puerto de Santa Maria Tel: 852711. Open 10.00am to 2.00pm Monday to Saturday). Another important museum is about to be opened in Jerez in the Plaza del Mercado. (See also Part Two, Chapter 11 for archaeological museum in Gibraltar.)

Beggars

Beggars in Spain are hard to avoid, especially for the foreign visitor who is a favourite target for that outstretched hand. Not all gypsies here are beggars by any means but many of the beggars, especially the professional, rent-a-baby type, are gypsies (women and children only). Drug addicts also go begging, usually from door to door with a suitable tear-jerking story. Amongst all the many beggars there may indeed be some genuinely desperate cases but a visitor will not be able to alleviate this with a couple of coins. Children are so often the tragic victims of the begging profession. In many cases they are drugged to keep them groggy and sickly-looking. Those that are sent out by themselves to beg often have strict instructions to bring home only money, not food or clothing. They tend to be very persistent, very rude and they make one feel more angry than sorry. If you make a general rule not to give money to beggars, the best way to deal with them is to look them straight in the eye and say 'No' firmly; they will get the message much more quickly that way than if you just look rather guiltily in the opposite direction.

On the other hand, there are plenty of youngsters who spend hours in the blazing sun standing by traffic lights, cleaning as many windscreens as they can before the lights turn green. They can be just as rude and persistent as the beggars and they may not leave your windscreen a great deal cleaner than it was before but they are at least offering a service for which they can reasonably expect to receive a tip.

There are also young men, often drug addicts, who act as 'parking attendants', directing you towards free parking spaces and guiding you as you park. Occasionally they can be helpful but usually their exaggerated 'help' is totally superfluous. If they have been helpful you may feel inclined to give them a tip but you are in no way obliged to give them money, whatever they may say to the contrary.

Birdwatching

The twice-yearly migration of millions of birds across the Straits of Gibraltar to breed in Europe makes Gibraltar itself and the area between Tarifa and Algeciras a must for keen bird-watchers. The Spring migration occurs from the end of February to May and the return takes place from August to November. Apart from the dramatic sight of these migrations to and from Africa, there is also a tremendous variety of sedentary species within the province owing to the diversity of natural habitats available; from coast, marshland and lake, to scrubland, forest and mountain.

Apart from the larger lakes and reservoirs, there are within the province some twelve smaller lakes called *lagunas* which are good spots for birdwatching if you can find your way to them and as long as they are not dried up by drought. Unfortunately there is no equivalent to an Ordnance Survey map to show you the exact position of these small lakes or the public footpaths that lead to them. You can just about make them out on a normal road map of Andalusia. The largest and most easily accessible is the **Laguna de Medina**, 10km from Jerez on the C440 road to Medina Sidonia. There are three near Espera which can be reached by taking the road from Espera to Arcos and about three kilometres from Espera on the left hand side of the road is a turning that leads to these lakes. Three more may be found about 10km north of Puerto de Santa Maria and they may be reached by taking the road to the Casino Bahia de Cadiz just outside Puerto. About 700m beyond the Casino a track leads off to the left towards the lakes. There are several more in the area between Puerto Real, Chiclana and Medina Sidonia. Excursions can also be made from Sanlucar into the Doñana National Park, a haven for many bird species (see Chapter 10).

A useful book on this subject might be: *Birdwatching in Southern Spain*, by Andy Paterson, published by Golf SA. But if your Spanish is good and you want exhaustive information, you could consult the *Guias Naturalistas de la Provincia de Cadiz*, published by the Diputacion de Cadiz and available in local libraries. Also available in Spanish is a new publication called *Guia de Aves de Jerez y la Provincia de Cadiz* (a guide to the birds of Jerez and the province of Cadiz), published by Editorial BUC with full colour photographs, available in local bookshops.

The Gibraltar Beach Hotel offers a special birdwatching holiday which, as well as talks and slides, includes trips into the province of Cadiz and a trip to the Doñana National Park. For more details about this hotel see Chapter 11.

Canoeing

If you bring your own canoe you can use it on several of the rivers or lakes in the province or along the coast in harbours or more sheltered bay areas. There are canoeing clubs in several towns of the province including Cadiz, Barbate, Los Barrios and Algeciras. The river Palmones (near Los Barrios) is said to be a little more challenging with more difficult currents than the river Barbate which is very easy flowing. In any case there are no really exciting rivers with spectacular rapids within the province. The river Guadarranque is another popular canoeing river near Algeciras and local enthusiasts also practise their sport on the Guadarranque reservoir and the Charcoredondo reservoir near Los Barrios. Canoeing competitions have been held on the Bornos reservoir which, along with the Arcos lake, is one of the best and most popular within the province.

The camp site called Camping Tavizna between El Bosque and Ubrique offers canoeing trips on Los Hurones reservoir using their own canoes (see Chapter 7 for details).

Customs allowances

When you leave home you can get whatever information you might need, either at the port or the airport, about duty free allowances for your return. This section is to remind people using the airport at Gibraltar that the customs allowances here are not necessarily the same as in England. If you fly into Gibraltar airport in order to spend a holiday on the Spanish side of the border, remember that you will have to go through the Gib customs on your way back to the aiport. Duty free allowances in Gibraltar are as follows: Tobacco products: 200 cigarettes or 100 cigarillos (cigars with a maximum weight each of 3 grammes), or 50 cigars or 250 grammes of smoking tobacco. Alcoholic beverages: spirits, liqueurs, cordials – 1 litre, or fortified wines (such as sherry) and sparkling wine – 2 litres and still wines (other than fortified wines) – 2 litres. Perfumes: 50 grammes. Toilet waters: 0.25 litre. Other goods: articles of any other description to a total value of £32.00.

Driving and car hire

Information for motorists
The minimum age for driving in both France and Spain is 18. You will need the following documentation and accessories:
• Your car registration document or written authority if the car is not in your name.
• A GB (or IRL) plate.
• Insurance.
• A Green Card is necessary and a Bail Bond is recommended though not essential.
• Red triangle(s): two if your vehicle is not fitted with hazard warning lights.
• A full driving licence.
• An International Driving Permit is advisable for driving in Spain.
• You must carry spare bulbs for headlights, side and rear lights.
It is advisable not to have a completely full tank of petrol when boarding a ferry. Remember that headlights should be adjusted to dip to the right, and the wearing of seat belts is compulsory in both France and Spain. If you want to check the speed limits on the various roads in France and Spain you could buy a copy of the *European Motoring Guide* for just a few pounds in your local bookshop.

Driving in Spain

Driving on the open roads in Spain is very much the same as in other parts of Europe. Spanish lorry drivers are usually very helpful, using their right indicator when they consider it safe for you to overtake and the left one to warn you that traffic is coming. There is little courtesy however amongst car drivers amd Spain has a high accident rate on its roads. Avoid driving long distances on the peak holiday dates, which are as follows:

– Beginning and end of Holy Week (Palm Sunday to Easter Sunday).
– Beginning of July.
– End of July, beginning of August.
– Around the 15th of August and the end of August.

These are dates when Spaniards go on holiday en masse, heading from the cities to the resorts, and the news is always full of the alarming number of accidents and deaths caused by careless driving.

In the province of Cadiz, driving becomes more complicated within the towns which tend to be criss-crossed by a maze of narrow one-way streets. Keep your eyes peeled for red Stop signs or triangular Give way or Yield signs which are often attached to the corner of a building quite high up on the wall. Theoretically, if there is no Stop sign you can go straight over the junction. If in doubt, slow down and sound your horn.

Spanish drivers sound their horns a lot so do not be intimidated by it. In fact, it has been said that in Spain the second is measured by the time it takes for the first horn to sound after the traffic lights have turned green. Driving through the narrow streets of a busy Andalusian town can be very frustrating. Lorries making deliveries to shops often have to stop in the middle of the road to unload their goods for want of parking space. Most people drive up on the pavement to get past if there is room. Pedestrians are in the habit of crossing the streets or walking in the road as if possessed of a death wish and mopeds nip in and out of traffic on all sides. Parking is a terrible problem in some of the town centres although pay and display parking zones have been introduced in many areas. Because of the narrowness of the streets you must not park too near a corner. Red and white or yellow paint on the kerb means 'no parking'. If you find your car has been towed away by the police or has had a clamp put on one wheel you must go to the local municipal police station (as opposed to the Civil Guard or the National Police) to pay the fine.

If you are driving through Seville or Malaga, to or from the airport, keep all handbags, cameras and so on well out of sight. Thieves on motorbikes are experts at grabbing anything they can through an open window or even throwing a brick through the window if they see something tempting. You could try sitting on your passport and travellers cheques.

Car hire

If you decide to fly to Spain and yet want to have a car at your disposal while over here, it is worth looking into the business of car hire well in advance since there are about as many variations on the theme as there are in the case of the flight itself.

If you want to hire a car for the whole of your stay it is not only more convenient but also cheaper to book and pay for the car before leaving. It is worth comparing a number of different companies and looking into the various types of rental. Some companies have a special agreement with particular airlines called Fly Drive. If you book your car at the same time as you buy your plane ticket, the car hire works out significantly cheaper than if you hire the same car on arrival at your destination. But there may be other systems that are more economical still. Hertz, for instance, have a rental system called 'Europe on Wheels' which can work out even better than their own Fly Drive system.

Tax on car rental in Spain has been reduced from 33 per cent to 12 per cent. No tax is charged on car rental in Gibraltar. This does not necessarily mean that it will be cheaper to hire a car in Gibraltar but check whether the prices you are quoted for Spain are VAT inclusive or not. There is no problem whatsoever about hiring a car in Gibraltar and driving it into Spain. In the same way, a car rented in Spain may be driven into Gibraltar. (Cars in Gibraltar are left hand drive as in Spain.) This is where a good travel agent can help you work out which combination of flight and car hire suits you best.

If you decide to wait and hire a car once you have arrived in Spain, there is a wide choice of car-hire companies. A good local travel agent should be able to help you work out the best deal for your particular needs. Different car-hire companies have different minimum ages for renting their cars. Most companies require you to have at least one year's driving experience and most will accept payment by any of the major credit cards.

Fishing

Sea fishing is extremely popular all along the coast and there are a great many good places to fish from. In fact you can fish just about anywhere along the coast except for the few areas closed off by the military and of course from crowded beaches in the summer. Many people fish, for instance, from the old sea walls in Cadiz, from the long stone jetties (called *el espigon*) in El Puerto de Santa Maria, from the Jose Carranza bridge across the bay between El Puerto de Santa María and Cadiz and from numerous other popular places. Officially you need a licence for sea fishing but in practise you would be hard put to find anyone who actually has one and you are very unlikely to be asked to produce one. However, for the record, licences may be obtained from the Delegacion de Agricultura, Isabel la Catolica 8, Cadiz. Tel: 227212. Licences cost 540 pesetas (for fishing off the coast), 1065 pesetas (for fishing from a boat) and 802 pesetas (for underwater fishing). If you can manage to be in the right place at the right time you can catch giltheads, sole, sea-bass and a great many different kinds of fish which are excellent to eat. You may also land a few eels and some ugly, slimy brown fish known as toads. Both are edible but most people pack up and go home if they land a couple of these. Grey mullet are also quite a common catch but in the Bay of Cadiz they are not considered good to eat as they tend to feed on waste in rivers such as the Guadalete.

Fishing from a boat anywhere along the coast can be very rewarding indeed. You can enquire about hiring boats from the sailing clubs in Sanlucar, Cadiz, El Puerto de Santa Maria, Sancti Petri, Cabo Roche and Barbate. In Bolonia Bay (south of Zahara de los Atunes), you can ask in the bars down on the beach. In Gibraltar you can enquire at the Marinas or in the tourist offices.

The most common kinds of bait used here are worms (*gusanas*), razor clams (*muergos*) and small crabs (*cangrejos*), all of which you can collect yourself from the beaches or buy from those who collect bait to sell. In Puerto de Santa Maria, for instance, bait can be bought under the archways opposite the river near the entrance to the town. In other seaside towns try the market place and ask for *carnada de pescar*. The larger worms (which live in a sort of tube, and are sometimes called *gusanas de sangre*, blood worms) are particularly good for fishing at night as they have a slightly phosphorescent glow in the water. For larger fish, sardines, pieces of mackerel, squid or cuttlefish may be used.

Underwater fishing is also very popular, especially along the coast between Tarifa and Conil where the water is exceptionally clear. It is also very cold so that a wet-suit is a must even in August. Underwater fishing using oxygen tanks is forbidden by law. The use of indicating buoys is mandatory for divers to warn nearby vessels of their presence. Bolonia Bay, just south of Zahara de los Atunes is a popular place for catching red grouper but you need to be able to dive right down to the caves they live in which can be 20 or 30 metres below the surface.

For fresh-water fishing you will need a special licence for non-residents which costs 1544 pesetas with an extra charge of 772 pesetas for trout fishing. You can get the licence by going to a savings bank in Jerez, the Caja de Ahorros San Fernando de Sevilla in the main street, and asking for the necessary form. Normally it would take about ten days to get the licence but most visitors will not be able to wait that long so you can take the form around to the nearby IARA offices in the Plaza Estevez where you should be able to get the licence on the spot (Tel: 331554). There is only one place within the province where you can catch trout and that is in the river that flows through El Bosque. The trout fishing season runs from the first Sunday in March to the 15th August. Once you have your licence you can fish in most of the lakes and rivers in the province. The most common catches are 'bogas', barbels, black bass and carp.

Gambling

In 1987 alone, Spaniards spent a massive 2.8 billion pesetas on the various forms of gambling, just the legalised ones, that is. Bingo is one of the greatest attractions. Salons seem to spring up as fast as cinemas are dying out. Bingo in Spain is a more sophisticated game than it is in Britain, for instance. The salons open around 5.00pm and close at three or four in the morning. Normal prizes are between 5000 and 15,000 pesetas and there are special prizes that can amount to anything from half a million to ten million pesetas. You have to be over 18 years of age and you must show your identity card or passport to be allowed in. The same goes for casinos like the Casino Bahia Cadiz in El Puerto de Santa Maria which, apart from its games rooms, also has a discotheque, show room, cinema, bar and restaurant.

Spain is only just waking up to the existence of problems such as gambling addiction but this must surely be a widespread disease in a country where there are so many different kinds of lotteries that the larger ones advertise on TV. People frequently come to your door selling tickets for all kinds of raffles, some of which are illegal. Then of course there are the football pools, horse racing pools and so on. The most noticeable form of gambling, for the visitor at least, is the

Lottery ticket sellers cry their wares loudly from many a street corner. This man, standing in traffic outside Sanlucar, could hardly fail to attract drivers' attention, resplendent in his bright yellow ONCE uniform. (Photo by Catherine Cavanaugh)

sale of lottery tickets in the streets. You will see two kinds of these tickets, the National Lottery and the ONCE coupons, the latter sold mostly by blind people or invalids working for the National Society for the Blind. You will hear them shouting out their numbers on street corners and competing with the beggars for your attention as you sit at a table enjoying your food.

Gestorias

A *gestoria* is an agency that deals with paperwork. The proliferation of *gestorias* in Spain is a result of the country's infamous system of bureaucracy. If you have any problems getting permits or with any sort of red tape, these agencies will do the running around for you and help you solve your paperwork problems. You can look them up in Yellow Pages.

Golf

At the time of writing there are eight golf courses open within the province, two being on the Sotogrande Estate near Gibraltar where there is also a 9-hole executive course, and the three are rated amongst the best in the world by the specialised press. There are plans to make two new courses here at Sotogrande.

Club de Golf Valderrama Postal address: Apartado 1, Sotogrande, Cadiz. Tel: 792775. Designed by Robert Trent Jones, the course was opened in 1975 but has since undergone an important refurbishment programme. 18 holes. Par 72. Green fees: 10,000 pesetas.

Sotogrande Golf Club Postal Address: Apartado 14, Sotogrande, Cadiz. Tel: 795050, 792050. Opened in 1964. Designed by Robert Trent Jones. 18 holes. Par 72. This is a private club but visitors are accepted, though they must telephone and book. Green fees: 8000 pesetas. Saturdays and Sundays 10,000 pesetas.

San Roque Golf Club Off the main N340 road just east of San Roque. Tel: 610649. Opened 1990. 18-hole course designed by Dave Thomas. Par 72. Green fees: 6000 pesetas. This club is the Southern European headquarters for the PGA Tour and hosts the TPC event. A 'Spanish village' is being built adjoining the course. Green fees: 8000 pesetas. There is a 40 per cent reduction in the green fees for residents of the Suites Hotel.

La Cañada Golf Club Located in the small town of Guadiaro and adjacent to the Valderrama course, is the Coast's first municipal

course. Opened in 1991 and designed by Robert Trent Jones. 9 holes.
Club de Golf Novo Sancti Petri Opened 1990. Beyond La Barrosa
on the coast near Chiclana, this is a new 27-hole course designed by
Severiano Ballesteros in the centre of a thousand acre residential
estate which, when completed will include several 4-star hotels. The
estate includes 4km of beach front. The course includes several small
lakes, higher rises with views of the Atlantic and it has been planted
with over 1000 trees of more than 30 different species. Green fees:
4500 pesetas for non-members (18 holes). Carretera La Barrosa. Tel:
405005.
Club de Golf Vistahermosa In the Vistahermosa residential area,
just outside El Puerto de Santa Maria on the road to Rota. Postal
address: Apartado 77, El Puerto de Santa Maria. Tel:850011. Opened
1955. 9 holes. Par 72. Green fees: 4000 pesetas for non members.
The club is currently awaiting planning permission to add a further
nine holes.
Club de Golf Costa de la Luz 14km from Chiclana on main road to
Conil. Opened 1983. 9 holes. Par 36. Green fees:1500 to 2000
pesetas.
Club de Golf Montecastillo Opened in 1992 this 18-hole course
designed by Jack Nicklaus is part of a large complex outside Jerez on
the road to Arcos de la Frontera, just behind the race track. The
complex includes a 4-star hotel, social club, various sports facilities
and an equestrian centre and polo club.

Apart from these courses there are several projects to build
residential areas around new golf courses within the province. One of
the most advanced of these projects at the time of writing is that of La
Alcaidesa which some believe promises to be one of the most
prestigious golf centres in Europe. It is to be a luxurious development
just six miles east of Gibraltar and will include three new
championship standard golf courses. The first course, designed by
Peter Alliss and Clive Clarke, should be ready for play by the time
this book is published. The building of Andalusian style apartments
and town houses as well as a full range of leisure facilities is already
underway.

In Arcos de la Frontera there are plans to build a complex called
The Arcos Golf Club which will be the province's second inland
course. This 18-hole course is to be designed by Dave Thomas and
will include a residential area and Club House.

Another project in the pipeline is La Ballena, a residential and
leisure complex to be built between Rota and Chipiona and which
will include an 18-hole golf course.

This is one way you might not have considered of viewing the local countryside. Parascending and hang-gliding are becoming more and more popular and this launch site above Algodonales was the venue for the 1991 National Championships.

Hang-gliding

If you enjoy this sport you can bring your own equipment and launch yourself from a number of high spots in the province. The most popular places are: Vejer, from a site called El Molino; the mountain behind the village of Facinas near Tarifa; the Sierra de Lijar, behind Algodonales. For this latter, one of the most popular spots, take the road to Coripe and then turning right towards La Muela you can find a wooden gate on the right hand side of the road which you can pass through to follow a track leading up to the top of the mountain. Here there is a launching site for parascending and another track leads up to a good area for launching hang-gliders. Since Algodonales is becoming such a popular place for these sports, the local authorities prefer people to get a permit from the Ayuntamiento although not everybody does. These permits are usually given to clubs and do not cost anything.

The area around Zahara de la Sierra, El Bosque and Grazalema is also popular. Within the Grazalema National Park you need permission to launch from spots such as the Puerto de Las Palomas, a mountain pass between Grazalema and Zahara which has a good space by the roadside to prepare your equipment. About 2km out of El Bosque on the road to Benamahoma, a path leads off to the right up to another popular launching site called the Cerro Albarracín, marked on maps as a high point of 977m. Permission may be obtained from the Agencia del Medio Ambiente, Avenida Ana de Viya 3, Cadiz. Tel: 274629, 274594, 27477, or from the National Park offices in El Bosque or Grazalema. (At the time of writing the Cerro Albarracín site has been restricted due to complaints by ecologists that hang-gliders were disturbing nesting vultures).

There are two clubs in the province whose members go in for hang-gliding and parascending. **The Club de Vuelo Libre de Cadiz** tend to just meet in situ, on whichever hilltop they have planned to launch from on a particular weekend. One of the club's members recently set a new Andalusian distance record by flying from Algodonales to Escúzas in the foothills of Sierra Nevada, Granada. You can get in touch with the following club members if you are interested in meeting up with them: Joaqui (who speaks English) Tel: 893112 or Harry (who, despite the name is Spanish but speaks German) Tel: 450310.

The other club is the **Escuela de Parapente ICARO**, which has its headquarters at Alameda del Rio 7, Chiclana. Tel: 403353. Members meet on Friday evenings after 8.30pm to make plans for weekend events. They have organised National Hang-gliding and Parascending Championships held at Algodonales and are also involved in the publication of a new *Guide* to the different places within the province that are of interest to hang-gliders and parascenders. At the time of writing the exact publication date of this guide is uncertain but you could find out whether or not it is available by contacting the ICARO club.

Horses

For horse lovers the town of Jerez de la Frontera is a must, first and foremost for its Royal School of Equestrian Art which is open all the year round and secondly for its week-long horse fair in the month of May (see under Jerez in Chapter 10 for details).

Holidays on horseback

The idea of exploring the local countryside on horseback is becoming increasingly popular and within the province there are several places that organise this type of holiday.

Rutas a Caballo SA have a pleasantly dilapidated, ivy-covered farmhouse with a swimming pool by the lake near Arcos de la Frontera. This is the starting point for their Atlantic Tours (lasting 8 or 13 days), which involve riding down to the Atlantic coast to Zahara de los Atunes, with overnight stops and meals on the way. They also offer an 8-day tour of the white villages visiting El Bosque, Zahara de la Sierra, Grazalema and Ronda. The farmhouse, El Santiscal, is also the finishing point for a 30-day tour that starts in the province of Segovia and passes through the provinces of Avila, Ciudad Real, Cordoba and Seville, spending the last few days in the province of Cadiz. For more information write to: Rutas a Caballo SA, Juan Bravo 21, 28006 Madrid. Tel: 2767629. Telex: 42867 AAIE.

Rancho Los Lobos near Jimena de la Frontera offers full board and lodging in a converted 100-year-old farmhouse. Visitors stay for one or two weeks and plan their own riding programme which can include hacks, day trips, moonlight rides or whatever. Instruction is provided for beginners. There is a nearby river where you can swim or fish. For further information write to: Wolf Zissler, Rancho Los Lobos, Estacion de Jimena de la Frontera, Cadiz. Tel: 680429.

Yeguada El Rosalejo between Villamartin and El Bosque offers two-week riding courses for youngsters (aged 8-15), including classes on the care and handling of horses. Maximum eight children per group. Prices include full board and lodging in a well-kept country house with swimming pool and tennis courts. Language ought not to be a problem since the owner speaks English and French. This might be a chance for parents to spend two weeks travelling in the area whilst their children enjoy a riding holiday. Courses for adults are also offered. For information write to: Señorita Isabel, El Rosalejo, Yeguada Duque de Ahumada, 11650 Villamartin, Cadiz. Tel: 730631.

Equitour is an organisation based in Barcelona that organises this kind of holiday in many areas. As well as being an agent for the aforementioned Rutas a Caballo holidays, they organise holidays for adults in the Yeguada del Rosalejo (Villamartin), mentioned above. They also offer holidays in a luxurious country house near Arcos de la Frontera on the road to Algar (Cortijo Faín, see Arcos in Chapter 7). Another interesting service they offer is to organise visits to the Horse Fair in Jerez, arranging accommodation in hotels, apartments or country houses and obtaining all the necessary tickets to get into the various shows and events. This can be done for groups of visitors or on an individual level and, considering how popular this fair is and how difficult it can be to find accommodation and tickets, this could well be an interesting offer. For details write to: Equitour, Juan Güell 163, 08028 Barcelona. Tel: (93)3394100.

Pure bred beauty

The Andalusian horse is the best known of all Spanish breeds and the most representative Andalusian horses are the ones that were bred some six hundred years ago in the Carthusian monastery of Jerez de la Frontera where Andalusian and Arab horses were crossed to produce this exceptional breed, *el caballo cartujano*. The purest Andalusian horses are a dapple grey colour with a bluish skin. They have an arched neck, with ears set wide apart and a very characteristic shaped head with protruding bones in the forehead. Their large and lively eyes sparkle with the intelligence that makes them so ideal for training in the complicated dance steps which they master with such impressive, elegant strength. The famous Lippizaner horses of the Spanish Riding School of Vienna are descended from this magnificent stock. It takes from four to six years of training for these horses to learn how to 'dance' but they reach the point of really feeling the music even to the extent of responding better to one type of music or another. A good horse can have a career of up to twenty years or more, that is after its years of training.

Riding schools

Apart from the aforementioned holidays on horseback, there are some good riding schools in the province where you can go for riding lessons or to hire horses on an hourly basis for trips into the local countryside or along the beaches. For instance:

Villa Julia Riding School About 2km outside of El Puerto de Santa Maria on the road to Sanlucar. Tel: 850627. Riding lessons, trips into the countryside (at least six riders), etc.

Escuela Hipica La Choza (annexed to restaurant Venta La Choza) Just outside of El Puerto de Santa Maria on the old road to Rota, signposted from the main road that goes around the top of the town. Tel: 541248.

El Cartujano Riding School Off main N1V road to Seville, near Jerez aiport. Director: Manuel de la Calle, Avenida Carrascal 17, Jerez de la Frontera. Tel: 307510. The school offers riding lessons including show jumping and dressage and organised treks into the local countryside on its special Carthusian horses (the famous Jerez breed).

Centro Hípico La Guindaleta Higuereta 28, Rota.

Centro Hipico Ciudad de Chiclana Opposite Hotel Fuentemar on Fuente Amarga road, Chiclana. Tel: 402922. Address: Carretera Fuenteamarga 32, 11130 Chiclana. Riding classes, including classical dressage, hacks etc. Accommodation can be arranged for more intensive courses.

Picadero de Caballos Camargo Near Vejer on the road to Medina Sidonia.

Yeguada El Tesorillo Riding school near Arcos de la Frontera on the road known as Carretera de Jadramil. Tel: 701359. Director: Manuel Rodriguez. A special classical dressage show may be seen by appointment

   In Algodonales on the road to Ronda are some stables that offer riding classes and hacks as well as one and two-day trips into the

(Opposite) Top: *The slow and patient cork oak trees take several years to produce each crop, which is cut by hand and hauled through difficult terrain before being processed into something so easily discarded as a bottle stop.*

(Opposite) Bottom: *Cortijo Faín, near Arcos de la Frontera, is a fine example of a traditional Andalusian farmhouse. Converted now into a luxury hotel, it retains all of its rustic charm.*

sierra region, including routes through the Grazalema Park area. Accommodation can also be arranged. For further information phone: 137079 (am) or 138129, 137014 (pm).

Valderrama Equestrian Centre Behind the Hotel Sotogrande on the Sotogrande Estate near Gibraltar. Run by an Englishman it offers riding classes specialising in jumping and dressage and also hacks out into the surrounding countryside. There is an international arena where you can see show jumping and so on. Welsh ponies available for children. Tel: 792060.

Asociación Amigos del Caballo Finca la Milagrosa, San Fernando (on the road to Campo Soto). Tel: 890040. Horse hire, hacks, classes in riding, dressage and jumping.

Almoguera Stables Near Los Barrios on the old Algeciras road. Riding classes, day excursions. Riders tend to be 50 per cent Spanish, 50 per cent other nationalities. Tel: 660000.

The Montecastillo complex outside Jerez on the road to Arcos de la Frontera and behind the race track will eventually include an important equestrian centre and riding school under the management of Alvarvo Domecq (founder of the Royal Andalusian School of Equestrian Art) and Luis Astolfi (national and Olympic show jumping champion).

Hunting

Hunting is very popular all over Spain and no less so within the province of Cadiz. In order to hunt you would first need to obtain a temporary weapons permit from a Spanish Embassy or Consulate in your own country. Once in Spain you need a hunting licence (an A5 licence), valid for two months. This licence costs 11,564 pesetas plus an extra 5782 pesetas for big game hunting. You can obtain this licence in the same way you get the fishing licence as explained before in the section on fresh water fishing; take the necessary form straight to the IARA office in the Plaza Estevez in Jerez (Tel: 331554). Along with your hunting licence you will need hunting insurance. The organisation you are hunting with should be able to arrange this for you.

(Opposite) *Sunflowers and bottled sun – two very representative symbols of the province. The Tío Pepe sherry bottle surveys many of the local scenes.*

The best time of year for hunting is from mid October to mid February, though obviously the open season varies from species to species. Larger game in the province would include deer and wild boar and the main areas for this kind of hunting are around San Jose del Valle, Medina Sidonia, Facinas, Grazalema and Benaocaz. By writing to the Spanish Tourist Office in London you should be able to get a brochure about hunting in Spain with more detailed information about the open seasons for the different kinds of animals and birds.

La Almoraima is probably the best place for an organised hunt on a 16,000 hectare estate which is considered to be one of the best big game hunting reserves in Spain. See Chapter 8 for more details about this hotel and estate near Castellar de la Frontera. You do not have to be resident in the hotel to take part in a hunt.

The Hospedería del Convento de San Francisco in Vejer de la Frontera can organise hunting trips for groups of at least six people by prior arrangement (see Chapter 9, Vejer).

An organisation called **Agrobrokers SL**, based in Seville, organises hunts within the province of Cadiz. For more information contact them at Avenida Ramon y Cajal 10B, piso 5F. Tel: (95)4647908. Fax: (95)4659886. They may be able to arrange accommodation in traditional style country homes or farmhouses and they are also in the business of organising very 'typical' Andalusian events such as testing the bulls or an El Rocio style fiesta.

Another Seville based organisation that can offer hunting trips within the province of Cadiz is **Promociones Cinegeticas SA**. They can arrange to pick you up at the airport and take you to your hunting destination accompanied by a bilingual guide. They can also arrange your accommodation. For further information write to them at: Ciudad de Ronda Numero 6, primero izquierda, 41004 Seville. Tel: 4421567.

Language courses

If, apart from getting to know the area, you are interested in acquiring a knowledge of the language or improving your skills, there are several language schools which offer courses for foreigners together with organised trips to points of interest and other cultural activities. They usually offer to accommodate students either in hotels, apartments and so on or with local Spanish families. You can write for further information to any of the following addresses:

• The **University of Cadiz** offers Spanish courses for foreigners from mid July to mid August. Student accommodation is available for the duration of the course, including full board. For more information write to: Secretaria de los Cursos de Verano, Ancha 16, 11001 Cadiz. Tel: 223808, 225706 or 225705.

• Also in Cadiz capital is the **Centro de Estudios Hispanicos Gadir** at: Hibiscos 6 – primero C, 11008 Cadiz. Tel: 26O557.

• In Puerto de Santa Maria the Madrid based **Estudio Internacional Sampere** has recently opened an Academy which offers various Spanish courses at different levels: Estudio Internacional Sampere, Cielo 40, El Puerto de Santa Maria, 11500 (Cadiz). Tel: 872021. Telefax: 858630. Telex: 76191 EIPSM E.

• Also in Puerto de Santa Maria is a school called The **English Centre** which, apart from its normal curriculum for Spanish students, has a department called the Linan Language Centre offering various Spanish courses. Accommodation can be arranged in hotels, hostals or with Spanish families and cultural activities and excursions are also organised. For information and reservations write to: Español para Extranjeros, Colegio El Centro Inglés, Apartado de Correos 85, 11500 El Puerto de Santa Maria, Cadiz. Tel: 850560, 850111. Telex: 76256 DIEP E. Telefax: 855911.

• In the lovely little seaside town of Conil there is a language school called **Al-Andalus** offering intensive courses of four hours a day. Write to: Academia de Idiomas Al-Andalus, Carretera del Punto 9, Conil, 11140 Cadiz. Tel: 440552.

• Again in Conil is the **Academia Atlantico**. At the moment the school caters mainly to people coming from Germany but other nationalities are welcome. For information write to: Academia Atlantico, Federico Garcia Lorca 8, Conil, Cadiz. Tel: 441296.

Medical attention

In order for UK citizens to get treatment under the local Social Security Scheme they need a special form as discussed in Chapter 2 under Documentation. People from other EEC countries should check with their local authorities before leaving. If you require treatment you would need to go to the local **Ambulatorio** (or National Health Clinic) with the necessary documentation and see what is available.

If you prefer to go to a private clinic there is an organisation within the province called **Los Angeles Nocturnos Seguridad y Servicios**, (LANSYS) which has clinics in several towns where you can see a

GP or just about any sort of specialist you might need at fairly reasonable prices. A visit to one of their GPs costs around 3000 pesetas. They have clinics in the following towns:

Algeciras: Blas Infante 3. Tel : 663461.

Bornos: Plaza Orellana 5. Tel : 712379.

Chiclana: Alameda del Rio 15-primero. Tel: 400237.

Jerez de la Frontera: Por-Vera 29. Tel: 322150.

Prado del Rey: Vegardila 10. Tel: 723389.

El Puerto de Santa Maria: Micaela Aramburu 21. Tel: 871111.

Rota: Nuestra Señora del Rosario 1. Tel: 812650.

Sanlucar de Barrameda: Trasbola 31. Tel: 363904.

Ubrique: Peman 29. Tel: 111758.

Villamartin: General Franco 97. Tel: 730906.

LANSYS is affiliated to the Previasa insurance group offering the facilities of the European sickness insurance known in Spain as Mundi-Salud. There are of course a number of other private clinics: your hotel should be able to help you if you need information.

In Gibraltar you do not need the E111 form if you are a UK national, you just need to show your UK passport. You can get free hospital treatment in the public wards of **St Bernard's Hospital** and free treatment also at **Casemates Health Centre**. Visitors of other nationalities can also get free treatment at the health centre as long as they are residing in Gibraltar at the time. Medical treatment elsewhere, prescribed medicines and dental treatment must all be paid for, although on weekdays, in normal working hours you can get a tooth extracted at St Bernard's Hospital for a nominal charge.

Parascending

This sport is growing in popularity within the province and tends to be much related to hang-gliding, many of the popular high spots in the province being suitable for both types of sport. See the section on Hang-gliding for further details.

Passports, personal security and the police

If your passport should be lost or stolen whilst over here, the first thing you should do is to go to the nearest Police Station (Comisaria), to report the loss or theft. You should be given a report which you would then need to take to the British Consulate in Algeciras (or in Seville or Malaga if you are in one of those provinces at the time). You can get an emergency passport to travel home on for 1050 pesetas. The Consulate in Algeciras is in the Avenida de las Fuerzas Armadas 11. Tel: 661600. The **British Consulate** in Seville is in the Plaza Nueva 8b, Tel: (95)4228875. The Consulate in Malaga is in the Edificio Parcent, Duquesa de Parcent 8. Tel: (952)217571.

As far as personal security is concerned, common sense is the most basic requirement. The question of security while driving through Seville or Malaga has already been discussed (see Driving section in this chapter). These two cities have gained a rather bad reputation for this kind of problem for tourists. Within the province of Cadiz, however, there is nowhere that has a comparable reputation and cases of snatching things through car windows are not common here. Whilst driving through cities like these, you may decide to keep your doors locked and windows closed. Pay special attention to motorbikes and mopeds coming up alongside when stopped at traffic lights. However, it is certainly not worth getting paranoid; just make sure there is nothing tempting in view.

Obviously, the tourist will always be a favourite target for delinquents since the idea is that if he can afford to get here and stay here he must have plenty of money to spare. There are a few basic pieces of advice that are easy to follow without spoiling one's enjoyment of the place.

• Do not carry large sums of money on you at any time. Make use of traveller's cheques, Eurocheques, etc. and do not open up a wallet stuffed with notes in public.

• Do not leave luggage or any valuables in a parked car, especially if the car has a foreign number plate or a number plate from a different part of Spain. It is best to leave nothing, not even jackets or such in view.

• It is a good idea to leave your spare wheel locked inside the boot of your car unless you are able to park in a garage or central well lit area since thieves are expert at removing the spare wheels from their harness under the back of the car.

• If you do have something stolen, contact the nearest police station. Ask for certification of having reported the theft. This will be helpful to present to your insurance company.

There should be a service available in hotels of every category for guarding money and valuables belonging to guests. The same can be said of first class camp-sites.

There are three main kinds of **police** in Spain; the dark blue-uniformed National Police (Policia Nacional); the green-uniformed Civil Guard (Guardia Civil), responsible for guarding coasts and borders and for controlling traffic on the open roads; and the navy-blue uniformed Municipal Police (Policia Municipal) who are basically traffic controllers within the town limits.

If your car has been towed away or had a clamp put on one wheel for being parked in the wrong place, you need to find your way to the Municipal Police Station to pay the fine and get your car back. In the case of theft or other such problems you would go to the National Police Station (Comisaria).

Polo

The **Sotogrande Polo Club** at the Cortijo Paniagua on the Sotogrande Estate near Gibraltar was one of the first and is still one of the few polo clubs in the country. Horses may be hired for play from the **Valderrama Equestrian Centre**. The month of August is high season for polo at the Club and several important tournaments are held. In high season it is usually possible to play or watch games every weekend and out of season games are organised according to demand.

Another polo club is in the pipeline at the **Montecastillo Equestrian Centre** next to the new Montecastillo Country Club and Golf course outside Jerez.

Potholing

Within the area of the Grazalema National Park there are a number of holes and caves of interest to potholers, being as it is a limestone area. The most interesting ones are probably the Sima de Villaluenga, some 200m south of the village of the same name and the Sima del Cabo de Ronda or Sima del Republicano, about 4km south east of Villaluenga along a well marked path. Obviously, in order to explore and enjoy these or any other caves you would need to be in the company of people who know the area. There are several potholing clubs or groups within the province, the most important of which is probably the **Grupo de Investigaciones Espeleologicas XEREZ** (GIEX), Apartado de Correos 1745, 11400 Jerez de la Frontera. Members of this club have discovered and explored several caves in the area. Note: the Apartado de Correos address is a Post Office Box number. You could try writing to the club before coming to try and make contact and find out about possible excursions. (See also the note at the end of this chapter about the organisation Senda Aventura whose varied activities include potholing.)

Puenting

This sport or activity involves leaping off bridges attached to a rope which is tied to the opposite side of the bridge thus allowing you to swing under the bridge in a pendulum motion. Within the province of Cadiz the bridge at Algodonales is used for this and if you are crazy enough to want to try it you can do so by staying at the **Tavizna** camp site between El Bosque and Ubrique. Puenting is one of various activities offered by the site's organisers. Senda Aventura (see end of chapter) also organises puenting events, usually from a bridge on the road to Coripe, which is the C339 road off the N342 near Algodonales.

Racing

Vehicle racing
Outside Jerez de la Frontera, on the road to Arcos, is the relatively new track that was part of the Formula One racing circuit although the future of Formula One racing on this track is now uncertain.

If the Jerez racetrack has lost out in the Formula One field it has definitely gained great prestige as host of the Spanish Grand Prix motorcycle races. The most recent edition of the Grand Prix attracted some 250,000 spectators from all over Spain and abroad and the whole province buzzed with the sight and sound of thousands of motorbikes roaring towards Jerez for this annual event.

A new moto-cross circuit has recently been opened within the Jerez racetrack. For information about this and other types of racing, you may phone the track: Tel: 349812, 321755 or enquire in the tourist information office.

Horse racing
In the month of August Sanlucar de Barrameda is the scene of the traditional horse races that have been held here since 1845 and which were the first official horse races in Spain. The racetrack is an unusual one, 2000m along the beaches of Bajo de Guia and Las

(**Above and Opposite**) *If your dream is to own a hand-made Spanish guitar, you should find your way to the workshop of Valeriano Bernal in Algodonales. This unassuming man sells his guitars to professionals all over the world including such outstanding guitarists as Algeciras born Paco de Lucia.*

Piletas. A total of 24 races are held over a six-day period from 6pm until sunset – Sanlucar is famous for the beauty of its sunsets. Along the length of the race course children put up little stalls which accept small-time bets on the races. The whole affair is delightfully informal though possibly a little dangerous at times in that many of the spectators on the beach do not get out of the way until the horses are almost upon them, despite the warnings of the organisers.

Rock climbing

Although there are no really spectacular climbs within the province when you compare it to more mountainous regions, there are some places within the Grazalema National Park that might interest rock climbers, such as the Aguja Puerto de las Palomas near Grazalema itself. There is also a place near Punta Paloma (Tarifa) where climbers can go to train and the routes have already been marked out. If you are interested in rock climbing it is worth getting in touch with a club in Jerez whose members get together to organise climbs and treks in the Grazalema area or further afield: **Club Montañero Sierra del Pinar**. Postal address: Apartado de Correos 556. Club address: Ruiz Lopez 14. This is fairly central in Jerez in a little back street off the Calle Arcos. If you go along on a Friday evening at around 9.00pm (later in the summer months), you should find a group of people who will be happy to tell you about interesting places to go and any activities they have planned. Recently many of the club members are getting keen on mountain biking and they get together most weekends to take to the hills. Tel: 347288 and ask for Franki, one of the club's representatives. See also the information on Senda Aventura at the end of this chapter.

Shopping and souvenirs

Food

If you are on a self-catering holiday, the easiest way to shop for food is to go to one of the large super or hypermarkets where you should find everything you need all in the same place. There are some very good ones in the province, such as: **Pryca**, just outside El Puerto de Santa Maria on the road to Jerez; a brand new Pryca in the new Bahia Sur commercial and leisure complex in San Fernando; **Hipersol**, outside Chiclana on the way in from San Fernando or Puerto Real;

Hiper Cadiz, at the entrance to Cadiz as you come in from El Puerto de Santa Maria; **Hipercor**, just outside Jerez near the road to the airport; **Continente**, outside Jerez on the road to El Puerto de Santa Maria and also Continente Algeciras on the road to San Roque. These are usually open from 10.00am to 10.00pm, Monday to Saturday.

Alternatively, for fruit and vegetables, meat, poultry and fish, most towns have a central **market place** called the Plaza de Abastos, or Plaza del Mercado, inside which are many different stalls offering these fresh foodstuffs. Open 9.00am to 1.00pm, Monday to Saturday.

Small grocery shops and supermarkets tend to open morning and afternoon every day except Sunday afternoons. Some stay open from about 8.00am to 11.00pm but more normal hours are 8.30am to 2.00pm and 5.30pm to 9.00pm. All shops tend to take a longer lunch break in the really hot months. Andalusians are not in the habit of forming queues. In small shops, when there are a lot of people the thing to do is to ask, *Quien es la ultima/el ultimo?* (Who is last?), and it will be your turn after that person. You often have to assert yourself quite firmly to avoid queue jumpers.

Other shops
Opening times for shops other than food shops are usually: weekdays 9.00 or 9.30am to 1.00pm and from 5.00pm to 8.00pm. Saturdays, 9.00 or 9.30am to 2.00pm. In Gibraltar shops are usually open from 10.00am to 7.00pm on weekdays and from 10.00am to 1.00pm on Saturdays.

Street markets
Many towns hold a weekly street market selling mostly clothes, shoes, material, plants, jewellery and so on but not food. The most important ones in the province are as follows:
On Mondays in Jerez, Cadiz and Medina Sidonia.
On Tuesdays in Puerto de Santa Maria, Chiclana, Algeciras and Tarifa.
On Wednesdays in Sanlucar, Rota and La Linea.
On Thursdays in San Fernando, Algodonales and Barbate.
On Fridays in Puerto Real, Conil and Arcos.
On Sundays in San Roque.

Souvenirs
Shopping for souvenirs and gifts to take home can sometimes be rather frustrating and many of the more typically Spanish souvenirs, such as fans or the more traditional ceramics look totally out of place once you get them home.

One of the more obvious souvenirs or gifts from this region is sherry – one of the brands you have sampled during your stay. In Pryca, (supermarket in El Puerto de Santa Maria) there is a small souvenir shop that sells various things to do with sherry; specially engraved sherry glasses, small barrels, miniature bottles etc.

The British and Irish connection

You will not go far within the province of Cadiz without seeing the famous symbols of three major sherry firms standing on some hilltop, surveying the scene. One is the black bull of the Osborne Company which in fact advertises one of their brandies called Veterano. Another symbol is that of a sherry bottle wearing a flat Cordobese hat with a guitar by its side, painted in bright red, orange and yellow, which advertises the best selling Gonzalez Byass *fino* called Tio Pepe, described as 'Andalusian sun in a bottle'. The third and perhaps most famous symbol is that of a man entirely in black, wearing a cape and a wide-brimmed hat, holding up a glass of Sandeman sherry.

These and many of the other famous sherry houses were started up by British or Irishmen with an eye for good business. The Sandeman Bodegas in Jerez were founded in the eighteenth century by a Scotsman; the Osborne Bodegas in Puerto de Santa Maria were started up in the eighteenth century also by a young English banker from Devon called Thomas Osborne. The Gonzalez Byass firm in Jerez was founded in the nineteenth century by a Spaniard called Gonzalez in partnership with a Welshman called Byass. The first of the large sherry houses was actually founded by a Frenchman, Pedro Domecq, but there are many other names that are inescapably British or Irish. The Duff Gordon company in Puerto de Santa Maria was started up by Sir James Duff who was British Consul in Cadiz. An Irishman called William Garvey built the Bodegas San Patricio in Jerez and it was his son, Patrick Garvey, who was the first in the business to realise the potential of exporting dry *finos* in addition to the sweeter wines which were normally exported to other countries. The Terry family of the Terry Bodegas in Puerto originally came from Ireland too and, of course, the names of Alexander Williams and Arthur Humbert who founded the Williams and Humbert Bodegas in Jerez in 1877 could hardly sound more British. Harvey's of Bristol is another of the famous names associated with sherry. They bought their wines from local *bodegas* and shipped them in cask to Bristol to be blended and bottled over there for over a century and a half. Only relatively recently did they acquire their own vineyards and *bodegas* in Jerez by buying up those of an old firm called McKenzie and Company that had been founded by two Scotsmen.

In the food line, you might like to take some local honey. You may see some being sold by the roadside in the sierra region or you could buy the Pinsapar brand which also comes from this region. Unfortunately, other local delicacies such as the cured ham or the shellfish cannot be taken home...but then that is one good reason for coming back!

One souvenir that should last a little longer than your bottles of sherry would be music in the form of records or tapes. The province has given birth to some excellent musicians: Paco de Lucia from Algeciras and Manolo Sanlucar from (guess where!) Sanlucar, both well known guitarists whose music will remind you of these beautiful skies and the rhythm of Andalusia. Felipe Campuzano, a pianist from Cadiz is another one you may find it worth getting to know.

If you are willing to spend a little more, you can find some very acceptable original paintings by local artists of scenes that will remind you of the beauty and the light of this area on a drizzly day back home. Try asking in the tourist information offices about good places to find work by local artists.

Back on the music theme, a hand-made Spanish guitar from Algodonales might be the perfect gift for someone special, or a special treat for yourself. (See Algodonales in Chapter Seven).

Other suggestions are as follows: a hand crafted doll from the doll factory in Chiclana; a blanket or poncho from the traditional old factory in Grazalema; a rug or carpet from the factory in Arcos de la Frontera; wickerwork from Jerez de la Frontera; leather articles from Ubrique. All these articles are typical of the area and either handmade or made by traditional methods.

Surfing

This is a growing interest amongst young people in the province. Favourite beaches for surfing are those of Camposoto in San Fernando, Roche, El Palmar, Caños de Meca and Hierbabuena in Barbate.

Taxis

There are no private taxi companies in this part of Spain. Each taxi belongs to its driver and the local authorities give out the licences and establish the prices. Prices are the same throughout Andalusia. Taxis in the province of Cadiz are always white with a coloured stripe and perhaps the name and coat of arms of the town they come from on the side. At night time a small green light on the roof indicates that the taxi is free and during the day, a sign with the word 'Libre' on it will be shown in the front window. See the section on budgeting for your holiday in Chapter Two for information on prices.

Telephoning

To make a phone call from a public phone box, pick up the receiver and wait for a continuous dial tone. For calls within the same town, put at least three 5 peseta coins in the slot at the top of the set and dial the number. The coins fall automatically when the other person picks up the phone. For calls to another province, start with at least a 25 peseta coin and dial the provincial code followed by the number you require. There is no separate code for each town, only for each province. In this book telephone numbers are usually given without the provincial codes, though these appear in brackets in front of the number if supplied. For international calls use 25 and 100 peseta coins. Dial 07 and wait for a high-pitched dial tone. Dial the country code followed by the town code and then the number. When dialling the town code, omit the trunk access code for automatic trunk calls in the country you are calling. This is usually a zero. Example: call to outer London (081), customer number 847 0935, dial 07-(wait for tone)-44-81-8470935. For information, dial 003. For the international operator, dial 9198 (European countries); dial 9191 (other countries). For dial-a-clock, dial 093; local weather information, 094; for information about traffic and road conditions, 91-4417222. Country and provincial codes should be displayed in the phone box.

To phone Gibraltar from within the province of Cadiz dial 7 followed by the subscriber's number. From other parts of Spain dial 956 followed by 7 then the local number. To phone Spain from Gibraltar dial the provincial code followed by the subscriber's number.

In some towns, especially in tourist centres, there are small telephone exchanges in key places where you can make a call and pay afterwards, thus avoiding the frustration of queueing up for phone boxes that then may not work and having to have a lot of loose change for long distance calls.

Tips

The question of whether or not to leave tips is something that visitors tend to worry about unduly. The whole idea of a tip is that it is a voluntary extra given to a waiter, driver, chambermaid or suchlike when one is pleased with the service they have given. If it becomes compulsory then it is no longer a tip. People do tend to leave tips in Spain but not by any means always. The only time a tip could offend anybody is if it were a ridiculously small amount.

In bars the general practice is to leave a couple of coins on the bar or on the plate out of the change you are given. If the bill comes to something like 950 pesetas and you give a 1000 peseta note, then you can just leave without waiting for the change. In *ventas* and more particularly in restaurants one would leave between five and ten per cent of the bill. On the other hand, if you are not pleased with the food and the service, why leave a tip? All bars tend to have a common box into which all tips are put to be shared out equally between the employees later. If you see the words *servicio includio* on a bill it means service is included.

In the case of chambermaids, it depends how long you have been staying in the hotel. If you want to leave a tip after a few days, anything over 300 pesetas should be acceptable. With taxi-drivers, think in terms of ten per cent more or less.

Tourist information offices

These can be found in the following places:
- Algeciras: calle Juan de la Cierva. Tel: 600911.
- Arcos de la Frontera: calle Belen. Tel: 702264.
- Cadiz: Calderon de la Barca 1, (Plaza de Mina). Tel: 211313.
- Chiclana: Excmo Ayuntamiento, Constitución 3. Tel: 400050, 401050.
- Conil: calle Padre Ramirez. Tel:440501.
- El Puerto de Santa Maria: calle Guadalete. Tel: 483144, 483146.
- Jerez de la Frontera: Alameda Cristina 7. Tel:331150, 331162.
- La Linea de la Concepción: Avenida 20 de Abril. Tel: 769950.
- Medina Sidonia: Excmo Ayuntamiento, Plaza de España 1. Tel: 410005.
- Rota: Plaza Andalucia 3. Tel: 810100, 810104.
- Sanlucar de Barrameda: Calzada del Ejercito. Tel: 366110.
- Gibraltar: Cathedral Square. Tel: 76400.

Walking

Walking or rambling, known in Spanish as *senderismo*, is slowly becoming more popular amongst local people and there are certainly some very beautiful areas to walk in, most notably within the Grazalema National Park. There is a book available in local bookshops (in Spanish) called *Andar por el Macizo de Grazalema* by Luis Gilperez Fraile (published by Penthalon) which, apart from giving some general information about the area, describes 20 different itineraries for exploring the region, most of the routes being accessible to anyone who is reasonably fit and healthy. For some of them you need permission from the Agencia del Medio Ambiente in Cadiz (Avenida Ana de Viya 3. Cadiz. Tel: 274594, 274629) or from the park offices. Some of these walks are along marked paths and you should be able to get more information about them in the National Park offices in Grazalema (Calle Piedra 9), and in El Bosque (Avenida de Juan XXIII). According to Gilperez, walking in this mountain region does not involve the same risks as in some others, mainly because the whole area is relatively small and you are never very far from a road or a town. If you do get lost, the very low temperatures that can make other mountain regions so dangerous are not usually experienced here. As long as you have some basic notions of map reading and using a compass you should be able to enjoy this region in all its beauty. There are only a very few days in late January or early February when it is likely to snow but the mountains are very beautiful at these times. It is, however, not unusual for a bank of fog or mist to come down on you without warning, in which case you would either need to be very good with your map and compass or make a quick change of plans. In his book Gilperez recommends certain times of year for the different routes and advises not to try walking in the area in July, August and September because of the heat and the fact that one is not allowed into many of the more shady wooded areas because of the fire risk. In fact it can be quite difficult to get permission for certain routes as numbers are limited and you need to apply well in advance, especially if you plan to go at the weekend. Guides may be available for some of the routes.

Apart from the Grazalema sierra area there are few if any marked footpaths as such, however you can still explore a lot of areas on foot. For instance, it should be possible to walk along the coast between Sancti Petri and Tarifa although in a couple of places you will have to find your way around some military zones. If you are backpacking there are several campsites along the coast you could make for as well as all the hotels and hostals.

For further information you might like to get in touch with the **Club Montañero Sierra del Pinar** as described in the section on rock climbing or the organisation **Senda Aventura** described at the end of this chapter.

Waymark, which organises walking holidays in many parts of the world do one of their holidays here in the province offering accommodation in Jimena de la Frontera and walks in this area. They may include other walking holidays in the province in future holiday programmes. You can contact them at 44 Windsor Road, Slough SL1 2EJ. Tel: 0753 516477.

Windsurfing

This watersport can be practised anywhere along the coast or on the lakes and reservoirs but real enthusiasts will want to head for Tarifa which is gaining an international reputation as a windsurfer's paradise, especially for fun-boards. You can always be sure of the wind in Tarifa and several international competitions including World Championships are held here. (See Chapter Nine for more details). The Provincial Tourist Board has published an excellent *Windsurf Guide*, available in Spanish, English and German with maps and information about ideal spots and their classification. For a copy try writing to the Patronato Provincial de Turismo, Palacio de la Diputación, Plaza de España. Tel: 240161.

Yachting facilities and sailing clubs

Until recently, the Costa de la Luz had little to offer in the way of yacht harbours or marinas to those sailing from more northern parts of Europe or from the American continent to the Mediterranean. The yacht clubs of El Puerto de Santa Maria and Cadiz were the best equipped of the province but very modest by comparison to the facilities offered by so many of the Mediterranean marinas. The most important marinas in the area were Gibraltar's Marina Bay and Shepherd's Marina.

The new marina being built in El Puerto de Santa Maria, **Puerto Sherry**, is a Brent Walker development and when finished it will be one of the largest and most modern yacht harbours in Europe and will serve as a perfect base stop for all kinds of vessels on their way in or out of the Mediterranean. It is already an important base for the training of Olympic sailing teams from several different countries and for various major national and international regattas. Puerto Sherry has a floating dock for 800 boats with fresh water, electricity, fire extinguishers and hoses, all at the water's edge. There are also showers and toilets at strategic points around the harbour and a launderette, shops, supermarket, post office with telefax service and so on. Security includes closed circuit monitoring of the quays from the control tower. The control and communications centre will provide sophisticated navigational assistance 24 hours a day. There are also dry docking facilities which will eventually be able to house some 1500 vessels, with repair and maintenance workshops and a travelift capable of lifting vessels of up to 50 tons. Next to the marina is a large asphalt beach for the beaching and launching of lighter vessels. There are two first class hotels called the Yacht Club Hotel and the Racquet Club Hotel (the first is open, the latter is still under construction at the time of writing), with various sports facilities including squash, tennis, swimming pools (indoor and outdoor), saunas and more. There will eventually be some six different restaurants and cafeterias, discotheque and so on. The central club area with its hotel rooms and sports and recreational facilities, will be for members only but there will also be a seaside 'village' with shops, bars, restaurants and apartments, open to all visitors. This part promises to be very attractive. For non members, Puerto Sherry's prices will be comparable to other marinas in the area in the same way that a five-star hotel may be comparable to a three-star one. Hotel residents will be treated as Club members for the duration of their stay. At the time of writing, only part of the installations are finished and if you come into Puerto Sherry right now you might find yourself a bit cut off from shops, bars and so on as the town is some 3km away. (Address: Apartado de Correos 106. Tel: 870203, 870303. Fax: 853750.)

The **Real Club Nautico** on the Guadalete river is closer to the heart of El Puerto de Santa María and although much more modest than Puerto Sherry it has adequate facilities for a pleasant stay, including restaurant, tennis courts and swimming pool, and it is within easy walking distance of the town centre. Its simplicity may well be more appealing to some yachtsmen than the sophistication and inevitable expense of Puerto Sherry. There are mooring buoys in the river and a draught of 2-9 metres. (Address: Avenida de la Bajamar. Tel: 852527.)

There are now three sailing clubs in Cadiz: the **Club Nautico Alcazar**, a modest club in the fishing harbour whose members enjoy going out fishing and messing about in boats (Club headquarters: Plaza de San Lorenzo 2. Tel: 256914); the **Real Club Nautico de Cadiz**, which can take boats of up to 12 metres and has fuel available (Punta de San Felipe. Tel: 213262); and the new club, **Puerto America** which is just next to the Real Club Nautico (Tel: 229607/ 229500). This harbour has a draught of 5-8 metres and mooring for 270 boats. There are shower and toilet facilities as well as a restaurant in the Edificio Puerto America, the main club building.

Other sailing clubs may be found at Rota, Chipiona and Sanlucar (although in this latter you have to moor in the river and wait for a boatman to pick you up and take you to the shore) and also further down the coast at Sancti Petri, Cabo Roche and Barbate. The latter has pontoons for visiting yachts and a draught of 4.5–9 metres (Tel: 430587, 430016). Beware of tunny nets laid out in the Barbate area in the spring and summer. There should be a fishing boat at the end of the nets showing two inverted black cones, flying a black flag with the letter A by day and having two red or red and white lights on the mast by night. You must sail out to sea around these nets (see Chapter 9 for details about this tunny fishing).

The **Club Nautico** at Algeciras offers berths for visiting yachts and here there is a maximum draught of 4 metres. Then of course you come to Gibraltar with the two marinas already mentioned, **Marina Bay** and **Shepherd's Marina.** The latter is rather small and crowded and a little tight to get in and out of. Work is expected to start on a third marina in Gib in the area called Queensway, next to the Gun Wharf Yacht Centre which claims to be the largest and most comprehensive yacht facility for hundreds of miles in any direction.

After Gibraltar, the first of the Mediterranean marinas, with 535 berths and still just within the province of Cadiz, is **Puerto Sotogrande**, just beyond Sotogrande. Its yacht club is in a striking new three-storey building commanding wonderful views of Gibraltar and the African coast. It belongs to the Best Western hotel chain. Next to the club is the marina village with attractive apartments, shops, restaurants and so on. (For more information write to Club Maritimo Sotogrande, Apartado de Correos 3, 11310 Sotogrande, Cadiz. Tel: 7970200. Telex: 78198 PDSGE. Fax: 615337.)

For more information about local harbours and marinas, you can consult a pilot covering this area called *The Yachtsman's Guide to the Atlantic Coasts of Spain and Portugal* published by Imray, Laurie, Norie and Wilson Ltd (Wych House, St Ives, Huntingdon PE17 4BT; Tel: 0480 62114). There is another book called *Centreport*, *Gibraltar*, a guide to harbours and marinas from the Guadalquivir river (Seville) to Malaga on the coast of Spain and from Melilla to Agadir on the coast of North Africa (A.A. and D.M. Sloma, Gibraltar Books Ltd, London-Gibraltar. 1986 first edition). This includes information, to be updated on a yearly basis, about all the yacht clubs and marinas on the coasts of Cadiz. For those arriving in Gibraltar there is a useful guide available called *Yacht Scene* which contains specific information for yachtsmen as well as general information about Gibraltar.

Note: Senda Aventura is the name of a recently formed cooperative made up of a group of young people whose desire is to promote a more adventurous kind of tourism and they organise all sorts of trips and activities related to canoeing, walking, mountain biking, rock and mountain climbing, hang-gliding, parascending, potholing, puenting and so on. Trips are accompanied by qualified instructors or guides and they can provide equipment and obtain the necessary permits for activities that require them. You can get in touch with this group in Cadiz at the following address on Tuesdays, Thursdays and Fridays between 7.30pm and 9.30pm: Manzanares 4 bajo, near the Plaza de la Candelaria or ring 257048 on Tuesdays, Thursdays or Fridays between 4.00pm and 6.00pm.

FIVE

Food and drink

Andalusian cuisine is by no means world famous. Even the better known dishes such as gazpacho are neither known nor appreciated in all their great variety but the richness and diversity of the local cuisine is such that a whole book could be written on the food and drink of this province alone.

Andalusia is generally thought of as the 'fried food' region of Spain and Cadiz is certainly famous for its *pescaito frito* (little fried fish), but to limit the view to this one observation is to miss out on many gastronomic delights. Besides, there are those who would argue that such a reputation is due not to the fact that here food is fried more but that here it is fried much better. There is certainly an art involved in frying those fresh little fish in such a way that they do not taste of oil but rather retain all their juices and flavour within a crisp coating of flour.

Breakfast

Perhaps the best point to start talking about eating out in the province of Cadiz is at breakfast. Breakfast is the least important meal of the day here – indeed a great many people eat nothing at all and just start the day with a cup of strong coffee. The two most common types of breakfast here are coffee and toast and either coffee or hot chocolate with *churros*, fritters made with a stiff batter which is squeezed out into rings and deep fried. Spanish coffee is quite a bit stronger than British or American coffee. There are several different ways of ordering it: *cafe solo* (black coffee), *cafe con leche* (white coffee), *descafeinado* (hot milk with instant decaffeinated coffee), *manchado* (more milk than coffee), and *cortado* (more coffee than milk). You can of course have a cup of tea if you prefer but it is not easy to get a good cup of tea here.

Snails and wild asparagus are amongst the crops that can be collected freely from the countryside and sold at improvised street stalls such as this one to bring in a few extra pesetas. (Photo by Catherine Cavanaugh)

Tapas

Considering the fact that meals here are eaten much later than in other parts of Europe, and the fact that many people eat nothing for breakfast, you may well wonder how people survive until lunchtime. This is where that wonderful institution, the tapa, comes into play. This is one of the first and perhaps most delightful discoveries you will make when you start eating out in this part of Spain. Tapas are small portions of food of almost encyclopedic variety served in just about any bar as appetisers or snacks. Another name for them is *tentempie* – something to keep you on your feet. Tapas provide a wonderful way of sampling a wide variety of local dishes with minimum risk. Because they are small and relatively inexpensive, you can afford to try a variety of dishes that might otherwise intimidate you were you obliged to order a full course meal of the stuff.

The word tapa means a lid. In the days of Tartessos, earthenware jars whose long necks ended in a wide, flat lip, were used to store liquids in. This lip served as a base on which to place some sort of lid in order to protect the liquid contents from dust, sand and rain. By the nineteenth-century this protective lid had evolved into a slice of ham, cheese or some other morsel of food, placed on top of a glass of wine as the inn keeper carried it out to a thirsty gentleman riding up to the inn on his horse. This lid served the dual purpose of protecting the drink from the dust of the road as well as accompanying it as a tidbit.

Nowadays the tapa has graduated to its own little plate and has evolved from a simple slice of ham or cheese into an amazing variety of dishes. The late eating habit of Andalusians is one of the main reasons why the tapa has become such an important part of local daily life. In a town like Puerto de Santa Maria during the summer you can walk into a restaurant at one or even two o'clock in the morning and still expect to be served a three course meal. The tapa serves the purpose of filling those morning and afternoon gaps. It is also an indispensable element in the art of drinking the local wines. The local sherries need to be drunk with a certain amount of know-how and the tapa serves to temper the strength of the wine as well as to stimulate the palate for each fresh sip. It is said that Andalusians eat in order to be able to drink better, rather than vice-versa. Certainly, when you go into a bar and the barman enquires what you would like, you are expected to order your drink first. You will then be asked if you want any tapas.

Tapa-hopping

Tapear is a much used Spanish verb that does not officially exist. It is often translated as tapa-hopping, though it is in fact a more relaxed activity than this seems to imply. *Tapear* is a delightful way of spending time with friends, enjoying their company and their conversation, strolling from bar to bar, indulging the palate in a variety of tastes. The marvellous climate obviously helps such an activity since one can nearly always move freely from bar to bar without having to worry about scarves, gloves and umbrellas.

Four is said to be the ideal number of people for a *tapa* session. Four can comfortably join in the same conversation and can usually find room at the bar without too much difficulty. Seven is said to be the best number of *tapas* for one session. Ideally one should go for variety, never repeating a dish and alternating fish with meat, hot with cold, including something like a Russian salad half way through as a sort of interval.

If you want a larger serving of a particular dish then you ask for a *ración*. This is generally about five or six times as much as a tapa. There are some bars that only serve *raciones*. If a price list appears to be rather outrageous, it may be referring to these rather than tapas, though you can usually ask for *media ración* which is half.

Places to eat out

When it comes to the mid-day and evening meals, there are several kinds of places to eat out. Many people are quite happy to lunch and dine on tapas or *raciones*. Some ordinary bars also serve meals, the menu usually consisting of *platos combinados* – simple meals involving fried eggs, toasted sandwiches, omelettes, fried fish and the like. Otherwise you can go to a restaurant, a *venta* or a *mesón*.

• Restaurants have one to five fork ratings although four and five fork restaurants are very rare and will usually only be found in large cities. Both two and three fork restaurants can be extremely satisfying places to eat.

• A *venta* is usually an inn or bar in the country or on the outskirts of a town, where meals are served. You will often come across them in what appear to be totally isolated places and you wonder how on earth they do business, but because they are humble and relatively inexpensive establishments which nevertheless serve very passable meals, they are popular with workers who lunch away from home and with people who make day trips into the country.

• A *mesón* used to be an establishment that offered both food and lodging. Nowadays it is usually a restaurant in an old building resembling the old style taverns. As in the case of *ventas*, the kind of food served tends towards the more traditional local cuisine whereas some restaurants try to offer more exotic and unusual dishes.

Well...er...yes, delicious!

Menus translated into English are often good for a laugh – one can be offered some quite outrageous dishes! One of the best translations I have seen is a recipe for *gazpacho* from Vejer de la Frontera which reads as follows:

"Gazpacho: rustic usage in Vejer de la Frontera.

On the inside of a dornillo cup, pound with a mortar two tooth of garlic, one middling spoonful of salt, a piece of capiscum and one tomato not very big. When all are pounded well, bruise with the palm of the hand to a crumb of bread, to let down it very thin in the dornillo cup. After this, cast a spouting of olive and two of vinegar. Stir all very well and add a piece of onion very pricked, as much water as it permit until your taste is all right. At last, cast a crust of bread that sponge and some cucumber pricked...!"

Traditional stews and vegetables

Although there is an abundance of eating places throughout the province, without doubt one of the best places to sample the truly traditional local cuisine is in the homes of ordinary local people. Of course, the opportunity to do so may not arise but if it does you may discover some of the wonderful Andalusian *potajes* – a wide variety of stews based on chickpeas, dried beans or lentils.

Hanging hams

Jamon serrano, literally 'ham from the mountains', is a very common sight in bars and restaurants all over the country. It is rather expensive and is considered a great delicacy. You will see the hams hanging from the ceiling, often with what look like upside down plastic umbrellas stuck in the bottom to catch the drips of grease as they sweat. The hams come from several different regions of Spain and from different breeds of pig. The best ones come from the neighbouring province of Huelva and Jabugo is the most famous of the many towns that produce these hams. The very best ham, *jamon de pata negra*, comes from black haired Iberian pigs that feed on large acorns rather than fodder. The real connoisseurs believe that the best of the best comes from the left hind leg because, nine out of ten times that these pigs lie down, they apparently do so on their left side so that more fat is accumulated on this side of the body. Producing a good ham is as much of an art as producing a good wine. In Huelva the curing process involves first hanging the hams in attics to sweat in the mountain air and then transferring them to dark *bodegas* where the temperature and humidity are kept constant to finish the curing process much more slowly. They hang in these *bodegas* for at least eighteen months. The fact that *jamon serrano* is often translated as 'raw Spanish ham' tends to put foreigners off, but I would certainly encourage you to try it. A good ham, cut correctly – it should be sliced so thinly that the fatty parts are almost transparent – makes a very delicious accompaniment to the local sherries.

One of the most traditional of these local stews is called *berza*. It consists of chick-peas and dried beans with celery and swiss chard leaves. These are cooked in a pressure cooker together with a whole onion and a head of garlic for flavour, paprika, olive oil and the indispensable part of all these stews which is known as the *pringue* or *pringá*. This consists of a piece of pork, a piece of pork fat, a piece of chorizo (spicy sausage), sometimes a piece of *morcilla* (blood sausage) and a piece of Spanish ham. There are about as many varieties of *potajes* as there are housewives who cook them. You are more likely to find these traditional stews in country *ventas* than in restaurants. Obviously a local person does not go out to a restaurant to eat the same food he eats at home every day. So, be adventurous and try out some of the more unlikely looking inns – you may get some pleasant surprises.

Vegetables are rarely served separately in the same way as they are in England where 'meat and two veg' is the norm. In restaurants vegetables accompany meat and fish dishes more as decoration than as part of the meal itself. This fact often gives visitors the impression that the local people eat very few vegetables when in fact the contrary is true. Andalusian housewives have a fantastic repertoire of vegetable dishes using artichokes, pumpkin, cauliflowers, asparagus, aubergines and so on.

Fish and shellfish

One thing you will find in great abundance in *ventas*, *mesones* and restaurants, especially along the coast, is a tremendous variety of fish and shellfish. These make up another very important part of the local cuisine, Cadiz being as it is a coastal province with both Mediterranean and Atlantic waters.

Besugo (sea bream), *lubina* (sea bass), *dorada* (gilt-head), *urta* (a variety of gilt-head) and *pargo* (porgy) are some of the fish commonly found on local menus. The latter three have strong teeth and feed on all kinds of crustacea, especially small crabs, a fact which accounts for the delicate shellfish flavour these fish often have. There is not room here to go through the wide variety of fish available and the many different ways of preparing them; the best thing is to try them out.

Most visitors to the area discover quickly what *calamares* are – squid, most commonly cut into rings and fried in flour or batter. They can also be stuffed with a mixture of minced meat and other ingredients and cooked in a yellow sauce. *Chipirones* and *puntillitas* are also squid in two smaller sizes and they are usually cooked whole, either fried or in their ink. Along the same lines you will find *chocos* (small cuttlefish) and *pulpo* (octopus). The former can be fried or cooked in a typical stew with potatoes. They are also very good *a la plancha* with garlic, parsley and a little sherry. (You will see this term '*a la plancha*' frequently on menus as many foods are cooked this way. It is usually translated as grilled or broiled but in

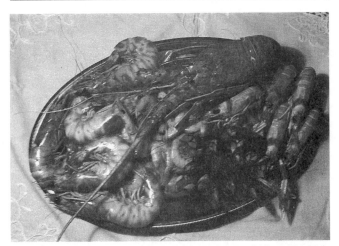

One of the best places to eat shellfish is on Puerto de Santa María's Ribera del Marisco, near the river. The famous Romerijo firm has been selling ready cooked shellfish here for well over twenty years and its highly successful shop on the Ribera sells over a hundred tons a year. (Photo by Richard Kearns)

actual fact the grill, as we understand it in Britain, is rarely used in this part of Spain. The *plancha* is a flat metal hot-plate on which food is cooked with a minimum amount of oil). Octopus is not eaten as much here as in other parts of Spain. It is usually served cold with tomato, onion and green pepper or sprinkled with paprika and oil. Fish roes are also served cold with a dressing or with that mixture of chopped tomato, onion and green pepper so typical of Cadiz called *piriñaca* or *picadillo*.

As far as shell fish are concerned, the variety is again tremendous. Amongst the best known are the large tiger prawns of Sanlucar. The *gamba* and the *langostino* are the two main kinds of prawn, the former being generally smaller and more delicate in taste and texture. Many people never try these prawns because they do not know how to eat them. You must of course eat them with your fingers: first, pull off the head. The head is generally considered to be the best part – do not actually eat it, just suck out the soft part – go on! Try it! Next, pull off the little legs and you will be able to peel off the body shell by pulling it back from the 'stomach' area. It really is easy once you get the hang of it. All the many different kinds of prawns, crabs and lobsters are quite delicious and what better place to sample them than in the province of Cadiz, especially in the town of Puerto de Santa Maria with its famous *cocederos de mariscos* (ready cooked shell-fish shops) by the park near the river.

Garlic, oil and sherry

One indispensible item in most Andalusian kitchens is a pestle and mortar used for making the *majado*. This is the secret to many of the stews (whether of meat, fish, chicken or game) which have such delicious sauces. If you ask a local housewife how to make some of the many different dishes, the answer will basically be the same for all of them: you fry a little onion, a little garlic and a little piece of stale bread. You grind these ingredients in the mortar, sometimes with a little nutmeg, a few fried almonds or some saffron. You start cooking the meat, chicken or whatever in olive oil and when it is hot, add a little sherry. Then add the *majado*, a couple of bay leaves, salt and a little stock and cook until tender. Grinding the onion and garlic in the mortar makes the sauce very smooth and the ground fried bread helps it to thicken. Considering that this is the world's sherry producing region, it is not surprising that sherry is used a lot in local dishes, one of the best known being *riñones al Jerez*, (kidneys in sherry). Olive oil is used liberally here but in a way that enhances the flavour of the food and the texture of the sauces without making them greasy. Garlic is another ingredient that British people tend to be very wary of but although it is a basic ingredient in so many of the local dishes, very few of them actually taste of garlic. It blends in with the other ingredients in a subtle way and only dishes *al ajillo*, such as the delicious *gambas al ajillo* (garlic prawns), have a strong garlic flavour.

Egg dishes

Eggs are eaten a lot over here and funnily enough many people will say that egg and chips is one of their favourite meals. *Huevos a la flamenca* is one of the best known of Andalusian egg dishes. These are eggs baked on top of a thick sauce of fried tomato with peas, ham, chorizo and a few other ingredients. One more important dish is *tortilla*. In Spain a tortilla is an omelette and can have many different fillings.

> ### The tortilla trick
> One of the best known egg dishes in Spain is *tortilla*. Here a *tortilla* is an omelette and can have many different fillings. Contrary to the impression given by all the English language recipes I have ever come across for it, a true *tortilla española* is simply a thick potato omelette. Its only ingredients are chunks of fried potato, salt and beaten egg. The omelettes are never put under the grill to cook the top side; when the underside is done you put a plate on top, turn the whole thing over so that the omelette stays on the plate and then slide it back into the frying pan, cooked side up, tucking the edges down to achieve a rounded effect. Typical of the province of Cadiz are *tortillas de camarones* but these are not made with eggs. They are more like very small savoury pancakes, fried with tiny whole shrimps and chopped onion in them.

Cold foods

In this category, Andalusia's most famous dish must surely be *gazpacho*. However in all Andalusia there may be as many as fifty variations on the theme of gazpacho, according to Jose Carlos Capel in his book about Andalusian cuisine. The basic requirement for a soup to be called gazpacho is that it contain garlic and bread ground together with salt, vinegar and olive oil. Apart from this, each town or village gives it its own personal touch. The best known gazpacho is the red or pinkish one made with garlic, green pepper, cucumber, tomato and bread with oil, salt and vinegar. This is commonly served in local bars and restaurants and it should be cold but not iced. It is usually served in the summer only, when it is truly refreshing, served with little pieces of chopped onion, green pepper, cucumber and bread.

Desserts and fruit

Desserts tend to be rather limited, sometimes disappointing and more or less the same ones are offered in the majority of eating places. In recent years some very delicious ice-cream desserts have come onto the market, such as iced melon and pineapple, to supplement the typical *tarta helada* (ice-cream cake) which comes in a variety of guises. Another common dessert is *flan* which is a simple caramel cream. Most restaurants offer a variety of cakes or tarts made locally.

A very typical dessert in the province called *tocino de cielo* originated in Puerto de Santa Maria. Egg whites used to be used in the sherry making process to clarify the wine and the amount of yolks that were therefore left over must have prompted somebody to invent this dessert. It is made basically from egg yolks and sugar and is therefore very rich and sweet but worth trying.

The alternative to this kind of sweet dessert is fresh fruit in season. From spring to autumn the variety can be tremendous and you will have an opportunity to try some fruits you may not have heard of before such as the cherimoya fruit, the persimmon and the medlar. If a fruit is offered *en almibar*, it simply means that it is tinned.

Sherry and other drinks

Now we come to the subject of drinking. Coffee, tea and hot chocolate have already been mentioned. Then of course there is water. Tap water here may taste slightly different to the tap water at home but there is no reason to be afraid of drinking it. In the mountains in Ubrique, Benaocaz and Grazalema, you can drink fresh spring water from fountains by the roadside. If you have any doubts about the water and if you are only here for a short stay then there is plenty of bottled mineral water available from bars, grocery shops and supermarkets. *Agua con gas* is carbonated and *agua sin gas* is still. *Zumo* is the general name for fruit juice and *refresco* is a collective name for fizzy orange, lemon, tonic etc. You usually ask for these by their brand name. *Cerveza* is beer although Spanish beer is pale like lager and gassier than other European beers. In some bars you can get bottles of *cerveza negra* (dark beer), or cans of European or American brands of beer and lager. If you want a small glass ask for *media copa*. There is a drink called bitter but it has nothing to do with beer. It is a bright red fizzy drink that tastes a bit like dental mouthwash.

Red wine is called *tinto* and a lot of very good red wine in Spain is extremely cheap, so do not be put off by low prices in the supermarkets. The real plonk here comes in bottles with plastic stoppers or in tetra-brik and even much of that is perfectly drinkable. A *tinto de verano* is a pleasant and quite refreshing drink of red plonk and fizzy lemonade served in tall glasses with ice in the summer. *Tinto* is also used to make the famous drink called *sangria*. For this, red wine is mixed with orangeade, lemonade, a little brandy and anything else you feel like throwing in together with a little sugar and plenty of chopped fresh fruit. Sangria is far more popular with tourists than it is with the local people. If you want white wine you have to ask for *vino blanco de mesa* to distinguish it from sherry.

Thank God for progress!

If, as well as visiting the more traditional parts of the sherry *bodegas* and seeing the wines in the old oak barrels in their silent, timeless rows, you visit one of the modern vinification plants where the wine may be fermented in temperature controlled stainless steel vats, you may feel a slight nostalgia for the old days when the grapes were trodden with nail-studded cowhide boots. However, most of the innovations introduced into the process of sherry production have been made not only to produce a greater quantity of wine but also to guarantee a high and consistent quality at the same time as ensuring the necessary standards of hygiene. One of the problems faced by previous generations of sherry producers was the taste and smell of mould that wine could sometimes have. This may have been due to poor disinfection of the containers. Olive oil was sometimes used to 'soak up' the mouldy taste but of course it did not mix with the wine. One recipe used to take the mouldy smell out of the containers was, to say the least, drastic. The following ingredients were dissolved in a quantity of warm water equivalent to a sixteenth of the barrel's capacity: four pounds of cooking salt, one pound of alum, a kind of white mineral salt and a small quantity of fresh cow's dung!

Last, but very far from least, we come to the wine the Moors called liquid sun or molten gold, the wine they grew to love despite the prohibition of their religion. Indeed all of the many civilisations that left their mark on the peninsula found their way sooner or later to the Bay of Cadiz in search of this golden wine which, according to the Greek historian Polibio, was jealously guarded in shining silver vessels. Sherry, as we call it, is the only Spanish wine that other countries have tried to imitate. The word sherry is derived from the name of the main sherry producing town, Jerez (pronounced Haireth). The British have always had a particular weakness for the sherries of this area, true sherry country being the triangle formed between Jerez, Puerto de Santa Maria and Sanlucar de Barrameda. Much has been written on the subject of Spanish sherry – and certainly, the sherry from this area is unique. The white *albariza* soil, rich in iron and lime, the *palomino* grape, the *solera* system of production and the climate of the region all contribute to this uniqueness.

Sherry does not have vintage years. The solera system basically involves the periodic blending of older wines with newer ones according to certain scales and percentages in order to produce wines of a consistent quality. The best way to get an idea of how sherry is made is to visit one or two *bodegas* (wineries). The tourist information offices in the three sherry towns will be able to inform you as to which *bodegas* may be visited and when. The other way to get to know the local sherries is of course to do a good bit of on the spot sampling! Much of the sherry sold in Britain is blended over there and here in sherry country you will find many labels you have not seen before. Finos (dry sherries) and olorosos are produced in Jerez and Puerto. The former is very pale, light and delicate, a very dry sherry and the one most commonly drunk by the local people. In a bar you ask for *un fino* or ask for it by its brand name. The special characteristics of the fino are largely the result of the *flor*, a special kind of yeast that is peculiar to this area and which forms spontaneously as a white film on the surface of certain wines soon after fermentation. This film gradually multiplies and becomes like a thick crust on top of the wine, giving it its unique flavour and bouquet. It only forms naturally on the lighter wines which then become finos or amontillados. When this flor does not develop, the wine becomes an oloroso. The oloroso wines have more body, a stronger bouquet, a darker colour and a higher level of alcohol (18-21% compared to a fino's 15%). Olorosos are naturally very dry but those shipped abroad are usually sweetened.

An amontillado is a fino that has aged without being subjected to the same periodic blending. It is not quite as pale or dry as a fino. It was really invented, or discovered, in the town of Montilla in the province of Cordoba. In the eighteenth-century a forgotten barrel of

(Opposite) Top: *In Carnival, anything goes and the best thing to do is to let your hair down (or roll your trouser leg up) and join in the fun. The ability to break out of dreary routine with explosions of alegría is an enviable trait of the Andalusian character. (Photo by Fernando Fernandez, supplied by the Fundación Gaditana del Carnaval)*

(Opposite) Bottom: *Rambling is fast growing in popularity in Spain and there are some great walks to do in many parts of the province, particularly in the Grazalema National Park. From several points, such as this one, you can see all the way to the coast, and from the highest point you can sometimes see the coast of North Africa.*

fino was found in the *bodegas* of the Conde de Corina. The barrel had been overlooked and therefore had not been through the usual blending stages. Sherry producers from Jerez liked the result and called it *fino amontillado* after the town of Montilla.

In Sanlucar de Barrameda finos develop into a very pale, dry sherry called manzanilla which has a flavour of its own, a very delicately salty flavour said to derive from the sea breezes. This wine apparently does not travel well so that the best place to appreciate it is in Sanlucar itself – try it with some tiger prawns in one of the Bajo de Guia restaurants while you watch the sun going down over Doñana.

Sherry sampling

Choosing a good sherry is more a question of choosing a good brand, since there is no such thing as vintage years or good and bad harvests, thanks to the *solera* system. In the case of fino, which is the sherry that most Spaniards drink, one looks at the colour, takes in the bouquet and tastes it slowly. The colour and bouquet are most important – indeed the professionals who sample the sherries in the different *bodegas* do not actually taste them but rather rely on their sense of smell. Sherry should ideally be served in long-necked glasses which are not filled right up. Again ideally, the glass should be held by its base between thumb and middle finger in order to swirl the wine gently round the glass and observe its colour and bouquet without warming it by the heat from the palm of your hand. It is also said that a bottle of fino, once opened, should be drunk in its entirety as the wine soon starts to lose its bouquet and, more slowly, its flavour. This is one reason why half bottles are available, especially during *feria* time.

The solera system of blending the sherries means that a particular brand and type should always taste the same and can be drunk without surprises. It is not a question of knowing which year had the

(Opposite) Top: *It is worth climbing the steps of the bell tower in the main square to get this view of Arcos, an appealing little town perched on a sheer sided rock, one of the gateways to the Sierra region.*

(Opposite) Bottom: *Like so many of the white villages, Olvera crowds around its little castle on a hilltop. From up in the castle you can contemplate the village and listen to the sounds of rural Andalusian life which carry so clearly over the immense silence.*

best harvest or anything along those lines. Part of the art of drinking sherry involves knowing which kinds to drink at which times of the day. For instance, the delicately pale and smooth finos and manzanillas are best sampled early and late in the day. In between, during the afternoon and early evening one can go in for the olorosos and amontillados, wines with more body and a higher alcoholic content.

SIX

History and traditions

A brief history of the province

With so much talk of inflation and other economic ills, it may be hard to think of an 'El Dorado'. This corner of Spain is as much beset by social and economic problems as is the rest of Europe and few can imagine that over three thousand years ago these lands were part of that fabled kingdom of Tartessus. But if you are on holiday here and are feeling mellowed by the warmth and the wine, you may well be able to imagine that mysterious kingdom to which King Solomon sent his ships to bring back 'gold and silver, ivory and apes and peacocks'. With the rest of the peninsula still in prehistoric darkness, the fertile valley of the Guadalquivir became the thriving centre of this, the earliest civilised state in Western Europe. Whether or not they were actually up to their eyes in milk and honey is something one can only guess at but they are thought to have been a peace-loving nation, given far more to commercial enterprise than to any thoughts of empire. They had their own system of letters and of laws written in verse; one imagines a lyrical and light-hearted people, qualities which appear to be all that remain today of this marvellous civilisation, lost to us now in a shroud of myth and legend.

An outpost of empires
Around the year 1100BC the Phoenicians, those famous merchants of antiquity, sailed through the Straits of Gibraltar and up the Atlantic coast until they discovered a large island. On one end they built a temple to Melkart (or Hercules) and on the other end they founded Gadir (Cadiz). This was one of a number of trading posts they set up along the coast as well as inland. They shared their colonising presence with the Greeks who also set up trading posts such as Puerto Menestheo (Puerto de Santa Maria), just across the bay from their rivals. Between them these two civilisations had a tremendous impact on the whole southern region of the peninsula. They were probably

responsible for the introduction of vines and olives to this area which, even today, depends heavily on both.

After Tyre fell to the Assyrians the Phoenician colonies were taken over by the Carthaginians who were far more ambitious than their predecessors. They were not content just to do business with Tartessus. They wanted it all and they took it. The State of Tartessus vanished from history like the legendary city of Atlantis. Despite the exploits of such familiar heroes as Hannibal and his famous elephants, the Carthaginians themselves were finally ousted by their longstanding enemies the Romans who drove them out of their last stronghold, Cadiz, in the year 206BC. Cadiz then became part of the Roman province called Baetica which covered the whole southern part of Spain and developed into the most culturally advanced part of the peninsula.

The tides of invasion

In the early part of the fifth century AD Barbarian tribes from the north began to invade the Iberian peninsula and Baetica was taken over by the Vandals from whom Andalusia took its name. Some years later the Visigoths, a Germanic people, took over most of Spain, driving the Vandals across the Straits of Gibraltar into North Africa. Towards the end of the seventh century the Visigothic monarchy started down a rather slippery road that was eventually to lead to the Islamic state of Al-andalus on Spanish soil.

The power struggles within the Visigothic empire reached the point of civil war when Roderick, Duke of Baetica, was acclaimed king instead of the rightful heir. The family of the latter sought help from the Muslims of North Africa who landed at Gibraltar in 711AD. They killed Roderick, defeated his army and went on to take over most of Spain. They stayed for over five centuries, a point not to be overlooked when considering the background of present-day Andalusians.

It was in the thirteenth century that the reconquest of this region by Christian troops from the north began in the Guadalquivir valley. The history of the province of Cadiz in this period is one of constant battles and uprisings. Towns fell to the Christians, were recaptured by the Moors, fell again to the Christians and so it went on until, one presumes, 'Divine Providence' decided whose side she was on and the Christians finally stood their ground. Many towns and villages in the province have the words *de la frontera* tacked on to the end of their names, which means that they were important strategic footholds along the frontier between Christian and Muslim

Salt has been collected in evaporation pools like these ever since Phoenician days although some of the marshy areas formerly used for this purpose have now been turned over to more profitable use as fish farms.

kingdoms. Many of the castles to be found in various stages of ruin all over the province date from these times.

The American connection

The final conquest of Granada, the last Moorish stronghold, in 1492 coincided with Columbus's first voyage of discovery. Seville and the seaport of Sanlucar de Barrameda, along with Cadiz and Puerto de Santa Maria, became thriving towns and attracted seamen and adventurers, businessmen, bankers and ship-builders from all over Spain and abroad. This was the beginning of a Golden Age in which some of the wealth and splendours of Tartessus returned fleetingly to these lands.

Over the next three centuries, voyages of discovery, conquest and exploitation of the Americas continued to set sail from these shores, much to the delight of the pirates that infested these waters and despite frequent interruptions and setbacks such as the humiliating loss of Gibraltar in 1704. Although such episodes of war and natural disasters like the plague were never very far from the pages of local history, the eighteenth century was for many a time of prosperity and the nineteenth appeared to be full of promise.

The Columbus saga

Few historical figures can claim such universal recognition as does that of the man we know as Christopher Columbus, 'discoverer of America', and few have been as controversial. In Spain he is known as Cristobal Colón but nobody is entirely sure who he was or where he came from. The most widely accepted version is that he originally came from Genova in Italy where he was born around 1451 and christened with the name of Christóforo Colombo. It is thought that he arrived in Spain from Portugal in the year 1485 and in 1488 he met the Duke of Medinacelli, lord of El Puerto de Santa Maria, who became his protector. Columbus lived in El Puerto as a guest in the Medinacelli palace between 1490 and 1491 and Medinacelli himself was so taken by his fantastic project that he wanted to sponsor the whole expedition himself. The Queen, however, intervened and invited Columbus to live at Court until the project had been studied in detail. Finally, Columbus set sail from Palos in the province of Huelva on 3rd August, 1492. The best known of the three ships that set sail on this first and most famous of voyages was the *Santa Maria*, belonging to Juan de la Cosa who lived in Puerto de Santa Maria. It was shipwrecked on the coast of Haiti on the 25th of December of that same year, after the initial discovery of the New World on October 12th. Columbus's second expedition set sail from the port of Cadiz in 1493 and the third sailed from Sanlucar de Barrameda in 1498, although on this occasion the departure was delayed because his crew all nipped off across the river to Doñana to go on the pilgrimage to El Rocio and refused to set sail until they had paid their respects to this most famous of Virgins! In 1502 Columbus sailed once again from the port of Cadiz on his fourth and final voyage during which he discovered the coast of what we now know as central America from Honduras to Panama, though Columbus himself still believed he was in Asia. After being shipwrecked on the coast of Jamaica he managed to return to the port of Sanlucar de Barrameda in 1504, the same year that his protector, Queen Isabel, died. Columbus himself died two years later at the age of 55.

Defeat and disillusionment

Hopes were short lived however. In 1805 the joint Franco-Spanish fleet sailed from Cadiz to meet its doom at the hands of Admiral Nelson. Those for whom Trafalgar was just the name of a famous square in London or a date in a tedious history book, can stand on the windswept shores of Cape Trafalgar and imagine the scene of smoke, flames and drowning men as others must have watched in fear and desperation a century and a half ago.

As shame and debris washed up along the coasts of Cadiz another war was brewing on northern horizons. The year 1808 saw the beginning of the War of Independence in which the French took over practically all of Spain with the exception of the town of Cadiz. For two and a half years Cadiz on its little island withstood the whole might of the Napoleonic forces which directed the siege from their base in Puerto de Santa Maria. The town became a symbol of freedom and in 1811 the Spanish Parliament, Las Cortes, was moved to safety there. In 1812 in this town under siege the first Spanish constitution was written and proclaimed.

The War of Independence left Andalusia weak and financially ruined. Meanwhile, the Spanish colonies in America had been making moves towards independence. In 1890, as a result of the war against the United States, the last Spanish colonies, Cuba, Puerto Rico and the Philippines, were lost. The twentieth century was ushered in under a cloud of gloom and disillusionment. The province of Cadiz which had lived the American adventure so intensely, which had seen such glittering wealth pass through its hands, looked around to discover that the only constant that remained after all those years was the poverty of the common people.

The early twentieth century was a period of acute political instability. The tremendous social injustices that existed, especially in the rural areas, gave rise to strong workers' movements and anarchist riots and turmoil. The year 1923 saw the coup and military dictatorship of Miguel Primo de Rivera, a Jerezano by birth, but the General resigned in 1930 having done little to solve the problems. The Republic declared in 1931 was greeted with optimism by many but political division and confusion still held sway. In the February elections of 1936 the left-wing Popular Front won a large majority.

Forty long, slow years

After these elections an army general named Francisco Franco Bahamonde was posted to the Canary Islands from where he joined in the preparations that were underway for a military insurrection. His mission was to lead the uprisen African army from Tetuan. Algeciras and Cadiz were two of the most important landing points for troops coming over from North Africa. To the local inhabitants, unable to put up any effective resistance, that 18th of July must have seemed like a twentieth-century re-enactment of the Moorish invasion. Cadiz did not therefore go through the trauma of the Civil War itself, being as it was one of the very first places in which the military coup triumphed. It did however suffer severe repression since Cadiz and its province were strongholds of the left-wing parties and labour unions. The general in charge of troops in Cadiz declared publicly that they would not leave a single republican or anyone who even smelled of left-wing alive. The fury of executions and imprisonments that followed show that his sense of smell must have been acute indeed.

Salute or run for the loo!

During the first six months after the outbreak of the Spanish civil war, thousands of people were imprisoned, tortured or executed. After that, the situation calmed down somewhat but life could still be very hazardous. The local prisons were so full of 'political' prisoners that the only way they could sleep was if everybody lay on his side. Some of the older locals still tell of one of the less dramatic dangers of living under the fascist régime. If you were walking down the street and happened to bump into a group of radical falangists, you were expected to hail them with that well-known raised arm salute. Anyone reluctant to do so was dragged off to the local headquarters and made to drink a large glass of castor oil before being turned out onto the street again. This treatment invariably had an immediate and embarrassing effect on the bowels, often before the unfortunate victim could reach a convenient loo!

The Civil War finally ended in 1939 with Franco as head of State. His dictatorship lasted until his death in 1975. The postwar years here in Cadiz were marked by desperate social conditions. Many who escaped the mass executions along the roadways and in the cemeteries died of starvation, whilst cargoes of foodstuffs could be seen in the Cadiz dockyards awaiting transport to Germany to supply Hitler's troops. The first rays of light came in the 1950s with the signing of the Spanish-American defence and trade agreement, which was followed by investment in Spanish industry and the beginning of the tourist boom. The most immediate result for the province of Cadiz was the building of the large Spanish/American naval base at Rota.

Rebirth of a nation

Franco's successor was King Juan Carlos and in June 1977 the first general elections in 40 years were held. The newborn democracy was very shaky on its feet until the general elections of 1982, in which the Socialist party under Felipe Gonzalez won an overwhelming majority. In the years of the transition King Juan Carlos proved himself to be an invaluable defender of democracy and the Spanish constitution and has become a much respected figure both in Spain and throughout the world.

*The penitents of Holy Week are nothing if not sinister... though for
many, as for this youngster, it may just be another game of dressing
up. (Photos courtesy of the Ayuntamiento de Jerez de la Frontera)*

Ferias and fiestas

The yearly cycle

December 24th (known here as **Noche Buena**), whilst marking with its warming glow the closing of the year, is also the starting point of the cycle of *ferias* and *fiestas* that are so very important a part of life in Andalusia. It is a gentle start that gets the ball rolling smoothly before tipping over the New Year into Carnival, Holy Week and Feria and sweeping right on through the summer until the autumn rains finally manage to put a damper on people's spirits – though never for long. These community celebrations are very much an expression of character. Superstition, sense of humour, earnest and often oppressive religious feeling, recklessness, gaiety, rivalry, loyalty, pride – all these intermingle in a curiously cohesive blend. The essence of carnival somehow creeps into everything to a greater or lesser extent as ancient pagan rites parade in their 'Christian' guises and people dress up, whether in carnival costumes, penitent's robes or the bright and flouncy flamenco dresses in fervent veneration of the gods or in impassioned celebration of life in spite of them.

Noche Buena is a quiet, family affair, one of the few festivities restricted to the home as families dine together on turkey and *turron* (nougat of many different varieties and flavours eaten especially at this time of year). Little marzipan figures, crumbly *polvorones*, honey coated *pestiños* and a variety of other sweet temptations are handed round the table in front of the television as the King makes his yearly speech and the soporific effect of over-indulgence sets in for some, whilst others prepare to go off to midnight mass. The following day, December 25th, is something of a non-event.

Parties known as *cotillones* are organised on **New Year's Eve** to welcome the coming year in bars, restaurants and discotheques. The champagne flows and out come silly party hats, plastic noses and *matasuegras*, those rolled up paper serpents you blow into. *Matasuegra* literally means mother-in-law killer! At the stroke of midnight one is supposed to eat twelve grapes, one with each chime of the clock – not an easy feat by any means!

The New Year never quite feels new, however, until you get past **Epiphany** on the 6th of January, which is, especially for the children, the most important date of this festive season. On the evening of the 5th many towns hold a parade of the so-called Three Kings and their entourage, who throw sweets to people lining the streets. It is traditionally they who leave presents for the children during the night. Then on the 6th, the Day of the Kings, everyone dresses up in their Sunday best and goes for a stroll in the parks and squares to give the children a chance to show off their new toys.

February fun

February does away with any lingering winter gloom with the explosive celebration of **Carnival**. In the past Carnival was related to the strict religious observance of Lent – a sort of last fling before fasting. Nowadays people are still very willing to have their fling but few remember the connection with the fasts and sacrifices of Lent. It must be said that Carnival here is not the same sort of wild extravaganza seen in other parts of the world. It is very much a family affair, a time when everyone gets together to do something different and have as much fun as possible. It is one of the most popular of all the year's festivities and one of the few in which the church plays no part.

Carnival is celebrated in many parts of the province but the best known are the ones held in Trebujena and Cadiz. The former is the best example of a country Carnival where the whole village turns out in fancy dress and the streets ring with the voices of the *murgas*, groups of singers, sometimes whole families complete with children, who go round the streets singing the kind of satirical songs so typical of Carnival. The songs allude to people and events that all are familiar with, the treatment given to each one depending to a large extent on what social class the singers belong to. The climax of the Trebujena Carnival comes with the burning of a figure known as 'Piti the Witch', thus marking the end of Carnival and the beginning of Lent.

Both in Trebujena and Cadiz Carnival is officially opened with a public announcement made by some well known figure of the Arts. The Carnival Queen is chosen and crowned, ready to take her place in the Sunday parade. In these and other towns Carnival is also preceded by an important song contest in which the different songs that will later be sung in the streets are heard in public for the first time. The four main musical groups are choirs, quartets, *comparsas* and *chirigotas*, the latter two being the most popular. Songs can be a kind of pot-pourri of well known songs of the past year, with different words, or original compositions within a very particular framework. They tend to have a quick marching rhythm and those who have an ear for such things may hear certain Afro-Cuban influences and samba rhythms. As with the *murgas* of Trebujena, the importance of the songs lies in the words – witty, satirical comments on outstanding people and events of the past year. Puns and allusions abound and it is difficult for the outsider to catch even the words, let alone their implications.

Carnival in the city of Cadiz dates from the fifteenth and sixteenth centuries, when large numbers of Italians took up residence there because of its connections with the New World. They brought with them much of their own lifestyle and, consequently, their own fiestas. In 1937 the Franco regime abolished Carnival in an effort to please the upper classes who were usually criticised and ridiculed during the celebrations. The Carnival proper was not reinstated until 1977, since which date it has also been revived in other towns of the province such as Puerto de Santa Maria. Now the Carnival in Cadiz lasts for ten days and a great many different activities are organised. During the last few days of Carnival, people throng the streets in fancy dress, throw confetti and paper streamers about and hit people on the head with squeaky plastic hammers! The *comparsas* and *chirigotas*, each group dressed in its own particular fancy dress, perform in the streets throughout the week. Even if you do not manage to catch any of the words you can sense their impact very strongly as the crowds laugh, cheer, whistle and applaud.

The end of Carnival in Cadiz is usually marked by a firework display in one part of the town and the breaking open of *piñatas* in two different squares in the old part of the town. The *piñatas* are huge pots suspended over the square filled with sweets and other surprises. In yet another square the celebrations reach a climax with the burning of the god Momo, a god taken from Greek mythology as the personification of jeering, criticism and sarcasm.

Penitence and pageantry

The next important event on the calendar is Easter, known here as **Semana Santa** or Holy Week. This is the most extravagant and the most solemn of the year's religious celebrations and although for many people it is just another holiday, the week is very much dominated by the religious processions. Throughout the week statues of Christ in varying postures of agony are taken in slow procession through the streets on special platforms, followed always by a sedate and elegant 'Virgin Mother', surrounded by candles and dressed in the richest of robes. These platforms are carried on the shoulders of men belonging to or recruited by the various fraternities. These fraternities are associations of devotees of a particular statue and they take charge of the statue's worship and all the celebrations held in its honour. There is often tremendous rivalry between fraternities, especially in the smaller villages such as Setenil de las Bodegas, where there are only two. The village can become completely divided, each fraternity trying to outdo the other in the magnificence of its processions. For this reason Setenil's Holy Week is one of the most colourful in the province.

The heavy platforms are manoeuvered with great skill in and out of the churches, up and down ramps and are often made to 'dance' in a swinging motion at some crucial point along the route. Otherwise the procession advances slowly to the beat of a drum, accompanied by penitents dressed in robes that inevitably remind you of the Ku Klux Klan. Wax from the large candles they carry drips onto the streets, which is why the wheels of your car may screech around corners for some time after Holy Week. Some of the penitents go barefoot or even on their knees, carrying crosses or dragging chains. As the processions go by, individuals from amongst the crowds lining the streets may sing *saetas*, which are short, fervent prayers, usually in praise of the Virgin, often spontaneous, sung in those harsh and tragic-sounding flamenco voices. In Arcos de la Frontera the processions are also accompanied by men dressed up as Roman soldiers. Many of the year's celebrations contain some grotesque and morbid elements but they are perhaps most striking in Holy Week.

Easter Sunday in many towns is more or less ignored and in others it is celebrated by far more obviously profane rituals. Many years ago, in some towns and villages people used to celebrate the macabre 'burning of Judas' in which a rag doll representing Judas Iscariot was made to pay, as it were, for the sins of the people and was hanged and then burnt in an attempt to destroy any evil that might be threatening the course of local events. In other villages 'Judas' was torn to pieces on the horns of a bull. Nowadays Easter Sunday is celebrated in some small towns by running bulls through the streets. The origins of these fiestas are similar to those involving 'Judas'. In this case the bull represented the evil but instead of destroying it, the people fled from it. The end result was the same, however, as the bull ended up being slaughtered anyway.

There are variations within the common theme of bull-running. Sometimes several bulls are run together through streets barricaded off for the purpose. People run in front of the bulls as far as the bull ring where the smaller ones are teased and played around with until they tire. The runners are mostly only men but a few women are starting to take part. This type of running is seen, for instance in the **Toro de la Cuerda**. A rope is tied around the horns of the bull and men run through the streets in front of it holding on to the rope. For them to drop the rope under any circumstance would, in former times, have been considered a public disgrace. The background to this type of celebration may be found in what used to be called the Toro Nupcial. In this wedding ritual, a rope was tied around the horns of the bull and the animal was led through the streets to the bride's door. There the bridegroom would stick *banderillas* into the bull's neck. The shedding of the bull's blood, with which the groom's clothes would be stained, was considered to represent the transference of the animal's sexual potency to the man (probably much to the dismay of the bride!). Somewhat less dramatic an explanation as to how the Toro de la Cuerda came to be celebrated is that at the turn of the century the practice was for a butcher to buy his stock outside of the town, tie a rope around the animal's horns and lead it through the town to his house, where the whole family would turn out to inspect the purchase. Many of the townspeople would follow him through the streets.

The Toro de la Cuerda is celebrated in several parts of the province on Easter Sunday or in ferias and fiestas. In other towns on similar dates the bull-running is known as a **Toro Embolao**. In this case the bull runs loose but has little leather bags or wooden balls put over the tips of the horns, or the tip of the horn may be cut off in an attempt to minimise the damage should an accident occur. When you hear a rocket go off you know that the bull is on its way.

As bulls are used in one way of another in so many of the ferias and fiestas throughout the province, it should perhaps be said at this point that these bulls can maim and kill and have done so on many occasions. Even if very small bulls are used, they can still do damage. Whilst certain precautions are taken for the runners' safety, a minimum of common sense is required. So unless you are still fairly sober, well able to run with a jostling crowd of youngsters, shin up lamp posts and leap tall buildings at a single bound, you would be foolish to try it. In 1986, for instance, two Americans were seriously injured in the bull running at Arcos de la Frontera whilst trying to get close up shots of the bull. The local papers politely described their behaviour as '*imprudente*'.

The frenzy of Feria

As soon as Holy Week is over the shop windows start to fill up with colourful flamenco dresses, shawls and all the trappings of **Feria** as if to try and chase off the sombre memory of the religious processions. The *ferias* originally started up around cattle markets. Buyers and sellers would camp around the market area to avoid too much coming and going from the town. Refreshment stalls were set up to cater for their needs and a good sale would be well and truly celebrated. The refreshment and celebrations side of things grew more and more each year until the cattle were more or less forgotten. Nowadays a *feria* consists of a fairground surrounded by streets lined with tents or booths of varying sizes where food and drink are served to the blaring sound of *sevillanas*, the music and dance typical of *ferias* in Andalusia. This is not strictly flamenco music or dance. It is the Andalusian variation of an ancient kind of Spanish song and dance called the *seguidilla*. It consists of four different movements and when danced properly it is supposed to represent the wooing of a young woman who dances with provocative movements and glances. What tends to happen at a *feria* though is that few men dance *sevillanas* well and even fewer dress up in the proper costume, so that on the whole you will see girls dancing together.

Each of the booths has a wooden platform to dance on and the main object of the *feria* is to drink and dance, day and night, defying sleep throughout the week. The booths are set up by bar owners, clubs, business associations and even the fraternities mentioned before in connection with Holy Week. You can walk past a booth with a name like 'Fraternity of the Afflicted Ones' and see how well they manage to forget their afflictions!

The Seville fair is the first one of the year after Holy Week. It is very well known and attracts famous people from all over Spain and abroad. Although this is the largest and most brilliantly splendid of all the *ferias* it is not really the best one for a foreigner to go to because it is a very exclusive affair. Parking is impossible and after walking a long distance to the fairground or waiting for hours for a taxi you will find that unless you have influential friends it will be very hard to join in the fun. The vast majority of the booths are private and you will probably have to get your refreshment from some seedy little side stall.

After Seville the *feria* moves on from town to town throughout the region. Within the province of Cadiz the best known fair is the Feria de Mayo or Feria del Caballo in Jerez. The latter name means Horse Fair and although you will see beautiful horses at many *ferias*, nowhere are they such a gorgeous sight as in Jerez, one of the most important horse breeding centres in Spain. Here again, true to the character of life in Jerez, the fair is a fairly elitist affair in that many of the booths are private too. You can get agencies to book everything for you to be able to spend the week in Jerez and get into all the various horse shows and events, which is probably the best way to go about it unless you already know the area well or have friends here. If you just want to join in the fun (although your ability to do so entirely will be limited by not knowing how to dance *sevillanas*), you would be best advised to go to one of the lesser known but equally representative fairs such as the ones held in Puerto de Santa Maria, Puerto Real, Rota or Sanlucar de Barrameda.

Feria is a vivid, noisy and frenzied affair, joyful on the surface but with tragic undertones. Armies of gipsy beggars follow the fairs from town to town pestering all comers to buy cigarettes or carnations or to give money for their sickly looking children. You can see a lot of poverty and desperation if you look beyond the swirling dancers and the bright lights of the fairground. The smaller the town, the more homely its *feria* and the more likely you are to feel welcome, though in the small mountain villages you may still be something of a novelty. A word of advice; do not wear your best shoes to a feria, they will get ruined; and ladies, do not drink too much liquid as finding a place to get rid of it can sometimes be embarrassingly difficult.

Saints, virgins and other curiosities

The next fiesta is another religious one, the celebration of **Corpus Christi**. In the larger towns of the province it is now purely a solemn, religious occasion in which the Host, or communion wafer, is taken in procession through the streets placed in a monstrance, a sort of glass vessel surrounded by a sun symbol and said by Roman Catholics to be the eye of God. The monstrance is carried on elaborate platforms – one of these in the cathedral in Cadiz is made of solid silver and weighs 900 kilos. Children who have been confirmed during the year walk in front throwing petals. Civil and military authorities walk behind with the religious authorities and the whole event is more or less ignored by the majority of the population, although it is a good excuse to put on a new dress and go out for a drink to see and be seen.

In the smaller mountain villages Corpus Christi is a very different affair. The whole village takes part in the decoration of the streets and in the religious celebration itself. In Zahara de la Sierra, El Gastor and Algodonales, Corpus Christi is one of the high points of the year. In Zahara and El Gastor the walls of the houses along the processional route are completely covered by a tapestry of sedge, poplar and eucalyptus branches. The men of the village collect the branches and decorate the streets and walls with them whilst the women hang beautiful lacy cloths and richly embroidered shawls or bedspreads from the balconies and decorate the little altars placed at intervals along the route. In these rural areas the procession is followed by a *velada*, a sort of street party with dancing in the main village square. In El Gastor this is probably the best date to see and hear the fascinating little Gastorian pipes being played.

Another kind of community celebration with a religious background is the *romeria*, which is a pilgrimage to a local shrine. It is a day for the whole community to get out of their everyday surroundings and do something different. Groups of people travel together on gaily decorated horse-drawn carts (others use more modern forms of transport), and join together for a meal and some general merrymaking in the open air around the shrine. The pilgrimages are organised by the fraternities, though the participants do not necessarily look for any great religious significance in the outing.

Fraternities from Sanlucar, Jerez, Rota, Puerto de Santa Maria and Puerto Real take part each year in the **Romeria de Rocio de Almonte**, known more commonly as El Rocio. This is one of the largest and best known *romerias* in Spain, held in the neighbouring province of Huelva. On the Thursday before Pentecost, pilgrims from the province of Cadiz are ferried across the Guadalquivir river at Sanlucar to travel on horseback, in horse-drawn carts or on foot through the Coto Doñana nature reserve to the shrine of the Virgin of Rocio. Over a million people from as far away as Madrid and Granada gather once a year to worship this particular Virgin. Far from being a solemn occasion, it is a time for great merrymaking as the pilgrims sing and dance, eat and drink through the four days and nights of the *romeria*.

The province of Cadiz has plenty of its own *romerias*, though none on the scale of the Rocio. Many of the towns and villages have local shrines to which the people go once a year to venerate various statues. The three most important of these pilgrimages are held in September in Villamartin, Alcala de los Gazules and Tarifa. Perhaps one of the most curious is the one held in Algeciras on the 15th of August. The statue of this particular Virgin is kept in an underwater cave at a depth of 17m out in the bay. A group of people go out to the site in boats, dive to bring up the statue and take it to the Rinconcillo beach. There it is cleaned up and enthroned to be venerated before being taken back to its watery bed for another year. On 16th July the coastal towns and villages celebrate the day of the **Virgen del Carmen**, patron of seamen and fishermen. The statue is taken in procession to the port where it is enthroned in a fishing boat and then taken round the bay accompanied by all the local fishing fleet, the boats being lit up and adorned for the occasion and salvoes of rockets and fireworks being let off at various intervals. Like many of the other religious celebrations, the roots of this fiesta go back long before the advent of Christianity and are planted deeply in maritime superstition.

In the month of August, the little mountain village of Benamahoma celebrates a fiesta that is not at all typical of this part of Spain. It is the **Fiesta of the Moors and Christians**, which re-enacts the struggles between these two factions at the time of the Reconquest. The local patron saint, San Antonio, is taken in procession through the streets, escorted by villagers dressed to represent the Christians. Along the route, the procession is repeatedly attacked by villagers representing the Moors who try to kidnap the saint. The first day of the fiesta ends in victory for the Moors. On the second day the roles are reversed and the Christians are the ones who lie in wait to attack the procession in an attempt to rescue the saint. The performance ends in victory for the Christians and fatal defeat for the Moors. In most other places the fiesta ends with the Moors converting to Christianity but here in Benamahoma they die at the hands of the Christians.

180 days of festivities!

Apart from the **Fiestas Patronales** which each town or village celebrates in honour of its patron saints or virgins, there is also a series of fiestas geared particularly towards the tourist sector. These are celebrated at peak holiday times and are designed to extol the virtues of particular products of the land or sea that are essential to the local economy. Most of these fiestas are of relatively recent origin and in most cases visitors are invited to sample the local products that give the fiestas their names. The **Fiesta de la Vendimia** in Jerez, held at the time of the grape harvest, was begun in 1948 when the sherry firms were looking for new markets for their wines. Each year the festivities are dedicated to a different town or country where Jerez sherry is drunk. Celebrities from those places are invited as guests of the sherry firms.

Along the same lines the **Fiestas del Guadalquivir** were started in Sanlucar de Barrameda in 1955, the idea being to promote the town itself. The fiestas include various cultural events as well as a bull fight and culminate in a literary competition. Both of these fiestas are in many respects fiestas of high society, the majority of the events being by invitation only. The general public are at best spectators. There are, however, other fiestas of this kind in which the whole town or village takes part. Such are the **Fiesta del Moscatel**

Many of those who make the annual pilgrimmage to El Rocío in the month of June, cross the Guadalquivir at Sanlucar. Horses, carriages and pligrims, all colourfully dressed, are packed onto a couple of ramshackle old ferries and dropped on the other shore to make their way to the shrine for a week or so of devout merrymaking. (Photo by Catherine Cavanaugh)

(Muscatel wine), in Chipiona; the **Fiesta de la Urta** (a kind of fish) in Rota; the **Fiestas de Verano** (for holidaymakers) in El Bosque; and the **Fiestas del Caracol** (snails), **del Gazpacho** (special Andalusian soup) and **del Pimiento** (peppers) in Medina Sidonia.

There are many others besides all the fiestas and celebrations mentioned here; in fact altogether, the different towns and villages of Cadiz celebrate 180 days of festivities between them! So you cannot go for long in this part of Spain without hearing the word *fiesta*. It refers to any kind of celebration, from a private party in the home to a national holiday. It can also refer to the bullfight. Fiesta is more than just a word: it is as integral a part of life in Andalusia as daily bread. Most of the fiestas have a strong religious influence, mixed always with lively celebration. The Virgin Mary is the mother goddess whose favour is constantly sought, a direct descendant of the Phoenician goddess Astarte whose temple was built in Cadiz three thousand years ago. The votive offerings that may still be seen in certain shrines of the province, similar to those offered to Astarte, are proof that old beliefs die hard. But though gods and goddesses may have become saints and virgins, fiesta will always be fiesta.

Calendar of events

A complete calendar of all the local *ferias* and fiestas of the province would be very long and somewhat tedious. The following version gives the main events in their different locations by months. The exact dates vary from year to year in the same way that Easter does. A star marks the ferias or fiestas that are likely to be of most interest when several similar events coincide. In the Tourist Information Offices you can obtain a Calendar of Fiestas for the current year which will give you the exact dates. Otherwise, you should be able to get accurate local information from your hotel reception desk.

Date	Festivity	Location
January 1st	Toro del Aguardiente (bull running)	Puerto Serrano
February/ March	Carnival	Cadiz*, Trebujena*, Ubrique Pto. Sta.Maria, Barbate, La Linea, Chiclana, Bornos, Arcos, San Fernando and others
March/April	Holy Week	All towns
	Easter Sunday with bull running	Arcos de la Frontera* Paterna, Vejer*, Los Barrios Benamahoma
May/June	Feria	Jerez de la Frontera*, Vejer, Rota*, Pto.Sta.Maria*, Jimena, Olvera, Sanlucar, Conil, Medina, Puerto Real* etc
	Corpus Christi	El Gastor*, Algodonales, Zahara de la Sierra
June 23rd	San Juan Bonfires	Barbate, Chiclana, El Bosque, some quarters of Cadiz, Vejer
July	Fiestas and Ferias del Carmen (around 16th)	Barbate*, La Linea, Chipiona, San Fernando, Setenil, Conil*, Chiclana, Grazalema* and all coastal towns
	Toro de la Cuerda (3rd Monday in month)	Grazalema

Date	Festivity	Location
	Fiestas (with bull running)	Bornos
August	Fiestas del Moscatel	Chipiona
	Feria and fiestas	El Gastor, Grazalema*, Zahara de la Sierra, Setenil, San Roque, Jimena, El Bosque, Rota Medina Sidonia, and many more
	Fiesta of the Moors and Christians	Benamahoma
	Toro de la Cuerda	Benaocaz
September	Feria de la Vendimia	Jerez de la Frontera
	Ferias and fiestas	Jimena, Villaluenga, Chipiona, Tarifa, Conil, Ubrique, Villamartin, Arcos etc

July and August are the busiest months for fiestas as this is the time of year when the many emigrants who have had to leave their native villages to find work in the larger cities or abroad come home to visit families and friends. Many of the *ferias* and fiestas that were traditionally celebrated at other times of the year have been moved to these months especially for the homecoming emigrants.

The bull fight

An arrogant looking matador in his brilliant 'suit of lights', swirling a cape in front of a huge black bull, has long been one of the most typical images associated with Spain. Many people come to Spain with preconceived ideas about the bull fight and very little knowledge. It must be said first of all that this is not a national sport – football is the national sport here as in so many other countries. The bull fight is not a sport at all, in fact it is not even a fight; it has been described as the playing out of a tragedy in which all the exchanges and movements between the man and the bull are part of an ancient ritual. Space does not allow here to go into all the details of what goes on in a *corrida de toros* (bull fight) but if you decide to go and see one then the ideal thing would be to go with someone who knows enough about it to explain what is going on. If this is not possible then you really should take the trouble to read something about it

Bull-breeding ranches tend to be out of sight down roads or tracks with signs that warn you to beware of brave bulls. This beautifully kept ranch house is easily visible however from the main C440 road.

beforehand. Much has been written on the subject but Hemingway's *Death in the Afternoon* (published by Penguin) is possibly still 'the best book ever written on the subject'. Hemingway's Spain however is a far cry from the Spain of the 1990s. For a shorter but nevertheless excellent exposition, try chapter 13 of Nicholas Luard's book *Andalucia* (published by Century Publishing, London).

When it first charges into the ring a *toro bravo* or brave bull has never before encountered a human being on foot. It is a highly intelligent animal and charges at the cape only as long as the matador can make him think that that is the target. As soon as the bull discovers the man behind the cape he will do his utmost to kill him, which is why no more than twenty minutes elapse between the time the bull first comes into the ring and the time it is killed. These bulls are formidable animals and far more dangerous than most visitors imagine. They have been bred purely for their fighting instinct and raised for the sole purpose of dying in the ring. The initial piercing of the bull's massive neck muscle, done by a man on horseback called a picador, is done in order to weaken that muscle and force the animal to lower its head with those lethal horns, without which it would be totally unmanageable. The barbed darts or *banderillas* that are then stuck into the neck area are not just for show. In theory they are placed to help counteract any tendency the bull may have to hook to one side or the other though, in practice, the man is usually too busy staying alive to place them quite so scientifically. This and all the passes done with the cape serve the basic purpose of tiring the bull, weakening his neck and back muscles and slowing him down to the point where the matador can kill him with the sword. For this, the front legs need to be together so that there is a space between the shoulderblades for the sword to go straight to the heart. When done properly, the sword goes in quickly and smoothly and the bull dies on the spot. If the matador is afraid or cannot get the sword in past the shoulderblades and just keeps stabbing at the animal, then it is a painful slaughter. When both the bull and the matador are brave and give a quality performance on a hot sunny day with no wind, then to many people it can be an exciting and moving spectacle. If the bull or the matador (or both) are weak and cowardly, then it can be a very sickening spectacle.

Another kind of matador is the *rejoneador* who runs and kills the bull on horseback. In this case the skill of the horse and rider is matched against the massive fury of the bull and the graceful movements of the horse, whose legs and body come within inches of the bull's horns time and time again, can be a breathtaking sight.

The tourist offices will be able to tell you where to buy tickets for a *corrida*. The bullrings in Jerez and Puerto de Santa Maria are the two most important ones in the province. The ring is divided into two main areas: *sol* (sun) and *sombra* (shade). The seats in the shade are more expensive, as are the ones closest to the ring. These two main areas are then divided into sections called *tendidos*, some of which start off in the sun but get into shade as the evening wears on (a *corrida* usually starts at 6.00pm). If you have fair skin it is worth getting a seat in the shade or high up under the little roof because sitting for three hours or more in the hot Andalusian sun could put paid to your holiday. In any case it is best not to sit too close to the ring your first time; farther back you get a better overall view of what is going on.

When you see a bull fight, especially if it is a bad one, it will undoubtedly seem cruel; and although this cannot be justified it is worth considering the fact that the bull you see in the ring has lived all his life roaming freely over large expanses of pastureland and has had little contact with man. The price he pays for this free and tranquil existence is a chance to do the very thing he was raised for – to defend his territory to the death in a ritual that will last no more than twenty minutes. Many a battery-raised animal from neighbouring European countries might well envy him his lot. There are millions of Spaniards who have never been to a bull fight and have no intention of going. There are many who are actively against it. It is definitely a minority interest. Spaniards in general do not dote over animals in the way the British, for instance, tend to and there are many cases of cruelty to animals that have nothing to do with the bull fight. Perhaps the main difference between cruelty to animals here and cruelty to animals in other European countries is that the Spanish are more open about it. Whatever your opinion of the *corrida* may be, it is a matter that belongs to Spain. To a foreigner who comes here and criticises it as being barbaric or uncivilised, a Spaniard could well turn around and say that in the *corrida* it is at least the bull that dies and occasionally the matador but never the spectators.

Flamenco – fire in the veins

Flamenco music and dance is something very profoundly Andalusian and the province of Cadiz, particularly the gipsy quarter of Jerez de la Frontera, is where flamenco has many of its roots. But even if you go to the recently opened Andalusian Flamenco Centre in Jerez (see Chapter 10), you will be hard put to find a simple definition of what flamenco really is. The centre offers an audio-visual presentation describing (in Spanish only at the moment) something of the background of this musical art form but one of the most important things about it is its very spontaneity; it is something that seems to pour from a deep well-spring of emotions within the performer.

The more official history of flamenco covers a period of only about two hundred years though its roots probably go right back to the days of Tartessos. Certainly from Roman times there are historical records of the 'dancing girls of Gadir'. Both the Jews and the Moors had their particular influence on the development of this music but the people who have had the greatest influence upon it and who today provide the truest representation of it are the gipsies. For an outsider it can be hard to grasp the depth of feeling, the intensity of the performance but you may be able to feel and enjoy its changing rhythms and moods. In the words of the Foundation's presentation, flamenco is at once 'rebellious and submissive, superficial and profound', pouring from the heart of a race of people whose history has at many times been marked by persecution, rejection and incomprehension. It is a 'song of love and hatred, somewhere between hope and despair, between joy and pain, in the face of life and death'.

As in the case of the bull fight, it is best to go at first to a real flamenco show with someone who knows what is going on. Try the local tourist offices for where to go to hear and see flamenco shows but remember that if it is a show put on specially for tourists it is likely be a watered down variety of flamenco.

The Route Guide

The provincial tourist office suggests four specific routes by which to explore the province of Cadiz: the Route of the White Villages, the Route of the Fighting Bull, the Atlantic Route, and the Route of the Wines. Although you may not choose to follow these routes exactly, they do make a useful starting point by dividing the province into four main areas. Part Two also contains a section on Gibraltar and the Mediterranean Coast.

With each town or village there is a list of places to stay and places to eat. These lists are not meant to be fully comprehensive or exclusive. The author has obviously not eaten in every restaurant in the province and those mentioned are simply suggestions. Where you stay and where you eat will depend very much on your own personal tastes and on your budget.

SEVEN

The route of the White Villages

This is perhaps the most picturesque of all the routes, starting at Arcos de la Frontera and taking in all the mountain villages in the north eastern part of the province. They are too many to explore in one day. You can make several easy day trips or spend two or three days in the area with overnight stops in Arcos, El Bosque, Grazalema, Zahara or Olvera. Whilst you are in the area you might like to do a slightly longer trip to Ronda, just over the border in Malaga, taking in some of the white villages on the way. Remember to start out with a full tank of petrol since filling stations are not always easy to find in these parts.

If you do not have a car at your disposal it is still possible to explore the white villages by bus, although you will need more time. The tourist information offices should be able to give you details of bus routes, and travel agencies will have information about special trips to the mountain villages. The main terminal for buses to this part of the province is the bus station in Jerez de la Frontera.

The gateway to this route is Arcos de la Frontera, also one of the most appealing little towns in the province.

Arcos de la Frontera

Driving along the N342 from Jerez, you begin to catch glimpses of Arcos in the distance; a cluster of houses, a castle and church towers, perched on top of a great rock, two sides of which are sheer cliff. The river Guadalete meanders peacefully past the foot of this yellowish coloured rock that has been inhabited from time immemorial. Legend has it that the town was founded by one of Noah's grandsons. The Romans had a settlement here and it was later the capital of a small Moorish Kingdom until it was finally reconquered in 1264. It then became one of the most important Christian strongholds in the region and its defensive walls, towers and fortress date from this period.

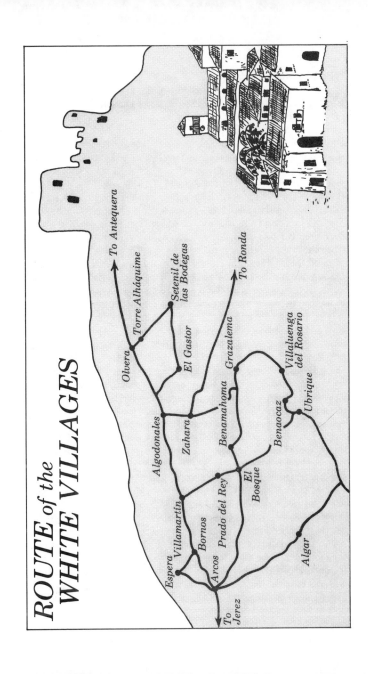

ROUTE of the WHITE VILLAGES

To Antequera

To Ronda

Torre Alháquime

Setenil de
las Bodegas

Olvera

El Gastor

Grazalema

Villaluenga
del Rosario

Algodonales

Zahara

Benamahoma

Ubrique

Benaocaz

Villamartín

Bornos

Prado del Rey

El
Bosque

Espera

Arcos

Algar

To
Jerez

What to see

You can drive through the lower part of the town and up some very narrow streets to the Plaza de España at the top. There is very little room for cars up here, so you may prefer to park at the bottom and exercise your leg muscles a little.

Parador: This state run hotel in a traditionally styled building is situated on one side of the square (Plaza de España); cool and peaceful, it is perched right on the edge of the cliff and is a good place to stop for a drink whilst enjoying the view.

Balcony: This square at the top of the town has the Parador on one side, the Town Hall and castle on another and the church on another. The fourth side of the square is a balcony on the edge of the cliff overlooking the River Guadalete, a superb view over the countryside.

Church: After a refreshment in the Parador it is worth making the extra effort to climb up the steep stairs of the bell tower of the Santa Maria church. This church is in the same square and to climb up inside the tower you go in through a small wooden door and climb up to the rooms where the caretaker lives. The caretaker is an elderly lady who gives the impression of being almost blind and very frail. However, she is not bothered about people going past and on up to the bell tower since they find themselves with a locked door at the top. She will bargain a good tip out of you before handing over the key – 100 pesetas per person should keep her happy – and while you are puffing your way up to the top and wondering how on earth she can manage with such steep stairs, she may well nip off down to get the milk on those deceptively elderly legs. Once you have the key, you can then carry on up the steps, past the ancient clock, coming out at the top where the huge bells hang, to contemplate a view even more commanding than the one from the cliff edge in the square below. These bells were amongst the first cast in Spain together with some others to be found in Toledo.

Castle: The best view of the castle is from a distance as you approach the town or from high up in the church bell tower. The castle is privately owned and not open to the public. It was rebuilt in 1430 and has been repaired fairly recently by the owners. Roman remains have been found in the foundations, including fragments of clay pitchers used to export olive oil to Rome. Local guides will tell you that it was bought for 30,000 pesetas at the turn of the century. Apparently it was once open to the public but things went missing and the experience was not repeated. The entrance is next to the Town Hall, up a little passageway but unfortunately you cannot go inside. A little way down the hill there is a bar called Al Caravan in what used to be the dungeons of the castle. Try the tapas there, they are good!

Guides: In the square you may be approached by somebody offering to guide you around the town. We were once approached by a seven-year-old boy who gave us a potted history of Arcos in verse as we walked. It was delivered at an incredible speed and addressed, apparently, to his feet. We were also followed about by a little gypsy girl who enquired in an innocent but insistent manner whether we had any dollars for her 'collection'.

Saint Peter, 'Mother of God'

One of the most farcical examples of religious rivalry on record has to be the dispute between the church of Saint Mary and the church of Saint Peter in Arcos de la Frontera. The dispute began in the mid sixteenth century when the church of Saint Mary was designated as the main parish church. The members of Saint Peter's were so put out by this that, in their responses to the litany, they would say the words 'Saint Peter, Mother of God' in order not to have to pronounce the name of the rival church!

The town: If you leave the main square and wander around this higher part of the town, past the other important and one time rival church of San Pedro, you will come to a sort of stone balcony which is another good vantage point from which to look out over the roof tops towards the Lago de Arcos, a small reservoir. Some well-meaning local may well point out an ancient sun clock high up on the wall of San Pedro but all you can see is a metal arrow stuck out at right angles to the wall. Your wanderings will also take you past some gorgeous patios and the openings to some very narrow streets that fall away so steeply as to give you the impression that by taking a step straight forward you could walk out into that wonderful Andalusian sky. You may also notice along one of the roads leading down from the town towards the lake some curious wooden doors set straight into the hillside. These are in fact the doors to cave dwellings, some of which are apparently still used.

The lake: You can reach the lake by taking the road to El Bosque and turning left into a somewhat dilapidated but not unattractive residential area called El Santiscal. Here there are apartments to rent, a camp site, hostal and *mesón*. You can practise windsurfing and canoeing on the lake if you have your own equipment and there is a funny little paddle boat known as the *Missispi* which does trips around the lake from the Mesón la Molinera in the summer and on Sundays and holidays during the rest of the year if the weather is fine.

There is a modest sailing club for people who have their own boats.

Local crafts: Near the Hotel El Convento in the high part of the town there is a shop that sells crafted rugs and carpets. This shop also has catalogues of the carpets made by a local factory. These are not hand crafted but the designs are original and the small company that produces and markets these carpets is called Naqsh, a Persian word that means 'design'. The carpets are made on mechanical looms but it is the personal touch of the craftsman working the loom that controls the colours and the design.

Wines: Both red and white table wines are produced in a local *bodega* and sold throughout the region. You will be able to sample these wines in most bars and restaurants in the province and if you like you can visit the *bodega* called La Vicaría. To find it, drive out of Arcos across the iron bridge over the Guadalete and when you come to a fork in the road, take the right hand road which leads to the Guadalcacín reservoir. Groups should telephone the head offices in Jerez to arrange a visit (Tel: 341265/343932) but if there are just two or three of you there should not be any problem about showing up at the *bodega* and asking to look around.

Accommodation

- Central

Parador Nacional Casa del Corregidor 3-star. Plaza de España. Tel: 700500. A traditionally Andalusian style building which has recently been renovated. DR 11,000–13,000 pesetas.

Hotel los Olivos 3-star. San Miguel 2. Tel: 700811. Small but attractive and comfortable, on the hillside as you go up towards the centre of town. DR 6050–7700 pesetas.

Hotel El Convento 1-star. Maldonado 2. Tel: 702333. Just two minutes walk from the square at the top of the town, this hotel is very small, only eight rooms, each with its own bathroom and balcony, but it has a homely sort of atmosphere. DR 5000-7000 pesetas.

- Outskirts

Cortijo Fain 3-star. On the road to Algar about 3km out of Arcos, this is a beautiful and luxurious seventeenth-century country house, set in a large olive grove with fireplaces in all the rooms, an attractive dining area and a swimming pool in the gardens. Highly recommendable for a genuine Andalusian setting in quiet and comfort. Tel: 701167. DR 20,000 pesetas.

Hotel el Lago 2-star. On the road to Ronda just at the turning off to

El Bosque. Tel: 701117. Recently refurbished and converted into a hotel with its own restaurant. Views over the Arcos reservoir. DR 7600-8600 pesetas.

Mesón La Molinera 2-star. In El Santiscal residential area by the lake with some little bungalow type rooms available by the lakeside. Take the road to El Bosque to get to El Santiscal. Tel: 700511. DR 4500 pesetas.

Hostal Voy-Voy 1-star. Avenida Ponce de Leon 9. This is the main road that skirts the town heading for Ronda. Tel: 701412. DR 5000 pesetas.

Hostal Malaga 1-star. Avenida Ponce de Leon. DR 3500-5500 pesetas.

• Camp site

Camping Arcos 1st class. In El Santiscal residential area near the lake. Newly planted trees. Capacity for 500 people. Cafeteria, bar and supermarket and all the usual facilities of a first class site. Open all year. Tel: 700514. Prices (a) 1555 pesetas, (b) 1035 pesetas.

Where to eat

Of the above hotels the Parador Nacional, the Hotel El Lago and Cortijo Fain each have a three fork restaurant while the Mesón la Molinera has a two fork restaurant. Probably the best known restaurant in the town is **El Convento**, formerly in the hotel of the same name but now in a new home of its own, a sixteenth-century mansion in the Calle Marques de Torresoto, very close to the square at the top of the town. This restaurant is not cheap but it is very good and it has won an important International Award to the Tourist and Hotel Industry for its typical Arcos cuisine.

Some other eating places are: Venta Pajuelo on the road to El Bosque; Meson El Brigadier, on the road to El Santiscal; Venta de Revertito near the crossroads on the road to El Bosque; El Kanguro Andaluz Carretera El Romeral km4.

There are several other bars, restaurants and *ventas* in and around the town, such as the Venta del Serrador in Junta de los Rios, 7km from Arcos, which has a play area for children. The local tourist office has a complete list of eating places within the town.

Algar

You can take several roads out of Arcos but the one to Algar is particularly scenic. It gradually becomes narrower and more and more twisty as you wind up and down and finally upwards again into this tiny village which appears at first to consist of just one street. Its full name is Santa Maria de Guadalupe de Algar and it was founded by a man from Jerez who had made his fortune in Mexico. On returning from Mexico with all his accumulated wealth, his ship was caught in a terrible storm. He prayed to the Virgin of Guadalupe, patron of Mexico, promising to found a town in her honour in the heart of the Sierra of Cadiz where the sea could never reach, if she would only spare his life and his fortune. When he got safely home he bought the land, divided it amongst local people and the town itself was founded in 1773. The lands are no longer well distributed; when the local people sold their lands in the past it all came into the hands of a few wealthy landowners. Nowadays there is very little work for the villagers who sometimes resort to poaching on the private game reserves. Collecting wild asparagus is another means of earning a few extra pesetas. When the landowners organise a hunt they employ beaters and it is still possible to hire a man and his dog or a man, dog and mule, as the lords of the land did back in the Middle Ages.

Algar is like an island in the mountains and is so quiet and peaceful, you can hear the birds singing in the main street. It is looking more prosperous lately and is well worth having a stroll around. It could be a good centre for tourism if the roads were improved. The nearby reservoir would be a good place for watersports but at the moment the road from Algar stops two kilometres short of it. There is one hostal here and you can camp in an area next to the municipal swimming pool. It could make a pleasant stop for cyclists or back-packers who are looking for quiet, out of the way places.

Espera

If you leave Arcos on the main N342 to Bornos, you can take a left turn onto the C343 to visit the little village of Espera. In the spring this road, like most roads in the province, is bordered by masses of brightly coloured wild flowers and you can see the village from a distance, crowded onto a little hill that rises above the gently rolling farmland round about. There is not much to do or see in Espera but it is worth climbing up the steep pathway to the half-ruined castle, el Castillo de Fatetar. From here you get a tremendous view and the peace and quiet is striking as the sounds of people working and the cries of children playing come to you clearly over the still, clear air. You can wander around the ruins of the castle but be careful, especially if you have children with you, as one part of the castle that still remains is a water cistern carved out of the rock; there are some gaping holes and plenty of loose stones about. Next to the castle is a shrine with a large iron door. Carrying its statue up and down this steep hill in one of the typical processions must certainly require a great deal of devotion.

As you walk down the steep, narrow streets past little red-tiled houses all piled on top of each other, you will probably see a lot of people just hanging around with nothing much to do, a typical sight in these rural areas where there is so little work; an area where donkeys and mules are still vital as beasts of burden and where time seems to pass so slowly.

The village has one pension which also serves food and a few other bars where you can sample the local cuisine.

Bornos

If, after leaving Arcos, you continue along the N342 road, the first little town you will come to is Bornos, spread out on the eastern slopes of a low range of hills. It commands a beautiful view over a large reservoir with the mountains in the background. You can enjoy windsurfing, canoeing and fishing here, with your own equipment, and there is an area near the lake where you may camp.

Bornos is another peaceful white village which depends largely on agriculture. The main point of interest in the town is the Palacio de las Ribera, a fortified palace with part of the original watch-tower and the chapel still intact. It has a cloistered patio and some beautiful and well kept gardens open to the public and in the first half of August it becomes the setting for a flamenco festival known as the Berza Flamenca. In fact, if you want to sample a tasty Andalusian *berza*, Bornos is a good place to do so.

Accommodation and restaurants
There is a two-star hostal called **Hostal Bornos**, Avenida San Jeronimo. Tel: 712289. DR 4500-5000 pesetas.

The modest dwellings of the quiet village of Bornos enjoy one of the richest views in the area on a clear blue day, across the lake to the distinctive shapes of the mountains beyond.

There are also some smaller pensions.

There are several bars where you can try the local dishes such as *berza*; try the Venta la Alegria on the main N432, the Bar Central, Bar Avenida, Mesón la Fragua or the Venta El Pinar.

Villamartín

The next town you come to on the N342 is Villamartín, founded in 1503 by people from other villages in the area who came here to these flatter lands to sow cotton. It is still very much an agricultural community although it has the curious distinction of being the place where Spain's first oil field was discovered. In 1918 a British company came to make the first perforations. They opened up a well and installed a derrick but an accident killed several people and the project was abandoned. Later, a German company came to investigate the possibilities and extracted some of the oil but then they too abandoned the idea.

In the Sierra de Pajarete, near the shrine of the Virgen de la Montaña on the road to Prado del Rey, are the ruins of the Castle of Matrera and also some Roman and Moorish ruins, though nothing very spectacular. The town itself is typical of the white villages with some attractive corners that can be better appreciated by wandering around the town on foot. Local craftwork includes some leatherwork and hand made saddles and harnesses. Villamartín also boasts one of the largest dicotheques in the province.

Accommodation
Hostal Izlu 1-star. Generalisimo Franco 43. Tel: 730280. DR 2400–2800 pesetas.
Hostal Nuestra Señora del Pilar Pasaje del Ambulatorio. Tel: 730427. Also has restaurant and public swimming pool.

Where to eat
Restaurante Montegloria On main Jerez road. Tel: 730895. Closes Mondays and 1st–10th June. Specialises in lamb and small game.
   Other eating places are Restaurante Bar Andaluz and Restaurante Bar Parada. There are plenty more bars within the town that serve tapas and meals.

Algodonales

Carrying on along the N342 you come to the village of Algodonales, another agricultural community dating from the sixteenth century. Its most prosperous period was after the Civil War when tobacco was rationed. The village devoted itself wholeheartedly to growing tobacco which was sold on the black market on a scale comparable to that of the tobacco smuggled from Gibraltar – in fact the village earned itself the nickname of *el pequeño* Gibraltar (little Gibraltar), until the fifties when the authorities clamped down on such activities.
   The main thing worth seeing in Algodonales is a little known guitar factory in a back street called Avenida Carrero Blanco. From the town's main square a narrow street leads downhill through an archway and brings you close to this workshop where a man called Valeriano Bernal and his wife make flamenco and classical guitars by hand which they sell to professionals all over Europe, particularly in Belgium and Germany. They also sell guitars to Japan and the United States but, incredibly, they are virtually unknown here in the province, except to those intimately involved in the flamenco world. One of their guitars takes about three months to make and can cost between 50,000 and 250,000 pesetas. They also make another instrument called a *bandurria*.
   Algodonales is also becoming a popular centre for people who enjoy hang-gliding and parascending. National championships of both these sports are held here and it is common to see bright spots of colour high

in the sky over the village as parascenders launch themselves from a special area up on the Sierra de Lijar (see Chapter Four).

Accommodation

The new **Hostal Sierra de Lijar** can be found in the street leading down through the archway off the main square and it is simple but attractive with a bar and restaurant. Address: Ronda 5. Tel: 137065. DR 3000 pesetas.

Where to eat

There are several bars and *ventas* apart from the Hostal Sierra de Lijar where you can try the local dishes such as gazpacho and vegetable stews known as *cocido*, or asparagus dishes: **Bar Los Amigos**, **Venta el Tikutin**, **Venta El Cortijo**, **Venta La Cueva**.

Olvera

The last town you come to on the N342 before reaching the province of Malaga is Olvera. It is typical of the white villages, one of the more picturesque ones with its appealing little semi-ruined castle perched high up on a rock, overlooking the town in a friendly rather than threatening manner. Far more imposing is the outsize church that tries to make up in size and grandeur for its inferior position on the hillside. This faded pink monstrosity only serves to highlight the charm of the Moorish castle that without doubt steals the scene.

When you find your way up the steep and narrow streets to the top of the town you may be able to park in the little square that houses the Town Hall and an old people's home directly beneath the castle and the church spires. You can visit the castle, which dates from the twelfth century, even if the entrance appears to be closed. Knock on the door of the house next to the entrance and you may be led through somebody's kitchen or asked to wait while the main entrance is unlocked, and then you can go into the castle up some very steep steps which leave you wondering how anybody ever managed to attack these places. Although it is in ruins, it is very impressive, as is the view down over the town and the surrounding fields and hills with the mountains in the background. Once again, the sounds of daily life and the song of birds are carried clearly to one's ears and it would be tempting to spend hours up here in the sunshine, amidst the peaceful scenery. The castle is on several levels with ever narrowing spiral stairways until you virtually have to squeeze up the last few

Of all the castles in the province, the one at Olvera is perhaps the most captivating. Others may be more spectacular but this one, perched on its craggy rock, has a very special charm.

steps to get out onto a flat roof top. Remember to give a tip to the person who let you in (100 pesetas per visitor should be acceptable).

Olvera has a certain air of prosperity about it thanks to the emigrants who have saved their money and come back to set up co-operatives or other small businesses and generally improve their native town. There are several pensions and a paved pedestrian street in the centre.

Accommodation
The following pensions are all fairly central: **Pension Cantalejo**, San Juan Bosco 16; **Pension Medina**, Sepulveda 6; and **Pension Maqueda**, Calvario 35. The new hotel is signposted on the way out of Olvera towards Antequera although it is still within the town:
Hotel Sierra y Cal 2-star. Avenida Nuestra Señora de los Remedios. Tel: 130303. The hotel has a restaurant and some rooms have a good view of the town. DR 3800-4800 pesetas.

Where to eat
There are several bars in the centre such as; **Restaurante Bar Manolo**, Plaza de Andalucia; **Bar Central**, Calle Llana; **Bar Peluso**, Calvario 11; **Bar Frenazo**, Avenida J. Besteiro; and there are also

some good ones on the way out of town on the road to Antequera. Some of the more typical local dishes are made with asparagus or spinach, rabbit or a speciality, *solomillo relleno* (stuffed sirloin steak).

Torre Alháquime

You may have glimpsed this tiny village from Olvera and you will drive past it on your way to Setenil. It almost looks like a toy village crowning its little hilltop and from a distance it does not even appear to have any streets. You can just make out the few remains of its Moorish castle next to the church although it is not possible to visit the site at the moment, indeed there is very little left to see. Opposite the entrance to the church is the Town Hall which looks almost like a miniature building from a model town, crammed into such a tiny place with a great air of importance about its well kept façade. The name Alháquime comes from an Arab word meaning 'the wise one' and it refers to a governor the village once had, famed throughout the region for his wisdom.

The Pension Casa Juan offers accommodation and food.

Setenil de las Bodegas

This is perhaps the most surprising village along this route and one of the few that cannot be seen from a distance. In fact, as you get closer to it you begin to wonder if you are on the right road but then you suddenly come across it and discover at once why it is so hidden from view. Instead of being perched on a hilltop like so many of the other villages, Setenil is crowded down into a little gorge cut by the river Guadalporcún. The river flows around a high rock on which the Moors built a fortress to defend the villagers who, in times of peace, lived in the caves in the gorge with their flocks in order to be closer to the fields. This fortress put up a fierce resistance to the reconquest and the name of the town derives from the Latin words *septem nihil* which mean 'seven nil', referring to the number of unsuccessful sieges undertaken by Christian troops. The resistance offered by this fortress and its Moorish inhabitants won such renown that Christian Knights and noblemen came from all over Spain and even from other parts of Europe to try their courage and their skills against these impregnable walls. Not until 1484 was the fortress finally taken by the Marquis of Cadiz and King Ferdinand, who had decided to use

(**Above and Over page**) *Most of the inhabitants of the coastal towns have never even heard of the fascinating village of Setenil de las Bodegas and yet, with its houses set into the very rock, it is certainly the most unusual of all the white villages.*

gunpowder on a massive scale, thus destroying much of the building with heavy artillery. When the Moors finally left Spain, the village lost its strategic importance. The noblemen left and it reverted to a peaceful, agricultural community.

Vines were once very important in the area and the grapes were pressed here in the village in underground *bodegas* with great vats in the floor which collected the juice from the grapes being trodden above – hence the full name of the village, Setenil de las Bodegas. The vines were wiped out by disease, however, and are no longer grown here. The village today is isolated by bad roads, drained by emigration, and has not yet realised its potential as a tourist attraction.

The most striking thing about the village is that so many of the houses are in fact caves in the rock with façades built up in the typical style of the Andalusian white villages. In some streets it looks as though the houses are actually holding up the mass of rock above them and in others the houses have a double roof, the tiles protected by the overhanging rock. One of the streets is like a tunnel with houses on both sides and a solid rock roof. There are several little bridges crossing the river Guadalporcún, which meanders around the

rock, the cave houses following its course, and there are plenty of steep streets and steps to climb up and down on either side of the gorge. Road signs are a little confusing here as some point to the town centre in a different direction to the historical centre but if you follow the different signs you will end up both times in the same place!

Setenil is so close to Ronda that you may want to cross over into the province of Malaga to see this famous town. Alternatively, from Setenil you can follow the little white road on the map that will eventually lead you to the village of El Gastor.

Accommodation
Hostal El Almendro 2-star. Carretera Setenil–Puerto del Monte, on the road to Ronda. Tel: 134029. In a picturesque location high on a hill about 800m out of the town, it has a swimming pool, tennis courts and an open air discotheque in the summer. DR 3500 pesetas.

Where to eat
There is the **Restaurante Bar Las Flores**, Avenida del Carmen, and several bars within the town; and the **Venta Huerta Primera** and **Venta Para si Puedes**, both on the road from Setenil to Alcalá del Valle.

El Gastor

This is yet another little white farming village on a hillside, dating back to the sixteenth century. The name comes from the word *castor* which means beaver; these animals used to abound in this area. There are many legends of bandits in these hills at the turn of the century; the villagers talk of one particularly famous one who lived in El Gastor and whose home is apparently still as it was when he lived there. Close to the town there is a dolmen known as the Giant's grave and also a Roman necropolis.

One peculiarity of this village is an instrument known as the *gaita gastoreña* or gastorian pipes. The instrument dates from at least the sixteenth century and developed out of the shepherds' pipes and it is still a curious and primitive instrument. It consists of a small wooden box (about 2 x 20cm), hollowed out with a hot wire, with three perforations on one side and one on the other. The mouthpiece is a small piece of fine reed which vibrates upon blowing and the soundbox is a cow's or goat's horn. It needs good lungs to play it, as each simple tune should be played in just one breath from start to finish. There are not many people who know how to play it but there is a special competition here on Corpus Christi day, and the instrument is also played during the December holiday period when people go carol singing. It is played in one or two of the neighbouring villages such as Algodonales, but El Gastor is the most likely place to see and hear it.

Where to eat
There are at least six or seven bars in this little village so you should not have to go very far to find some good country cooking.

Zahara de la Sierra

You will probably have seen this village already from the N342 road with the ruins of its thirteenth-century Moorish castle perched high up on a rock. From a distance you can also see a white, sixteenth-century clock tower crowded with the rest of the buildings around the base of a large rock and on the other side a curious white-painted cemetery that almost looks as if it is hanging in mid air. The village has its origins back in Roman times although its name is an Arab word that means 'flower'. Its important strategic position made it the object of several sieges during the reconquest. It was taken by the Christians in 1407 but the Moors recaptured it in 1481 and all the Christian inhabitants had their throats cut. A year later the Christians took it again and this time managed to hold on to it.

The steep climb up to the castle is not for the faint hearted, nor for sweltering summer days. All that remains at the top is a square tower in which a staircase leads up into pitch darkness. But of course from here you get yet another magnificent view. There are some beautiful places to walk around this area and the road that leads up towards Grazalema is impressive; there is a popular place at the top for hang-gliding. The local scenery will be altered soon when a new reservoir under construction is finished. This will flood the area known as Arroyomolinos where there are some interesting caves and places to walk. However, there are plans to build a water sports and recreational centre on the lakeside and this could be an important attraction to add to the beauty of this sierra region and its fascinating villages.

Accommodation

Despite being such a small place, Zahara, in the heart of the Grazalema National Park, has some very reasonable, albeit modest, accommodation.

Hostal Marques de Zahara 2-star. San Juan 3. Tel: 137261. DR 3750–4250 pesetas. Tastefully decorated, family run hostal in restored sixteenth-century house.

Hostal los Estribos 1-star. Fuerte 3. Tel: 137445. DR 3000 pesetas. You can also find rooms in the **Venta Los Tadeos**, **Pension Gonzalo** and **Fonda el Tajo**.

There is a camping area called Las Cobatillas off the road to Grazalema; 3^1/$_2$km from Zahara on the left hand side there is a forest track you can drive along for 3 km. At the end of this track you walk another 300m to the camping area. There is drinking water, tables, benches and barbecues as well as a rubbish collecting service.

Where to eat

Here again, you do not have to go very far to find somewhere to eat. Apart from the hostals and the *venta* already mentioned, there are at least four or five more bars where you can try local specialities.

Grazalema

This mountain village is considered to be the most typical of all the white villages along this route and although it has a harsher climate than other parts of the province, it is without doubt one of the most beautiful places to see in the whole area. Clean and well preserved, at 823m above sea level, the village has very little modern architecture and its streets and houses are just as one imagines an Andalusian village to be. Until very recently there were notices in the main streets stating that the penalty for spitting or causing a disturbance in the public thoroughfare was a 500 peseta fine! The village, clinging on to a steep hillside, has an open-air swimming pool by the edge of a cliff and a large terrace area with balconies hanging, as it were, in thin air, offering a marvellous view.

Grazalema is now a quiet, peaceful village with a permanent population of 2600 but in the last century it was a busy industrial town with a population that at one time reached 20,000. Some of the older villagers still remember the more prosperous days of the textile industry.

Although the town dates back to Roman times, it was the Moors who gave it this special legacy by bringing with them their textile crafts and passing their skills on to the Christians before finally being expelled in 1571. In the seventeenth and eighteenth centuries the local industry grew, everything of course being made by hand, especially the famous woollen blankets. At the start of the nineteenth century the town already had 10,000 inhabitants but a cholera epidemic decimated the population and isolated the town. The French invasion of 1810 claimed more lives and resulted in the destruction of much of the local industry's means of production. In 1825 the first primitive textile machines began to arrive, giving a great boost to the industry which at that time sold its products all over Spain and even abroad. Most of the working population depended directly or indirectly on the industry since only one tenth of the rocky terrain round about is suitable for agriculture. The social changes of the late nineteenth century brought an end to this period of prosperity. Rising wages forced up the cost of the products and a lack of investment to modernise the factories made it impossible for them to compete with the more industrialised areas like Catalonia. As the factories closed down, families emigrated and now there are only two small textile mills left, kept up more as a tradition than anything else, though they could be the seed of a revival of the industry.

Just above Grazalema's petrol station are the workshops of Artesanía Textil S.A. where many different articles are made by traditional methods and where you can see a museum of the old textile machinery. Apart from the famous woollen blankets, they make ponchos, jackets, scarves, shawls and rugs as well as handbags and purses out of wool and finished with leather from Ubrique. You can buy these articles at the workshop itself or from a shop in the main village square.

As you go out of the village past the Hostal Grazalema, there is a road to the left which leads back to the C339 linking Ronda and Algodonales. The only other remaining workshop is down this road on the right. It dates from the last century and the machinery still works on energy generated by a watermill. They make blankets and ponchos from local wool and can produce about 200 blankets a year, though in the summer there is often not enough water in the river to turn the wheel. You can buy the blankets from a house in the main square of the village, though be prepared for prices that reflect the amount of time and effort that goes into each one.

Meanwhile, Grazalema depends quietly on tourism for survival. The National Park is an attraction for those who enjoy the countryside and there are many routes one can explore. If you climb up to the highest points on a clear day you can see both the Atlantic and the Mediterranean and even the mountains of North Africa. The best way to explore the park is on foot and the best time of year is the winter or spring since the summer months can be too hot for walking any distance. There are many different animal and bird species within the park including one last elderly pair of Golden Eagles and some important colonies of vultures. There are also a large number of species of bats. To check whether you need permission to walk some of the different recommended routes within the park you can get in touch with the main office in Cadiz (Agencia de Medio Ambiente, Avenida Ana de Viya 3) but there are also park offices in Grazalema (Piedra 9) and in El Bosque (Avenida Juan XXIII). It is quite difficult to get permission to visit the *pinsapar* (the famous forest of Spanish firs) and some other areas, especially at weekends, as numbers are quite strictly limited. See Chapter Four for information about groups that organise walks in the area.

Dangers of the ice trade

If you walk in the highest areas of the *pinsapar* near Grazalema you may come across some very old constructions known as snow wells. These were deep wells made to trap the snow which was packed down into blocks of ice to be transported on the backs of mules and sold in the surrounding towns. In those days it was a dangerous business for these beasts of burden negotiating steep and narrow paths and they often slipped and fell down the mountainsides. Even today it is possible to find skeletons of mules or donkeys amongst the forest of fir trees. It seems incredible that ice was transported by the Duke of Medina Sidonia's muleteers from these wells as far as the Doñana reserve, 150km away across the Guadalquivir river, to supply ice for King Philip IV's hunting parties.

Accommodation

Hostal Grazalema 2-star. This hostal is a bit spartan in its decoration but at the same time very attractive and has a lovely view and a small pool in the garden. DR 5040–5940 pesetas.

You can also find accommodation in the Hostal Garcia within the village. Some new tourist apartments are being built behind the Hostal Grazalema. When finished these should be available to rent. Ask in the information office in the Town Hall (Ayuntamiento).

On the way into Grazalema from El Bosque by the side of the road is a camp site called Tajo Rodillo. There are showers, toilets and a bar here.

Where to eat

The Hostal Grazalema has a reasonable restaurant serving some good country cooking and there are several bars and restaurants within the village.

The Costa de la Cal

The provincial tourist board once launched a campaign to get people more interested in visiting the country and mountain villages along the Route of the White Villages with the catch phrase, 'Come to the mountains, discover the Whitewash Coast'. The uniform whiteness of these ancient villages is one of the most typical images associated with Andalusia although in fact the mid-June ritual of lime-washing the walls is not such an ancient tradition as one might think. Whitewash is made by mixing calcium oxide, obtained by burning raw lime rock, with water, and it serves as an excellent disinfectant. Relatively recent government measures were in fact responsible for introducing the widespread use of whitewash both inside and on the outside of dwellings in an effort to improve conditions of hygiene and limit the spread of disease. At the beginning of the summer, when the rains are all over, out come the buckets of whitewash and on goes this year's layer, covering up the cracks and stains and, over the years, rounding off the corners and building up a sort of thick crust that can actually help waterproof a building. When it is being brushed on the lime-wash is actually transparent but as it dries it takes on that brilliant whiteness that so characterises the villages of this part of Spain.

Benamahoma

If you leave Grazalema and take the road to El Bosque, you will pass the tiny village of Benamahoma which in August celebrates its Moors and Christians festival, unique in this part of Spain. It is worth stopping to look at this attractive village where three small streams are born, joining together to start the river that flows through El Bosque. You can leave your car here in Benamahoma and walk around the village. On one road you will come to a fresh water stream that flows out of the mountain and down below you will see the hatcheries of a trout farm where you can buy the fish fresh out of the water. Beyond this is a public swimming pool with a bar and gardens. The water in the pool comes from the mountain spring so it is quite cool! After seeing the village you can walk along an attractive pathway by the river to El Bosque. This is a popular spot for picnics and campers and there are some parts of the river deep enough to bathe in. Unfortunately, not everyone is as careful about litter as one would hope, but it is an easy walk and an ideal picnic area, especially on a weekday early or late in the season when you will find the place more secluded.

One of Benamahoma's sources of income is a small chair-making craft industry.

Accommodation

It is possible to rent accommodation within this tiny village, houses with fireplaces for a cosy winter weekend or a holiday at any other time of the year. You can try asking in the local bars about renting these houses but for peak holiday dates you would need to book in advance.

There is also a camping area known as Los Linares, 500m from the village along a path called El Camino del Nacimiento which is the road that leads to the swimming pool. There is drinking water here and a rubbish collecting service, although work is underway to convert this into an official second class site with showers, toilets and so on and room for some 30 caravans and 60–70 tents.

Another camping area called Los Llanos del Campo can be found off the road to Grazalema on the left hand side. It is signposted so you should not have any trouble finding it. There is no drinking water here.

El Bosque

The village of El Bosque, whilst not as striking as Grazalema, is the most important of the sierra villages for tourism. Its position in a river valley just 300m above sea level gives it a rather more sheltered climate and it was the first village in the area to build a public swimming-pool. It has a camping area, a very pleasant two-star hotel and apartments to rent. People come here to hunt, to fish on Europe's southernmost trout fishing reserve and generally to enjoy the surroundings. It is a good base from which to explore the rest of the sierra region.

The name El Bosque means the wood or forest. It was the richness of the wildlife in this area that first attracted the Duke of Arcos to build a country house here from which to hunt. The nobles brought with them a large contingent of servants for whom housing had to be provided and gradually a little village grew up. In the eighteenth century the nobles came less and less to hunt and the village became more and more independent. It continued to grow until the arrival of the Napoleonic forces in 1810. The villagers rebelled and attacked a group of French soldiers. The French retaliated by burning and completely davastating the village. Although El Bosque was rebuilt, its subsequent history was marked until quite recently by acute poverty. It began to be important as a tourist centre when people from the larger towns started to buy cars and were therefore able to explore a little further afield at weekends. El Bosque has well kept streets with fountains of fresh mountain water and a friendly, open atmosphere. There are also trout hatcheries here as in Benamahoma.

Accommodation

Hotel Las Truchas 2-star. Avenida de la Diputacion 1. Tel: 723086. DR 4375-5160 pesetas. This peaceful hotel is really very attractive, in keeping with the traditional Andalusian style.

There are apartments and houses to rent which you can find out about through estate agencies or by asking in the local bars.

There is supposed to be a camping area called La Torrecilla just off the road to Ubrique with water, showers and toilet facilities, though at the time of writing it is not open. According to the local council it should be open 'soon'.

There is a first class camp site called Camping Tavizna 7km from El Bosque on the road to Ubrique. It is easily visible from the bridge over the river Tavizna and has young trees with earth and gravel underfoot. There is a supermarket, bar and restaurant with a social room for campers. Camping equipment can be hired and there are some little wooden cabins for rent that sleep two people. You can also hire mountain bikes and canoes and the camp site offers guided walking or biking tours, canoeing trips on the nearby Hurones reservoir, rock climbing for beginners and 'puenting' for the more adventurous (see also Chapter Four). Prices: (a) 1525 pesetas, (b) 1050 pesetas.

Where to eat

The Hotel Las Truchas has a restaurant where you can try the local trout and apart from this there are *mesones*, *ventas* and restaurants such as the **Restaurante Calvillo** in the Avenida de la Diputacion; the **Venta Julian** in the same Avenue or the **Restaurante Los Nogales** on the road to Ubrique.

Prado del Rey

About 7km from El Bosque is the village of Prado del Rey, which means, 'the King's meadow'. It was founded in the eighteenth century during the reign of Carlos III as part of a plan to colonise and repopulate parts of Andalusia. Each family that came to settle here was given a plot of land, a mare, a pair of pigs and a pair of goats, on the condition that they would cultivate the land. This accounts for the rather artificial structure of the village with its parallel streets and geometrical layout so unlike the rest of the white villages with their intricate jumble of houses and streets.

Some twenty years ago a group of leather workers from Ubrique came and set up an industry here which has since grown and expanded. A furniture making industry was also started by carpenters who moved here from Benamahoma. Bee-keeping is another important activity in the village and there are plans to instal a factory to pack and sell their own honey. All in all it is a hard-working and relatively prosperous village and there are a lot of bars and discotheques, three swimming pools and a very lively atmosphere.

Not far from Prado del Rey on an estate called La Cabeza is a place where there are natural springs with a high concentration of salt. It is a most unexpected place to find a saltworks operating by the same methods of evaporation as those used in the sea saltworks of San Fernando and Chiclana. On the same estate are the ruins of yet another Roman town, Iptuci, but again, there is little to see. Any pieces of interest are either in the Cadiz archaeological museum or in private hands.

Accommodation
The **Hostal Los Cuatro Vientos** is on the road to Arcos; the **Hostal del Carmen** is on the Villamartín-Ubrique road; the **Hostal El Mirador** and pension **La Laguna** are within the town.

Where to eat
You can try the local specialities in many places such as the **Restaurante Los Cuatro Vientos** on the road to Arcos or the **Venta Nueva** on the Villamartín–Ubrique road.

Villaluenga del Rosario

If you leave Grazalema by the lower road that joins the C3331 to Ubrique, you will pass this tiny village, 870m above sea level, the highest village in the province, with fresh natural springs and an underground river that can be heard in the main village square. Here the roofs of the houses are not flat as in most of the towns and villages of the province but sloping because of the possibility of snow in winter. There are several caves in this area, some with stalactites and stalagmites (see Chapter Four, Potholing).

The population of Villaluenga is small because it is very hard to make a decent living here. Its altitude means that the winters are harsh and cold and it has long been no more than a forgotten village in the mountains. The beautiful countryside, the fresh, healthy air and the peaceful solitude are, however, beginning to attract tourists. All new buildings must keep to the traditional styles but the village now has a swimming-pool, tennis courts and a restaurant bar. Its small bull ring built on the rock of the mountainside is said, jokingly, to have the greatest seating capacity in the whole of Spain because by climbing up the mountainside and choosing a suitable rock to sit on thousands of people could get a bird's eye view of the bull fight.

Accommodation

The **Hostal Restaurante Villaluenga** is a large building on the main road that runs past the village. There is no sign outside indicating that this is actually a hostal though the size and layout make it fairly clear. When asked why there was no sign outside, the owner replied that the wind kept knocking it down. Perhaps by the time you get there he will have tried painting the name of the Hostal on its lovely white exterior walls! Tel: 461912. DR 3600–5000 pesetas.

Where to eat

In the Hostal, or you could try the **Meson Restaurante La Cancela**, easy to find in the centre of the village.

Benaocaz

The little village of Benaocaz, founded by the Moors in the eighth century, is in many ways similar to its neighbour, Villaluenga. It too has hard winters, warm dry summers, beautiful scenery, healthy air and delicious fresh water springs. There is also a historical museum of the Sierra here. This village can be the starting point for some beautiful walks through these mountains.

In Benaocaz, as in other villages of the Sierra, fresh mountain water is almost as readily available as the fresh mountain air.

Accommodation
There are rooms available in the **Bar Las Vegas** and in various apartments and houses in and around the village.

Apartamentos Sananton 1-star. Plaza de Sananton 5, Tel: 110764. Price: 4400–5500 pesetas.

There is also a camp site in the village and there are two camping areas with drinking water, near Benaocaz on the road to Grazalema.

Where to eat

Again, considering the size of the village, you do not need to go far to find somewhere to eat and there are several bars where you can try some of the local stews or some of the spicy sausages typical of the Sierra region.

Ubrique

From Benaocaz the road leads downhill to Ubrique, one of the most prosperous towns of the Sierra, crowded into a valley and surrounded by mountains. The town has some attractive streets and corners but being down in a valley it gets less light and sunshine than some other towns. The river Ubrique has its source right here in the town and here too there are natural springs of fresh drinking water.

The town owes its relative prosperity to a leather industry that employs a large proportion of the population in over a hundred workshops. Even in Roman times the town exported tanned leather to the capital of the Empire. In the eighteenth century the local industry produced mainly little leather bags called *precisos* used by muleteers to keep their tobacco, tinderbox and flints in, but nowadays Ubrique produces a wide variety of goods from bags, wallets and suitcases to jackets, skirts and so on. If you visit Ubrique you will have no trouble finding these leather goods as they constitute the town's greatest attraction.

Off the road from Benaocaz are the ruins of another Roman town, Ocurris, but there is not very much to see (see Chapter Four, Archaeology). The same can be said of the ruined Moorish castle, the Castillo de Fatima, also in this area. The road from Ubrique to the Puerto de Galiz crossroads is a picturesque route through pine woods and cork forests.

Accommodation

Hostal Ocurris 2-star. Avenida Solis Pascual 49. Tel: 110973. DR 3750 pesetas. This is a passable though not very attractive hostal.

There are also four Pensions in the town and houses to rent.

Most of the churches that local guide books would have you visit are large, ornate and gloomy. This one, in the tiny village of Torre Alháquime, looks decidedly Mexican. You half expect the Magnificent Seven to start shooting from the bell tower!

Where to eat

Ubrique seems to be so concerned with selling you its leather goods that it forgets that shoppers like to rest and take some pleasant refreshment whilst they think over what they are going to buy. Whilst walking round the streets you really do see very few interesting looking bars or restaurants. There is one restaurant in the centre called **Briston's** which specialises in local game but you might do better to try one of the *ventas* outside the town like the **Venta El Chorizo** on the road to Cortes de la Frontera. A lot of young people in Ubrique tend to congregate in a bar called **Jazz Tamos** (the name is a play on words) at 9a Calvo Sotelo, about the only place particularly geared to young people. Some of the local people find Ubrique a little claustrophobic, being stuck down in a valley, penned in by the mountains and a heat trap in the summer. For visitors, however, it is well worth the trip and Ubrique is an essential stopping place along this beautiful route of the white villages.

EIGHT

The route of the Fighting Bull

This route covers the central, lower lying part of the province between Jerez and Algeciras. It will not take you to see bull fights but rather the natural habitat of the Spanish fighting bull. You can see these animals grazing freely over wide expanses of terrain which, many argue, could be put to more profitable use. Defenders of the *corrida* (bull fight) argue that, ironically, the survival of these animals depends on the survival of the *corrida*. These bulls never existed as wild animals; they have been bred deliberately for their aggression, not to be raised for beef and no farmer would raise them at all were it not for the *corrida*. Not all the animals you see grazing in these fields will end up in the ring by any means, only those which have proven their worth in terms of courage and determination at the yearly testings of the young stock. The bulls' pastures are shared by all kinds of birds, animals, wild flowers and butterflies and one of the best times to travel this route is in the spring when the pastures are a mass of colour with great expanses of purple or bright yellow flowers and the countryside is still green after the winter rains.

There are no big towns on this route; the most important ones are Medina Sidonia, Alcalá de los Gazules and Jimena de la Frontera and then there is the spectacular hilltop village within a castle, Castellar de la Frontera. The rest of the villages are quiet rural communities. On this route the greatest attraction is the landscape which, as always, offers a rich variety of details on which to feast the eye. It is possible to travel at least along the main routes by bus although the driver will obviously not be interested in stopping to admire the scenery. Ask in tourist offices for information. The main terminal is in Jerez.

The route basically follows the C440 from Jerez to Los Barrios and then takes you back to Jerez on the C3331 past Jimena de la Frontera to the crossroads of Puerto de Galiz from where the road to Jerez becomes the CA 503, 502 and 501 respectively. Within this area there are however many other roads and tiny villages, any of which can be rewarding if your intention is simply to explore and enjoy the

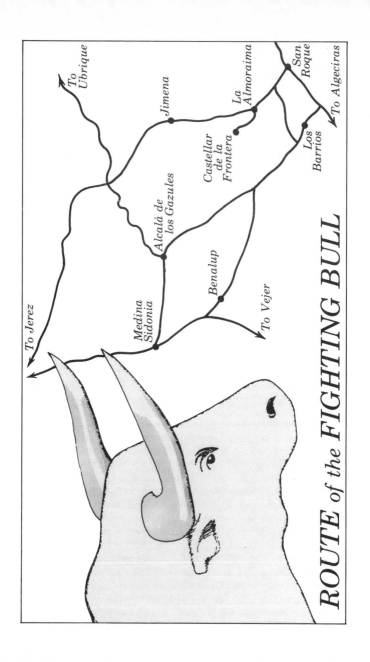

ROUTE of the FIGHTING BULL

This archway at Medina Sidonia is a perfect example of the simple but striking beauty of the Moorish architecture of which, sadly, relatively little has been preserved. (Photo by Catherine Cavanaugh)

countryside. There are plenty of sights to surprise and fascinate: storks nesting in giant cactus plants, long horned cattle looking like something out of a western movie, hairy wild pigs running across the road, primitive dwellings made of sticks and straw and shaped like haystacks, cork and eucalyptus trees, ruined towers and castles standing forlornly on many a hilltop, and an abundance of birds and flowers. One example of an off the route road is the CA221 going off to the right from the C440 just before Los Barrios (if you are heading south). At the beginning of the road there is a sign stating that the road surface is in a bad state of repair, which turns out to be a rather optimistic assessment of the situation as the road is truly appalling, its myriad potholes being far worse for your car than a simple dirt track. However, it takes you through some very beautiful scenery and would be a wonderful route to walk along in the spring time or early autumn.

Medina Sidonia

This is a quiet, white Andalusian town up on a hill some 300m above sea level. It was founded by the Phoenicians shortly after they founded Cadiz, the name Sidonia probably deriving from the Phoenician city of Sidon. In the Gothic period it was the head of a very large diocese and hundreds of priests served in the church here. The name Medina is a legacy of the Moorish occupation, as is the *alfajor*, a kind of cake made out of toasted almonds, honey and spices, produced in the local convents and in what are very much small family businesses. Medina was once the cake making centre of the Arab world and many of the recipes used today have been passed down from generation to generation. They tend to be fairly dry cakes made with almonds, egg yolks and various spices, such as the marzipan figures and *polvorones* typical of the Christmas season.

The land around is given over to agriculture, bull-breeding and private game reserves and there is a high level of unemployment in the town. From the top of the hill you can see the dockyards of Puerto Real which is where many of the men aspire to work using Medina basically as a dormitory town. Tourism is once again a hope for the future and more and more people are visiting this ancient town which is smartening itself up and making an effort to attract more visitors. There are plans to build a three-star hotel which will make an important contribution to the tourist sector since, at the moment, there are only two or three small pensions in the town.

The town's main monument is its sixteenth-century **church** which at one time was more important than the cathedral of Cadiz. Now it is rather dilapidated, a typical rural church full of statues and relics. At the main entrance to the church is a patio with columns and mausoleums. You might find it worth climbing the 132 narrow spiral steps of the bell tower for an even better view of the surrounding countryside.

Next to the church are the ruins of a Moorish **castle** but there is little left to see. There is a plaque on one wall saying that Doña Blanca de Borbon, wife of Peter the Cruel, was imprisoned here and killed in 1361 but the same story is attached to a little tower on the outskirts of Puerto de Santa Maria called the castle of Doña Blanca.

Probably the most pleasing sights in Medina, apart from the panoramic views, are the Moorish style **archways**: the Arco de la Pastora, in what were once the town's defensive walls and the recently restored Arco de Belén. A third remaining archway is known as the Puerta del Sol.

On the outskirts of Medina there is a **hermitage**, the Ermita de los Santos with Visigothic remains dating from the year 630AD

Accommodation
Pension Sidon Plaza España 6. Tel: 410035. Right in the centre of the town. DR 2500 pesetas.

Where to eat
Mesón Bar Machín Local cuisine in an interesting setting with beautiful views, in the top part of the town in the church square.
Restaurante Bar Cadiz Plaza de España 7. In the town's main square, this bar serves good food and has an attractive vine covered patio.
Venta El Castillo Calle Castillo.
Restaurante El Duque Carretera Medina-Chiclana. Local dishes.
Venta La Duquesa On road to Benalup. Tel: 410836. Speciality in game, asparagus and fresh fish.
Restaurante La Tejera On the road to Paterna de Ribera. Typical local cuisine.

The Benalup road

After Medina Sidonia one route you can follow is the road to Vejer and then take the turning off to go through Benalup, a small agricultural village. Beyond the village you will see signposts to the **Tajo de Las Figuras** which is a small cave with prehistoric cave paintings and which may be visited. Once you reach the place on the road where signs direct you up towards the cave you can walk up to it and you will find a guard there who will show you round. There are also signs directing you to the ruins of an old monastery, **El Monasterio San Jose del Cuervo**, lost in this beautiful part of the Andalusian 'outback'. The monastery may be visited on the first three Wednesdays and the last Saturday of each month. If you phone the Benalup Town Hall (Tel: 424129) you can arrange to walk to the monastery with a guide as it is on private land. It is about a 3km walk from the road and there is no charge for the visit.

Alcalá de los Gazules

This is the next of the border towns along what was the frontier between Moorish and Christian kingdoms. It may originally have been a Phoenician settlement like Medina but it certainly dates from Moorish times when it was a military stronghold. The soldiers took to farming in times of peace and that was how the town grew up. At one time it had a population of 12,000 but by the twentieth century its rather primitive agriculture could not compete. Emigration en masse was the only solution as was the case in so many towns and villages of Andalusia in the fifties and sixties. The population is down to some 6000 and the town is still stagnating with a high level of unemployment and underdeveloped agriculture. Perhaps many of the locals would be quite happy to see the fighting bulls disappear and their pastures turned over to modern methods of agriculture that could bring more work and wealth to the area.

Alcalá is a very picturesque little town with a church and a ruined castle in its higher part like Medina but there is not really a great deal to see. It makes a good staging post along a scenic route and if you stop for a while and wander through some of its tranquil streets, you can hear a marvellous silence overflowing with the sounds of birds, animals, bees and goatbells.

Brightly coloured flowers highlighted against the whitewash – one of the most typical images associated with the white villages. In the semi-abandoned fortress village of Castellar de la Frontera, a profusion of flowers seems bent on taking over the narrow, unpeopled streets.

Eh, Toro!

On your travels around the province you are more than likely to see some of the great black fighting bulls grazing in their pastures. In spring time they can sometimes be seen resting in fields ablaze with yellow and purple flowers, with just their head and horns visible above the mass of brilliant colour. Seen from a distance in such peaceful and ruminative stances, they may not seem to be particularly impressive. If you should happen to come face to face with a large and angry bull at one of the local bull running events, however, you would be quick to change your mind. These magnificent creatures are loved and highly respected by all true aficionados who describe them above all as 'noble'. The bull's indisputable courage is believed to be inherited from the female of the species, the male contributing only the physical strength. They are short sighted but have exceptionally acute hearing and over short distances can run faster than a racehorse. They can also be tremendous jumpers and many are the anecdotes about bulls jumping over the barrier into the corridor around the ring or even into the crowds, goring anyone they happened to find in their way. One bull named Granizo jumped the barrier 22 times and another called Bonito jumped it eight times without touching the boards! A fighting bull always attacks head on and in a face to face fight there is no animal that can match him.

Accommodation

Hotel San Jorge 2-star. Paseo de la Playa. Tel: 420252. DR 4000 pesetas.
Hostal Pizarro 2-star. Paseo de la Playa 9. Tel: 420103. DR 4000 pesetas.

(Opposite) Top: *If you have time to see only one or two villages in the province, this spectacular village-in-a-fortress, old Castellar, should be one of them.*
(Opposite) Bottom: *These giant trees by the sea walls of Cadiz give the impression of being almost as ancient as this ancient city itself, though in fact they are probably less than a hundred years old.*

Where to eat
Restaurante Pizarro Paseo de la Playa 9. Menu includes wild boar and other game.
In other bars and *ventas* you should be able to try some of the local specialities such as *gazpacho caliente*, asparagus with eggs or venison.

La Almoraima

If you are not heading for Algeciras, Gibraltar or some other spot on the coast, you can avoid the busy main road by taking the CA512 just a bit before Los Barrios, joining up with the C3331 to head back north again. Just before you get to the village of Nuevo Castellar is the entrance to La Almoraima. This ancient convent was founded in 1603 and in 1868 it came into the hands of the Medinacelli family who transformed it into a luxurious country mansion. In 1972 it became the property of the Rumasa holding which was expropriated by the government in 1982, since which time it has been under the administration of ICONA (nature conservation institute). The mansion now has 17 bedrooms, some with fire places, two dining rooms, sitting rooms, a billiards room, library and chapel. Guests eat together at long tables, a set menu of the day. La Almoraima was, until its expropriation, the largest private landed estate in Europe with 16,000 hectares of land including a reservoir. During their stay guests can tour the estate by Land Rover or on horseback and observe the deer and other animals that live here in their natural habitat. Hunting and fishing can be practised in the proper seasons; guides and equipment can be hired. There is also a swimming pool, tennis courts and a mini golf course. (You do not have to be resident in the hotel to be able to hunt, fish, go horseriding or tour the estate by Land Rover.)
Casa Convento La Almoraima Castellar de la Frontera. Tel: 693002, 693050. DR 12,000 pesetas.

(Opposite) *The sandstone cliffs near Conil seem to take on new shapes each year and although one or two of the beaches are losing their sand, this is still a very impressive stretch of coastline.*

Castellar de la Frontera

If you carry on along a little side road past La Almoraima it will take you on a laboriously twisting road up to old Castellar, a thirteenth-century Moorish fortress on top of a huge rock overlooking the Straits of Gibraltar. The old village of Castellar is inside this fortress. Despite the beauty of the place it must have been a very harsh existence and in 1956 the Ministry of Agriculture built a whole new village at the bottom of the hill: Nuevo Castellar. The idea was to convert the old village into a Parador but unfortunately funds ran out – it would surely have been one of the most impressive Paradors in the country. The villagers moved en masse and the fortress village was left to the birds, the animals and the wind. It was later discovered by a group of hippies, predominantly Germans, who moved in, painted psychedelic graffiti on the walls, slept all day and spent the nights partying and living as lords of the castle. On our first visit we gave a lift up the steep, winding road to a young German couple who described Castellar as a little German village. I stood by the castle looking over at Gibraltar in the distance and wondered how many of the local Spaniards knew or cared about this little invasion.

A more recent visit was somewhat more heartening. There were no groups of people sitting around listlessly in broken down old vans, stoned out of their minds but, rather, signs of restoration of some of the buildings within the fortress. Hopefully it will not just be left to crumble for, despite its difficult access, it is a wonderful, haunting place to visit.

Jimena de la Frontera

Some twenty kilometres beyond Castellar you come to yet another ancient frontier town around the skirts of a hill whose top is also crowned by a ruined castle. This castle is like a mosaic of the remains of successive civilisations that have inhabited the place. Jimena possibly dates right back to the kingdom of Tartessus. Cave paintings found nearby dating back to 1000BC represent Phoenician and Greek ships similar to other paintings found in Nineveh. The castle was rebuilt in Roman times and then again by the Moors as part of a line of defence that stretched from Gibraltar to Olvera. From the top of the hill you can still see Gibraltar and it is fascinating to see how that line of defence worked: it went from Gibraltar to Castellar and Jimena, then to the Castillo de Fatima near Ubrique, Zahara de la

Sierra and Olvera (see Route of the White Villages). Another line of defence went through Jimena, Alcalá de los Gazules and Medina with several other castles and watch-towers you may have seen along this route that are not always marked on the map. This route of the fighting bull was once a real war zone, the route of the fighting Moors and Christians.

Of bungs, plugs and stoppers

Spain is the second largest cork producing country after Portugal, and Cadiz is the province with the highest density of cork trees, most of which grow on the Almoraima estate, especially around Castellar, Jimena and Alcalá de los Gazules. Cork bark is cut from the trees once every nine or ten years between the months of June and September so that each year a different part of the forest is harvested. The best cork comes from trees over twenty-five years old which have a diameter of over 25cm. Most of the cork produced in the province is of a relatively low quality and it is mainly used for making bottle corks and agglomerates. Once the cork bark reaches the factories where it is to be processed it is boiled in water for about 40 minutes to eliminate the impurities and to soften it, making it more pliable. Then the rougher parts are scraped off and the cork is classified according to its quality. The making of corks for bottles used to employ a great many people in the province in the days when they were made by hand, but nowadays the whole process is mechanised.

Jimena is now the centre of the cork producing area of the Gibraltar hinterland but there is no local industry to process the cork. Despite its typically Andalusian aspect, Jimena is a surprisingly cosmopolitan town as quite a few foreigners have settled here.

Accommodation

Hostal El Anon Consuelo 37. Tel: 640113. In a large old house in the town with an attractive terrace, swimming pool bar and restaurant. DR 4000 pesetas.

Rancho Los Lobos (see Horses section in Chapter Four). Tel: 680429. DR 4000 pesetas.

The rest of the route

From Jimena you follow the road signposted Jerez and Ubrique which takes you very briefly through part of the province of Malaga, up to the crossroads of **Puerto de Galiz** where there is a *venta* at which you can get a reasonable meal. On this road, although officially within the province of Malaga, there is a place called **La Sauceda** where you can camp. It is not a camp site as such but there are cold showers, toilets (which may not be very pleasant), and also some wooden cabins which can be rented for 600 pesetas a day (sleeping 8–10 people). It is all very basic and is sometimes used for school outings and camps but it is in a very beautiful spot. Off the road to Jerez, after Puerto de Galiz, there is a road to the right signposted **Charco de los Hurones** which takes you up to a reservoir. By the dam there is what looks like a miniature village, a group of little houses once used by those building the dam and now only used for holidays. One can swim and fish in the reservoir but there is little shade near the water's edge. Before you get up to the dam there is a place where the river forms large pools amongst the rocks and it is a popular place for picnics and weekend campers.

This is a good route to bring a picnic on as *ventas* are relatively few and far between but there are plenty of places to stop for your own little private feast.

NINE

The Atlantic route

This route starts in the busy capital of Cadiz and follows the coastal road south as far as Tarifa, as far south indeed as one can get in Europe. The beauty of this route lies not so much in the quiet charm of country villages but in the rather more savage beauty of some 100km of Atlantic coastline. The waters along this coast are cold all the year round and in some places there are strong and dangerous currents in the sea. There are long stretches of white-golden sands scoured clean by the wind and there are sheltered coves that are hard to get to amongst crumbling sandstone cliffs. You really need a car to explore this route, unless you are cycling or back-packing, but if you have already been to the Costa del Sol or other better known beach resorts in Spain, this part of the Costa de la Luz will surely surprise and delight you, for whereas the Mediterranean coastline is cramped and tame, this part of the Atlantic coast is wide open, wild and challenging.

If you do not have a car it is still possible to get to the coastal towns and villages by bus, the main terminals for the Atlantic route being those of Cadiz and Algeciras. The tourist information offices should be able to help you with timetables.

Cadiz, the capital

Founded by the Phoenicians in 1104BC on an island near the coast, Cadiz has always been a city dependent on the sea and upon maritime trade, whether with the Mediterranean countries, Africa, northern Europe or the New World. In the days of Julius Ceasar it was one of the most important cities of the Roman Empire. During the Moorish occupation however it was little more than an insignificant fishing village. Columbus's second and fourth voyages to the New World set out from the port of Cadiz and the town's important strategic position was both its making, in terms of trade, and, on several occasions, its breaking, thanks to the frequent attacks it suffered. The eighteenth

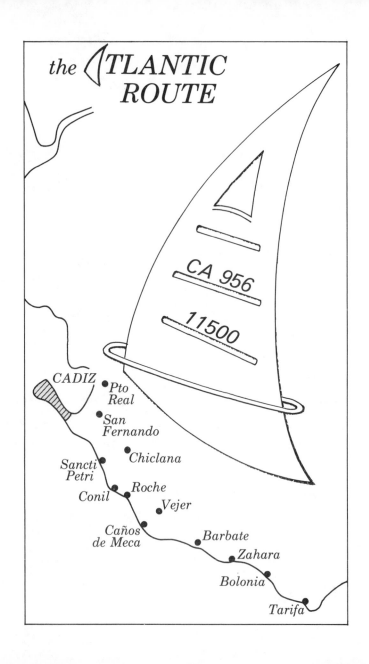

the ⟨ATLANTIC ROUTE

CA 956
11500

CADIZ
● Pto Real
● San Fernando
● Chiclana
Sancti Petri ●
Conil ● Roche
● Vejer
Caños de Meca ●
● Barbate
● Zahara
Bolonia ●
Tarifa ●

century was the city's golden age and the old part of the town as it stands now basically dates from this period. In the nineteenth century Cadiz played an important role in the political, cultural and ideological life of the nation, but the final loss of Spain's colonies in 1898 cut off much of the city's maritime trade and brought the more glorious chapters of its history to a close. Twentieth-century Cadiz consists of a somewhat dilapidated old city area on the far end of what is really a small island and a crowded, more modern part that has filled all the remaining land leaving no more room to build and grow. From across the bay in El Puerto de Santa Maria, the silhouette of the city at dusk is reminiscent of a giant steamer facing out towards the open seas but with too heavy a load to be able to break free and set sail.

The best way to see the old part of Cadiz is on foot. Driving around the city can be a nightmare and parking can be even worse, so the best thing to do is to put on a comfortable pair of shoes and take to the streets at a steady pace with frequent stops for rest and refreshment. If you come into Cadiz by car just keep on driving until you pass through the old city walls (**Las Puertas de Tierra**) and head downhill to the right towards the docks. After passing a fountain you will come to a small park area underneath which is a car park which would be a good place to leave your car. If you come into Cadiz by ferry or by train you will arrive in more or less the same area and if you come by bus, make sure you stay on the bus until you get to this part of the town. The main square opposite the docks is called the **Plaza de San Juan de Dios** and by taking the first street on the right as you face the square you come into a long, straight pedestrian street called the Calle San Francisco which will take you into the main shopping area in this part of the town.

Tourist information office

If you can find your way to the Plaza de Mina (a little further on from the end of the Calle San Francisco), you will find this office where you will be able to get yourself a street map of the city and any other leaflets or information you might find interesting. There is also a municipal tourist office in the Calle Marqués de Valdeiñigo, one of the side streets off the Calle San Francisco. You should be able to get a street map here too.

Museums

In the Plaza de Mina, very close to the tourist information office, are the Archaeological Museum and the Fine Arts Museum, housed in the one building under the name **Museo de Cadiz** and they are well worth a visit. Amongst the more important pieces in the archaeological section are some ancient Phoenician sarcophagi or stone coffins, a Roman statue of the Emperor Trajan and many interesting pieces brought up from the sea bed from sunken galleons and so on. In the art section there is an important collection of paintings by Zurbarán as well as paintings by Murillo and other Spanish baroque painters. A third section of the museum contains a collection of puppets from the famous Tía Norica puppet company which dates back to the eighteenth century. Open 9.30am to 2.00pm Tuesday to Sunday. Closed Mondays and public holidays. Entrance free for members of EEC on presentation of passport. Other nationalities: 250 pesetas.

Next to the church of San Felipe Neri is the **Museo Histórico Municipal** which contains, among other exhibits, a scale model of the city of Cadiz in the eighteenth century. Open 9.00am to 1.00pm and 5.00pm to 7.00pm Tuesday to Friday and 9.00am to 1.00pm on Saturdays and Sundays. Closed Mondays and public holidays. Tel: 221788. Entrance: free.

Forming part of the old sea walls near the Parque Genovés at the far end of Cadiz is the recently inaugurated **Museo del Mar** which offers exhibitions on maritime themes such as the *almadrabas*, the ancient method of tunny fishing described in this route guide (see Barbate). These exhibitions are changed periodically. Open every day 10.00am to 1.30pm and 5.00pm to 6.30pm. Entrance: free. Tel: 222474.

Sea walls

If you leave the Plaza de Mina by the Calle Zorilla it will bring you out to the sea walls and you can walk along these as far as the **Parque Genovés** with its botanical gardens. This is a truly lovely part of Cadiz and the sea walls are quite impressive, with their balconies overlooking the bay and little round stone sentry boxes that will remind you immediately (if you have seen them) of the ones on the walls of old San Juan in Puerto Rico. Another impressive sight in this part of the city are the enormous *ficus rubiginosa* trees that originally came from Australia. Their great size gives the impression that they must be very ancient but they are probably no more than ninety years old. Amongst the other unusual trees to be seen in the botanical gardens are a few examples of the truly ancient dragon tree, found only here and in the Canary Islands.

Firs, ficus and dragon trees

There are several varieties of trees that give a very characteristic touch to the local scenery; bushy-headed pine trees along the coast, palm trees with their particularly exotic flavour, cork trees and eucalyptus trees with their characteristic kinds of bark, or the tall and sombre cypress trees which so often mark the site of a cemetery. (The reason for this is that the roots of the cypress tree go straight downwards without spreading out and therefore do not disturb the occupants of the graves.) For something more unusual a trip to the Grazalema nature reserve will give you a chance to see the *pinsapar*, a grove of Spanish fir trees of a species found nowhere else in western Europe. Despite their uniqueness, these trees are not nearly as spectacular as the enormous *ficus rubiginosa* trees to be found at the far end of the city of Cadiz, two outside the hospital Mora and others near the old sea walls. They came originally from Australia and their great size gives the impression that they must be hundreds of years old, though they are probably no more than ninety. Amongst other unusual trees to seen in the botanical gardens at the far end of Cadiz as well as in one or two other parts of the city are a few examples of the truly ancient dragon tree with its blood-like resin, found only here and in the Canary Islands. A dragon tree can live for over a thousand years.

The **Puertas de Tierra** are the old city walls at the entrance to the old part of Cadiz. On Saturdays, Sundays and public holidays one can walk along the top of these walls to get one more view of Cadiz. The gates are open from 10.00am to 10.00pm.

Castle

If you carry on walking around the edge of the city you will come to a sheltered little beach called La Caleta and the castle of **San Sebastian** at the end of a stone causeway leading out into the sea. The castle belongs to the military and you cannot walk out to it, though there has been talk of turning it into a museum.

Streets and squares

From this point you can head back into the town, past the Hospital de Mora with two more of those enormous trees outside (*ficus rubiginosa*), and down the Calle Moreno de Mora through the quarter known as the **Barrio de la Viña**. In the famous **Tio de la Tiza** square, open air barbecues are held on summer evenings. Leading off this square is the Calle San Jose that takes you past the **San Felipe**

If you drive into Cadiz you will not have reached the old part of the city until you pass this ancient dragon tree and go through the seventeenth century walls, known as Puertas de Tierra. (Photo by Catherine Cavanaugh)

Neri church where the Spanish constituent parliament was held during those years under siege by the Napoleonic forces. From here you can take any one of a number of streets, either to head towards the **Plaza de San Antonio** or in another direction, towards the central market place. The fish market in Cadiz is quite impressive for its quantity and variety of fresh fish.

Palatial houses

In its days of glory, particularly in the eighteenth-century, a lot of very grand houses were built in Cadiz by shipowners and others who were prospering from the trade with the New World. Several of these palatial houses are still in good condition or have been renovated recently. The old part of Cadiz is one of the best preserved eighteenth century cities in Spain, with its narrow streets and tall houses, built like that partly due to lack of space, partly to keep as sheltered as possible from winds. The local tourist office publishes a leaflet detailing the main characteristics of these houses and giving a complete list of them by streets, noting their different styles. The oldest of them is a baroque style building dating from the early seventeenth century called **Casa Marquina** in the Plaza de Fray

Felix, numero 1. In the Plaza de San Antonio there are two more very attractive and typical ones, recently renovated, at numbers one and five in the square, and one that may be visited is the **Palacio de Mora** at 26 Calle Ancha. This great house dates from 1862 and has three floors and a little lookout tower like so many of these houses so that ship owners could watch out for returning ships. Open Saturdays only from 10.00am to 2.00pm.

The Cathedral, its museum and El Populo

From the market area it is a short walk to the cathedral, whose domes you will probably have seen several times from a distance. The first stone of this cathedral was laid in 1722 but the building was not finished until 1838, over a century later. It has recently been restored and if the main doors are not open you can visit it by walking up the side to the museum. As one would expect, the cathedral museum contains many paintings, statues and relics typical of the Roman Catholic religion, including a silver monstrance on an enormous silver platform weighing 900 kilos, which is carried round the streets on Corpus Christi day. Then of course there is the inevitable 'piece of the cross of Christ'. From the museum you can go into the cathedral itself and down into the crypt where the famous composer from Cadiz, Manuel de Falla, is buried. Down here in the crypt you are below sea level and can hear the sound of the waves breaking against the sea walls. The crypt has a curious echo and a sound made in the centre can be echoed up to fifteen times.

The jumble of houses next to the cathedral, known as the **Barrio del Populo**, is the oldest standing part of the city, dating from the Middle Ages. From here it is a short distance back to the Plaza de San Juan de Dios and your car, the ferry, a bus or a train. If you are driving back out of the city you could do so along the sea road which takes you to the more modern, tourist sector of the town with some good bars and restaurants as well as take-away type eating places, serving pizza, fried chicken and so on. The beach along here, the **Playa de la Victoria**, has been greatly improved with many tons of new sand.

On Tuesdays, Wednesdays and Thursdays in the summer, the local tourist information board offers guided tours of the old part of the town. This walk around the city lasts about two hours and is free of charge. It starts from the Plaza de España, by the monument to the Spanish parliament, Las Cortes. For further information about these tours, ask in the tourist information offices.

Also in the summer months, on Thursday evenings, there is a boat trip available around the bay, leaving from the docks where the ferry from El Puerto de Santa María comes in, near the railway station, at 10.30pm. Price: 500 pesetas.

Ferry service

A company called Catsline runs a catamaran ferry service from Cadiz docks to Tangiers, Seville and Villareal de San Antonio (in Portugal). For further information phone 226917 or enquire in any local travel agency.

Accommodation

There are a large number of hotels, hostals and so on in the capital but the overall standard is not as high as one might expect at the time of writing. There are however several new hotels in the pipeline which, when finished, will greatly improve the city's touristic image. The best hotel at the moment is probably the **Hotel Atlantico** at the very far end of the city which belongs to the Parador chain. It is a good quality hotel in a lovely setting by the old sea walls but from here you need at least half an hour to drive through the city and get out onto the main road if you want to do day trips to other towns. There are several in-between sort of hotels and on the lower end of the scale, some fairly grotty accommodation. The following is a small selection of what is available:

Hotel Atlantico 3-star. Parque Genovés 9. Tel: 226905. A modern building in an attractive setting as described. DR 11,000–12,500 pesetas.

Hotel Francia y Paris 3-star. Plaza San Francisco 2. Tel: 222348. In the centre of the old part of town, a fairly old hotel, renovated in 1991. DR 6500–7500 pesetas.

Isecotel Touristic Apartments 3-star. Paseo Maritimo. On the sea front in the more modern section of town. Tel: 255401. Apartment 4400–6100 pesetas.

Hotel Regio 2-star. Ana de Viya 11. Tel: 279331. A modern building on the main avenue that takes you to the older part of the city. DR 6000–7500 pesetas.

Hotel Regio II 2-star. Avenida Andalucia 79. Tel: 253008. On the same avenue as its sister hotel. DR 7000–8500 pesetas.

Hotel San Remo 2-star. Paseo Maritimo 3. Tel: 252202. On sea front in modern part of town. DR 6300–8400 pesetas.

Hostal Del Duque 2-star. Ancha 13. Tel: 222777. In the centre of the old part of the city on a pedestrian shopping street. DR 3000–3500 pesetas.

There are many more one and two star hostals and pensions. The tourist information office should be able to give you a complete list.

Where to eat

Restaurante El Faro San Felix 15. One of the best restaurants in the province.

Meson del Duque Paseo Maritimo 12. Menu includes some home cooking type dishes.

Restaurante Achuri Plocia 15. Closed Sunday, Tuesday and Wednesday nights. Basque cooking.

Restaurante La Costera Paseo Maritimo (corner of Calle Dr Fleming). Large outdoor area and attractive bar for tapas. Mostly Galician and Basque style cooking.

Restaurante El Brocal Avenida de Jose Leon de Carranza 4 (at the entrance to Cadiz almost opposite the football stadium).

Restaurante El Candil Javier de Burgos, near the Municipal cinema in the centre of old Cadiz. If you get tired of fish, this restaurant serves good meat dishes and is famous for its garlic chicken.

Restaurante La Marea Paseo Maritimo.

Restaurante Curro El Cojo Paseo Maritimo. Specialising in meat, hams, etc.

Ventorillo del Chato On road to San Fernando. Has been a restaurant for over two centuries and is still very popular.

Apart from those mentioned there are a great many more restaurants and bars; some in the old part of town are very old and traditional, often attractively so.

San Fernando

Driving out of Cadiz southwards along what is in fact the last stretch of the N1V from Madrid, you come to the town of San Fernando. If you look at a map you will see that the town is in fact on an island, the **Isla de Leon**, surrounded by sea and marshland and joined to Cadiz only by this road along a thin strip of land. San Fernando is a naval town, the base of La Carraca being one of Spain's more important naval bases and a lot of young men do their stint of military service here.

Ships have been built here since Roman times. The surrounding marshy area contains a network of evaporation pools making up the largest saltworks in Spain although salt production by these ancient methods is really a thing of the past. Nowadays fish farming is becoming a far more important industry. San Fernando is an ancient town which has played its own significant role in the history of this area but the presence of the naval forces has prevented it so far from playing a significant role as a tourist resort. The local beach is within the militarised zone and, until recently, the people of San Fernando could only use it at certain times during the summer months. Otherwise they had to go to Cadiz or Chiclana to enjoy the beach. Now the beach of **Camposoto** is permanently open to the public. It is a long beach on the edge of the marshlands, exposed to the Atlantic waves and popular with surfers.

San Fernando has its own quiet charm and many people who want to rent an apartment in the Cadiz area opt for San Fernando as it is close by and summer rentals are more reasonably priced here than in Cadiz itself.

Bahia Sur
On the outskirts of San Fernando a new centre called Bahia Sur is being built at the time of writing. This is an ambitious project designed as a commercial and leisure centre, the largest in Andalusia. It covers an area of 220,000 square metres and will include all kinds of specialised shops, a large supermarket and so on as well as housing, a hotel, a beach club, a sports centre with an Olympic sized stadium and swimming pool, a concert hall, discotheque, multi cinemas, a fairground, bars, restaurants and more. It will have been at least partially opened by the time this book goes to print.

Accommodation
Hotel Sal y Mar 3-star. Plaza del Ejercito 32. Tel: 883440. In the centre of San Fernando, a fairly old hotel, not up to the same standard as some of the newer three-star hotels in other towns. DR 4800–7200 pesetas.
Hotel Roma 2-star. Calle Real 52. Tel: 881372. Also central; small but passable. DR 5800 pesetas.

Where to eat
Venta de Vargas On N1V road. Closed Mondays. Very popular thanks to its good food and reasonable prices.
Los Tarantos On main N1V road. Decorated in style of a traditional Andalusian farmhouse. Closed Sundays. Regional cuisine.

San Fernando is well known for the fish caught in the estuaries and marshy areas round about which have their own special flavour. Also typical of San Fernando are its *cañaillas*, a kind of sea snail – in fact the people of San Fernando are known in the rest of the province as *cañaillas* (not to be confused with *canalla* which would be an insult!). Another local speciality are *bocas de la isla* which are the pincers of a particular kind of crab which can actually grow new ones!

Puerto Real

Between San Fernando and El Puerto de Santa Maria, on the innermost shores of the bay, is the small town of Puerto Real. Originally Roman, it was rebuilt by the Catholic monarchs towards the end of the fifteenth century. Amidst pine forests and marshland it now has an artificially made beach and quite a bit is being done to 'do up' the town which remains, however, fairly insignificant in terms of the tourist sector.

There are a few very popular restaurants here such as **La Marina**, **El Dorado** or the attractive **Jardin de Canileja**, that serve very fresh fish.

Chiclana

Driving out of San Fernando you turn right down the N340 to Chiclana. A new bypass around the town has made a tremendous difference to Chiclana which used to be a dreadful bottleneck in the summer, particularly on a Sunday as many people from Puerto Real, San Fernando and other towns headed for the beaches further south.

Chiclana itself is a friendly town sprawling untidily around a small hill with a dome shaped hermitage on the top. It is a relatively properous town with several furniture factories and stores, salt producers and *bodegas* producing white wines called *pastos*. Its most famous industry however is the **Marin doll factory**, founded in 1928 by Jose Marin Verdugo and run very much as a family business giving work to a great many people, particularly women, in Chiclana. Though the best known dolls are probably the flamenco dancers, the factory now produces some 400 different models including some very beautiful historical figures made of porcelain. You can visit the factory (Calle Rivero 16, not far from the central market place) and see an exhibition of the dolls but you will not actually see them being made there as most of the work is carried out in local homes, some women specialising in the hair, others in the clothes, others in the faces and so on. Some of the more complicated dolls can pass through a hundred different pairs of hands before being completed so that they are very much a product of local craftsmanship. These dolls are sold all over Spain and in many parts of the world, particularly Japan, Italy and the USA. They have won many national and international prizes.

La Barrosa

Although Chiclana itself is not on the coast you can go through the town following signs to La Barrosa and you will drive through a growing tourist area with plenty of villas and small country houses until you reach La Barrosa beach, 8km of sand bordered by the typical pine groves. There is quite a bit of development going on in this area but there are no blocks of flats and everything is spread out over an area with plenty of beach and trees for everyone. Along one stretch of the beach however a rather unfortunate, unattractive promenade has been built which seems to have caused the loss of much of the sand from that section of the beach. From this beach you can see the island of **Sancti Petri** with the remains of its thirteenth-century castle and lighthouse. This was the site of the ancient temple of Melkart founded by the Phoenicians about three thousand years ago on what was then the other end of the island of Cadiz. You cannot see anything of the temple, any remains there might be would be underwater, but as you lie in the sun looking out over the waves, you might turn your mind to imagining that pagan temple, filled with the richest of treasures and visited in its days of grandeur by those old school friends of ours, Hannibal and Julius Ceasar.

Sancti Petri

On your way from Chiclana to La Barrosa you will pass a road leading to the tiny village of Sancti Petri. Sancti Petri is a ghost village. It was built to house the workers of a tuna canning factory but when the factory closed down in 1971, the people had to move away. The only life there now is provided by a small yacht harbour as this is a port of refuge for small boats. They can only come in at high tide because of dangerous sand bars at the entrance. It is a curious place to stroll around, rather sadly peaceful with overgrown streets that would have been filled with children playing. The tuna fish weather vane on top of the old factory is a poignant reminder of these fish, one of the greatest catches along this coast since the days of Tartessus, and on the front of the abandoned church you can still see the painted tiles depicting Saint Peter (Sancti Petri), the fisherman, with a huge tuna fish behind him.

Sorry Ladies!

The ancient temple of Melkart, founded by the Phoenicians on the western end of the island of Gadir (where the little island of Sancti Petri is today), was in its day an important centre of pilgrimage. Adopted later by successive civilisations, it was believed to hold the ashes of Hercules himself along with unimaginable treasures and in its day it received such illustrious visitors as Julius Caesar. It was here that Hasdrubal, the Carthaginian general, swore his nine-year-old son Hannibal to eternal hatred of the Roman enemy. There was said to be an inscription on the entrance columns barring entry to pigs and women!

Boat trips and fishing

In the months of July and August a ferry boat called *Ciudad de Chiclana* makes trips from Sancti Petri. It makes three trips a day leaving at 12.00am, 4.00pm and 6.00pm and has room for up to 72 passengers, with a small bar and toilet facilities on board. Each trip follows a different route, one taking you out around the island of Sancti Petri, and another going inland towards San Fernando up the channel known as Caño de Sancti Petri which is within the Bay of Cadiz natural park. The third trip takes you up the same channel, coming out into the bay of Cadiz and passing under the Carranza bridge to dock in Puerto de Santa Maria. Prices: adults 600 pesetas, children 400 pesetas. For further information phone 401659 or contact the Viajes Rico travel agency in Chiclana at Puerto Jose Antonio 17. Tel: 400570. This ferry boat can also be chartered privately for groups.

On Saturdays you can join this same boat, *Ciudad de Chiclana*, for a fishing trip leaving at 8.30am and returning at 2.30pm. Price: 5000 pesetas. For further information, as above.

Novo Sancti Petri

This is a huge new touristic complex being built around a 27-hole golf course designed by Severiano Ballesteros. Several top quality hotels are being built, two are open already and others will be open soon. The residential areas being built within this complex are very attractive modern houses but in typical Andalusian style and there are no blocks of flats or high rise buildings of any sort. (See also Golf section in Chapter Four).

Accommodation

Hotel Fuentemar 3-star. Carretera Fuente Amarga. Tel: 400216. This is an unexpectedly good quality hotel in a rather difficult to find location, badly signposted on the road to Fuente Amarga, a thermal spring. It is a tall, modern building with swimming pool and tennis courts. It offers medicinal baths and various thermal water treatments said to be good for certain skin disorders, rheumatism and so on. You can write for further information to Apartado de Correos 1, Chiclana de la Frontera. DR 6050–7260 pesetas.

Ideal Hotel 2-star. Plaza Andalucia 9. Tel: 403906. Next to the river (which is actually no more than a rather murky little stream); an attractive building close to the main road, the hotel has one floor exclusively for non-smokers. DR 12,000 pesetas.

Hostal Villa 2-star. Virgen del Carmen 14. Tel: 400512. DR 3500 pesetas. In Novo Sancti Petri

Hotel Royal Andalus Golf 4-star. Urbanización Novo Sancti Petri. Tel: 405550, 405050. Fax: 405350. Very attractive new hotel belonging to the Royaltur chain like the Hotel Royal Sherry Park in Jerez. Very modern exterior, typical Andalusian interior with indoor and outdoor pools, sports facilities, activities for children including crèche. The hotel is also right on the beautiful La Barrosa beach. DR 12,000–22,000 pesetas.

Hotel Costa Golf 4-star. Urbanización Novo Sancti Petri. Tel: 494535. Fax: 494626. For bookings ring 530581. Andalusian style two storey buildings with extensive garden areas, one indoor and two outdoor swimming pools, a putting green, conference rooms, a cafeteria and restaurants. DR 12,500–24,000 pesetas. Prices vary considerably according to the season; out of season there are some very interesting offers.

Soon to be opened in this same residential area are the **Hotel Playa La Barrosa** and the **Aparthotel Nelson Golf** with 300 apartments, both 4-star.

Camp sites

Camping La Barrosa 2nd-class. Tel: 403605. Open 1st June–30th September. Capacity for 800 people. On road to La Barrosa beach, turn left up a track through the pine woods and past various private houses. Large swimming pool, children's play area, restaurant. Prices: (a) 2420 pesetas, (b) 1650 pesetas.

Camping La Rana Verde 1st-class. Opened 1991 with first class amenities. Pago de la Rana, on the new road to La Barrosa. Tel: 530248/531061. With swimming pool, roller skating rink, artificial

lake and various sports facilities, children's play area, restaurant etc.
Prices: (a) 2450 pesetas, (b) 1650 pesetas.

Where to eat

Within the town itself there are not all that many bars to eat in except,
for instance, the **Cerro del Trigo** in the street going uphill from the
central church or the **Bar Capricho** at Jose Antonio 13 which is well
known for its shellfish. There are a few other bars in the centre but the
majority of restaurants and *ventas* are in the outlying areas on the
road to La Barrosa and along various side roads and even along tracks
amongst the pine woods. You have to be prepared to explore a little.

El Sanatorio San Antonio 5. Here you can sample all the locally
produced wines along with some good meat dishes.

El Santuario de las Carnes San Antonio 7. Tel: 400215. Good
barbecued meats.

Restaurante Bulerías On the road to La Barrosa. Tel: 405710.
Spanish and international cuisine.

El Azor On the beach front at La Barrosa Tel: 400746. Specialising
in fish and sea food.

Los Faroles On main Cadiz–Malaga road, near Costa de la Luz golf
course. Specialising in local fish and sea food.

Restaurante Popeye On road to La Barrosa. Tel: 400424. Very
popular for its fish dishes and game in season.

Restaurante Los Drogos On the road to La Barrosa.

La Rana Verde On the new road to La Barrosa. See above (camp
sites) for other facilities. A good place to go with children.

Club Nautico Sancti Petri in the abandoned village of Sancti Petri,
the restaurant of this little sailing club is popular for fresh fish dishes.

Roche

South of Chiclana as you carry on down the N340 you will come to
the entrance of a fairly new residential area called Roche. This is a
developing area of mostly private villas amidst acres of pine forest
close to the beach, the **Playa del Puerco**, which is a continuation of
La Barrosa. This is another long stretch of wide open sands where the
water is clean and clear and the bottom of the sea bed as you walk out
is extraordinarily smooth and free of stones. From the far end of the
residential area you can follow a rough track through the trees along
the cliff tops as far as **Cabo Roche** with its lighthouse and small
fishing harbour.

Conil

A little further on you come to the turning off to Conil, a pretty but unassuming white fishing village at the mouth of the river Salado. You drive through the more modern part and then downhill through an archway into those typically Moorish streets, narrow and twisting with low, white houses and colourful flowers and patios. Conil has been a fishing village since Roman or even Phoenician times. In recent years the fishing industry has brought little money into the town. There is no longer any tuna fishing here and until very recently the fishing fleet had no proper harbour. They had to launch their boats from Los Bateles beach when the weather allowed, which was generally only 100–150 days in the year. You can still occasionally see huge, old fashioned rowing boats with six men at the oars, straining through the Atlantic waves to lay out or bring in the trammel nets. The variety of fish in these waters is great but the catches are often small.

Beaches

Tourism is now the town's main hope for the future and although the industry is only just starting to develop, the population doubles in the summer months. The town itself is very attractive and the beaches are along the same lines as those already mentioned but between Roche and Conil there is a stretch of coastline made up of crumbling sandstone cliffs with some lovely, secluded little coves at their foot. If you drive into the top part of Conil, follow signs to the Hotel Flamenco and then drive on beyond the hotel along an unmade track, you will be able to drive up onto the top of these cliffs and explore a little. Climbing down to these coves can be a little tricky and in some places dangerous and the rapid erosion of the rocks can dramatically change the path of access from one year to the next, but as long as you are not too laden down with sun umbrellas, ice boxes, small children and the like, you should find it worth the effort. These are ideal little beaches from which to fish, snorkel or scuba dive. Do be careful though – apart from being cold these waters can surprise you with strong currents so that it is unwise to go very far from the shore unless you know the waters well.

Between the beaches of Conil and Vejer are seven kilometres of open, lonely sands known after the little hamlet of **El Palmar**. Here you will not find any convenient shops, any deck chairs for hire or young men marching up and down the beach selling cold drinks at exorbitant prices. You might find some surfers or windsurfers because there is nearly always a fairly strong wind and some good waves. One thing you should certainly find is peace and solitude in the kind of natural setting that can bring one to meditate on the smallness of man in the face of that immense sky and ocean that stretch out before you to where, once upon a time, unfortunate sailors used to fall off the edge of the world.

Accommodation

Hotel Flamenco 3-star. Fuente del Gallo. Tel: 440711. Open from Easter to 31st October. Attractive modern building on the beach with swimming pool, tennis courts, mini golf, children's play area. DR 7000–10,500 pesetas.

Hotel Espada 2-star. Carretera El Punto (in higher part of town). Tel: 440780. DR 7500 pesetas.

Hostal Tres Jotas Only one-star but looks as good as the previous one. San Sebastian 27. Tel: 440450. DR 4175-6150 pesetas.

Cortijo de la Fontanilla AT 3-keys. Hijuela del Ojo. Postal address: Apartado 4. Tel: 441024. Touristic apartments in a very attractive setting with pool. There is a great variety of apartments and prices so it would be best to write for details.

Aparthotel La Gaviota AT 2-keys. Plaza Nuestra Señora de las Virtudes 10. Tel: 440836. Attractive, modern building in traditional Andalusian style in the higher part of the town. Again it is best to write for details.

There are at least eight more hostals and pensions in Conil though space does not allow for them all to be included here.

Camp sites

Pinar Tula 1st-class. Rincon Juan Arias. Km20 Cadiz–Malaga road. Tel: 445500. Access off N340 road. Open 15th June–15th September. Capacity for 400 people. New installations with swimming pool. Prices: (a) 1900 pesetas, (b) 1375 pesetas.

Cala del Aceite 2nd-class. Roche Viejo. Postal address: Apartado de Correos 34. Tel: 440972. Open all year. Capacity for 510 people. Attractive setting, 250m from a quiet sandy cove. Modern installations. Prices: (a) 2405 pesetas, (b) 1765 pesetas.

Fuente del Gallo 2nd-class. In Fuente del Gallo area, near Hotel Flamenco. Postal address: Apartado de correos 48. Tel: 440137. Open 15th March–15th October. Capacity for 600 people. Has all the basic facilities in good condition. Close to small beaches. Prices: (a) 2080 pesetas, (b) 1440 pesetas.

Roche 2nd-class. In area called Pago del Zorro. Open 1st June-15th

September. Capacity for 500 people. Tel: 442216. Prices: (a) 1905 pesetas, (b) 1415 pesetas.
Los Eucaliptos 2nd-class. On road in to Conil. Tel: 441272. Open all year. Capacity for 486 people. Prices: (a) 2080 pesetas, (b) 1440 pesetas.

Where to eat
Restaurante La Fontanilla Calle La Fontanilla. Specialities: fish and seafood.
Restaurante La Gaviota International cuisine, particularly German dishes, as well as local fish dishes.

Vejer de la Frontera

South of Conil on the N340 you come to the very picturesque Moorish town of Vejer de la Frontera, perched up high on a hill-top, overlooking the river Barbate. This is a beautiful white village that can best be enjoyed on foot, exploring the narrow streets, the main church and the castle area, climbing up to the ancient windmills, delighting in the typical contrast of the bright flowers against the white walls, the dazzling blue skies and panoramic views. There are a few souvenir shops, so far in fairly good taste. One hopes that they will not proliferate to spoil the simplicity of these picturesque streets. On certain days of the year, preserving an ancient tradition, women of the town dress in a costume called *la cobijada* which covers them in black from head to foot with a heavy black veil held over the face leaving only one eye uncovered.

Accommodation
Hotel Convento de San Francisco 3-star. La Plazuela. Tel: 451001. In a seventeenth-century convent which contains a Roman mosaic dating from the second century. DR 10,000 pesetas. Hunting parties can be arranged for groups of at least six. Horse riding is also available.
Pension La Janda 2-star. Cerro Clarinas. Tel: 450142. DR 3000–3500 pesetas.
La Posada 2-star pensión. Los Remedios, 21. Tel: 450258. In the centre of Vejer. DR 3000–3500 pesetas.
Motel La Barca de Vejer 1-star. Off N340 km36. Tel: 450369. DR 4200 pesetas.
Antiguo Meson de la Barca 1-star. Barca de Vejer. Tel: 450390. DR 2500 pesetas.

Camp sites
Camping Vejer 1st-class. Off main N340 road. Tel: 450098. Open all year. Swimming pool. Prices: 850 pesetas per adult, 613 pesetas per child.
Los Molinos 2nd-class. Just off main 340 road about 1km past Vejer. Tel: 450988. Open all year. Capacity for 288 people. Swimming pool. Prices: (a) 2500 pesetas, (b) 1750 pesetas.

Where to eat
Restaurante El Refectorio in the Hotel Convento de San Francisco. 2-forks. The chapel next to the convent has been turned into a tapas bar.
Restaurante El Quijote 2-forks. Avenida Andalucia. Follow sign to the windmills, Los Molinos.
Restaurante La Posada 2-forks. Los Remedios 19.
Restaurante El Paso down on the main road by the turning off to Vejer and Caños de Meca.
Venta Pinto 2-forks. Barca de Vejer. Has been roadside inn for nearly 100 years. Fresh fish from Barbate and Conil as well as good game dishes.
Restaurante Infante 2-forks. Barca de Vejer.

Trafalgar

If you drive from Vejer towards the coast following signs to Caños de Meca you will see a lighthouse standing solitarily on a small headland. This is in fact Cape Trafalgar. To have stood on these shores on that windy October day back in 1805 and to have witnessed that now famous battle in which Nelson lost his life and Spain lost her navy, must have been both spectacular and terrifying. There is nothing there now to remind one of that fateful day, except perhaps the empty echoes of the wind.

Caños de Meca

This is a small tourist resort that takes its name from a particularly well known spot on this coastline between Vejer and Barbate which is made up of sandstone cliffs that stand over three hundred feet above the Atlantic waves. It is possible to walk from this resort along the cliff tops to Barbate. From the highest part you can get a marvellous view of the town and coastline beyond and even of the mountains around Tangiers on a clear day. At the bottom of the cliffs nearer Caños de Meca are several little coves where you can camp. The one that gives the resort its name is not really a beach but a beautiful spot where fresh water streams (called *caños*) cascade from the cliffs down into the sea and large rocks eroded from the sandstone stick up out of the water. Apart from its natural beauty it is well known locally as a favourite haunt for nudists. There are bars, restaurants and apartments here but the place has its own peculiar atmosphere – one that does not fit with the beauty of the surroundings and it could not be described as a family holiday resort. A lot of young people involved in the drug culture tend to congregate here in the summer. It is the only place of its sort along this coast.

Campsites in Caños de Meca area
Camping Caños de Meca 2nd-class. Close to Cape Trafalgar. Tel: 450405. Open Easter to October. Capacity for 500 people. 600m from a fairly sheltered beach. Prices: (a) 2140 pesetas, (b) 1430 pesetas.
Camping Camaleon 2nd-class. Very close to Caños de Meca beach. Open all year. Capacity for 560 people. Prices: (a) 2030 pesetas, (b) 1445 pesetas.

Barbate

From Caños de Meca you can also drive to Barbate along a new road that takes you through the magnificent pine forests which, along with the cliffs along this section of coast, are within a protected area, the **Parque Natural Acantilado y Pinar de Barbate**. The difficult access to these cliffs makes them a favourite nesting site for many birds. As you drive down from the pine forests to the town of Barbate you pass a beautiful beach on your right known as the **Playa de Yerbabuena** that stretches from the harbour around to the cliffs on the right hand side. On the other side of the harbour is the start of the main beach of Barbate which is also spectacularly beautiful with equally clean, clear water and the most fantastic shades of blue in sea and sky.

Barbate is another quiet, unspoilt fishing village, one of the last places where tunny fishing is still practised by the ancient method of the *almadrabas*. It takes place between April and July when the tunny fish are migrating. A wall of netting is strung out to sea from the shore, weighted and anchored to the sea bed with a total of 150,000 kilos of chains and 150 anchors. It takes two months to set out this labyrinth of nets, an art handed down from generation to generation since the eighteenth century. Another two months are needed to take in all the nets again after some sixty days of fishing. The labyrinth of netting is designed to lead the tunny fish into a purse-seine, a kind of corral of nets with a floor to it from which they cannot escape. The wall of netting starts at the beach and finishes with the corral some three and a half miles from the coast. As the tuna fish swim up the coast, they come across this barrier and turn out to sea to find a way around it. They swim into the purse-seine and become trapped inside. When the captain of the *almadraba* considers there are enough fish caught in this corral, some eight to ten boats surround it and start drawing up the floor of the netting, first by hand and then on pulleys. As the bottom of the purse-seine comes up, the fish are forced to the surface. These fish can weigh anything up to 450 kilos (over a thousand pounds). The fishermen waiting in the boats stab the fish with special hooks or harpoons and haul them over the side of the boat. The surface of the water inside the corral appears to boil with so many fish thrashing about and after an hour or so the sea is red with their blood. When there are only a few fish left in the nets and they can no longer be reached with the hooks, some of the fishermen get into the water, walking over the taut netting and bring in the last of the fish. There are only two canning factories left in Barbate but ironically they do not can these tuna fish caught right here on their shores since the whole catch is immediately bought up by a Japanese firm that has two or three factory ships moored in Barbate throughout the tunny-fishing season. The local factories can frozen fish brought in from the Canary Islands. Were it not for the Japanese's love of raw fish and the special flavour of these tuna fish, which can fetch up to 22,000 pesetas per kilo in a Tokio market, these *almadrabas* would probably have died out by now. Conil, Zahara and Tarifa also have teams of fishermen who fish these magnificent tunny fish by the *almadraba* method.

Barbate is just beginning to wake up to the touristic potential of its beautiful beaches. There are some one-star hotels in the town and a few hostals. A new marina with some 580 berths is in the pipeline. It is expected to be the second largest marina on this stretch of coast after Puerto Sherry although it is not possible to say yet how soon it will be built. There are also plans to build new hotels and a first class camp site near the Yerbabuena beach. These changes to the town will do much for its difficult economic situation and should add to rather than detract from its charm. There are also plans to start running a ferry service from Barbate to Tangiers in Morocco and to Faro in

Portugal. Meanwhile, Barbate is a small and thoroughly authentic Andalusian fishing town. If you are looking for sun and sand in 'the real Spain' then this would be one good place to come.

Accommodation
Hotel Atlantico 1-star. Avenida Generalisimo 13. Tel: 430050. DR 4500–7500 pesetas.
Hotel Gran Sol 1-star. Calle Sanchez Rodriguez. Tel: 443008. DR 5000–7800 pesetas.
Hostal Sevilla 2-star. Padre Lopez Benitez 12. Tel: 432383. DR 4500–8000 pesetas.
Hostal Daniel 1-star. Avenida Generalisimo 89 Bis. Tel: 430322. DR 1800–2900 pesetas.

Where to eat
Restaurante Torres Avenida Atlantico. Good fish dishes with special emphasis on tuna.
Restaurante Gadir Padre Castrillon 15. Basque cuisine.

Zahara de los Atunes

Some ten kilometres down the coast is the tiny fishing village of Zahara de los Atunes whose only claim to fame is as the birthplace of Francisco Rivera Paquirri, the much loved bullfighter who died after a bad goring in 1984. Driving through the village, past the unfortunately hideous shell of an unfinished hotel and then past the more attractive Hotel Atlanterra, you come to a group of houses on the hillside known as the Germans' houses. Rumour has it that this little settlement was originally built by army officers who fled from Germany after the Second World War. Whether or not this is the case, one can certainly imagine that 40 years ago this far flung corner of Spain would have seemed like the end of the world.

From amongst these villas a man-made stairway leads steeply down to the beach where there are large rocks to dive or fish from. The sand is coarse and the sea is strong, cold and wonderfully clear. You can dive for sea-urchins and eat them raw on the beach – delicious! Although it can be very windy here at times this must be one of the most beautiful beaches in the whole of Spain and it is definitely 'unspoilt'.

Driving even further along this road you come to a lighthouse where the road ends and from here you can see Tarifa and the coast of North Africa and, just down beyond the lighthouse, an amazingly solitary, beautiful beach that can only be reached by boat or by a long scramble around the coast. In fact this beach is within a military zone and if you did reach it you might well be asked to leave. As is the case with all the beaches along this stretch of coast, the sea is very strong with dangerous currents. The only beach with a lifeguard service is the Playa del Carmen in the town of Barbate; on the other stretches of coast you are on your own with the waves so do be careful, especially if you are snorkelling or diving.

Accommodation
Hotel Atlanterra Sol 4-star. Urbanización Cabo de Plata. Tel: 432608. Open 1st May to 31st October. A luxurious hotel with swimming pool, tennis courts and so on. DR 11,400–17,800 pesetas.
Hotel Gran Sol 2-star. Avenida de la Playa. Tel: 443009. New and attractive hotel right on the beach with beautiful views from rooftop terrace and balconies. DR 4950–6800 pesetas.
Hostal Antonio 2-star. Urbanización Quebranta-Micho. Tel: 431214. DR 3500–6500 pesetas.
Pension Nicolas 2-star. Maria Luisa 13. Tel: 431174. Modest but very pleasant. Bar and restaurant. DR 3700–4800 pesetas.
Hostal Castro 1-star. Calle Dolores Sanchez Rodriguez. Tel: 430248. DR 3500–5500 pesetas.

Camp site
Bahia de la Plata 1st-class. Just beyond Zahara on the road to Atlanterra. Tel: 432412. Open all year. Capacity for 350 people. This is a new site right on the beach with new installations and newly planted trees that as yet do not offer an abundance of shade. Prices: (a) 2575 pesetas, (b) 1725 pesetas.

Where to eat
Restaurante Antonio in hostal of same name.
Cortijo de la Plata Urbanización Atlanterra. Beautiful views of sea from dining rooms.
Restaurante Hotel Gran Sol (see above).
   The **Pension Nicolas** serves some good meals and there are a few other bars in the village which are not too difficult to find.

Beaches between Zahara and Tarifa

The next main beach along the coast after Zahara is one known as **Bolonia**. Driving along the N340, about 5km after the village of

Facinas, there is a turning to the right signposted **Ruinas de Claudio Baelo**. This takes you up and down a winding road that is sometimes so infested with enormous grasshoppers that you drive over them like a brown carpet and hear them banging against the bottom of your car in suicidal leaps. The road takes you down to a beautiful bay with a small cluster of bars and houses around the ruins of a Roman town that is being excavated and partially reconstructed. These are the most spectacular Roman remains in the province of Cadiz. In its day this was one of the most important fishing communities in the southern part of the peninsula and fish was salted here for exportation to other parts of the empire. You can go on a guided tour of the town to see its streets, squares and patios, its amphitheatre and its thermal baths (or at least what is left of them). Official visiting times are displayed near the entrance. There are some five guided tours a day from Tuesday to Saturday between 10.00am and 6.00pm. Entrance: 250 pesetas for non Spanish visitors. Group visits may be arranged through the archaeological museum in Cadiz. The ruins actually continue down onto the beach and into the sea.

If you do a little snorkelling, and this is a perfect place to do it, you will see white painted markers on the sandy bottom of the crystal clear water. It is exhausting to think of the Romans building their town in this rocky heat – no doubt they got someone else to do it – but they certainly chose a gorgeous spot. Bolonia only needs a fringe of coconut palms to, make it look quite Caribbean. As with the other beaches along this stretch of coast, the wind can sometimes be uncomfortable and the water is always cold so that if you want to do much snorkelling you will really need a wetsuit. There are a few bars near the ruins where you can get a drink and something to eat and maybe find a fisherman to take you out fishing in his boat. You may see some of the divers with their enormously long flippers and harpoons who come here to catch *mero* (red grouper). These fish are sold to restaurants throughout the province as a highly rated dish although there is a suspiciously large amount of 'mero' on menus everywhere considering the limited numbers that can be caught by divers.

Accommodation

The first three listed are relatively new but very simple hostals, open during the summer season only.
Hostal Bellavista Tel: 684718. DR 3000 pesetas.
Apartamentos Miramar 2 bedroomed apartment: 6000 pesetas. Double room with bathroom: 3000 pesetas.

Hostal Don Pedro DR 2500 pesetas.
Hotel San Jose del Valle 2-star. Carretera N340, Cruce de Bolonia.
Tel: 645122/645092. This is also new and is of a good standard for a
2-star hotel, with air conditioning and TV in all the rooms and a bar
and restaurant on the ground floor. It is on the main 340 road just at
the turning off to Bolonia and is open all year round. DR 6000–8000
pesetas.

One of the last beaches on this section of the Costa de la Luz is
Punta Paloma, signposted from the main N340 road. Between
Bolonia and Punta Paloma there is a section of beach closed off by
the military, but if you park on the main beach you can wander quite
far around the coast to find more secluded spots. Whilst Punta
Paloma may well be one of the windiest beaches in Spain it has got to
be one of the wildest and most beautiful, especially on days when
you can see the coast of North Africa. It is a very popular spot for
windsurfers.

Tarifa

Between Punta Paloma and Tarifa there are several campsites, hostals
and restaurants and along this stretch of coast you will see many
windsurfers in the summer, for Tarifa is known as the Wind Capital
of Europe. It is said by other inhabitants of the province to be the
town with the highest rate of lunacy in Spain. Living farther up the
coast, in the relative shelter of the Bay of Cadiz for instance, on one
of those incredible days of Levante when you have to hang on to your
children with both hands to stop them from being grabbed by the
wind and slammed against a wall, it is easy to think, 'Gosh! They
must be going crazy in Tarifa!'. But wind is the friend of the
windsurfer and Tarifa offers its modest shops and bars to the many
windsurf enthusiasts who spend countless hours racing the waves.
World championships are held here and it is a fantastic place to use a
fun-board. Shop windows are also filled with wet-suits and diving
equipment as this is an important centre for scuba divers too.

Although the Levante wind can be terrible, it by no means blows
here all the time. I have been camping many times in this area and
have not once coincided with a day of Levante. If you enjoy camping
and going to the beach you will enjoy this area – sitting outside your
tent on the hillside, grilling a freshly caught fish over the fire, sipping
some good cheap Spanish wine and enjoying a fantastic view over
the Straits of Gibraltar to the African coastline, watching ships go by.

Tarifa itself is rather a dreary little town, useful for campers in the area to do their basic shopping but not the sort of place you would go specially to see. It does have one of the best preserved castles in the area dating from the tenth century, the **Castillo de Guzman El Bueno**. It is still used for military purposes but can be visited between 9.30am and 1.30pm from Sundays to Wednesdays and on public holidays. Tarifa has always been strategically important, dominating as it does the passage of ships between the Atlantic and the Mediterranean. The Moorish King of Granada once offered the Christian King six fortresses and 'enough gold to buy a kingdom' in exchange for the town of Tarifa. Today, however, the military presence here is fairly low key.

A hydrofoil service runs between Tarifa and Tangiers which is another reason why tourists pass through the town but again they do not usually come for the town itself. However, the presence of so many windsurfers in the area makes for a young and lively atmosphere in and around Tarifa in its bars and in the various camp sites and hotels.

Accommodation

Hotel Balcon de España 3-star. Carretera Cadiz–Malaga km76. Tel: 684326. On the beach. Open 1st April–31st October. The rooms are 'bungalows' surrounded by garden areas. DR 6500–9000 pesetas.

Hotel Dos Mares 2-star. Carretera Cadiz–Malaga km795. Postal address: Apartado 80, Tarifa. Tel: 684035. Open all year. On the beach. DR 8000–9500 pesetas.

Hotel Hurricane 2-star. Carretera Cadiz–Malaga km77. Tel: 684919. On the beach. Windsurf school. DR 9000–14,000 pesetas.

Meson de Sancho 2-star. Carretera Cadiz–Malaga km94. Swimming pool. DR 5200-6100 pesetas.

Hotel La Codorniz 1-star. Carretera Cadiz–Malaga km77. Tel: 684744. On the beach. DR 4900–7000 pesetas.

Cortijo las Piñas Touristic apartments. 1-star. Carretera Cadiz–Malaga km74. Tel: 685136. On beach. DR 5900 pesetas.

Hotel La Ensenada 2-star. Postal address: Apartado 108, Tarifa. On the beach on main 340 road. Tel: 643587. DR 4000–8000 pesetas.

Hosteria Tarifa 2-star pension. Amador de los Rios 22. Tel: 684076. Open 1st April–31st October. DR 3500–4500 pesetas.

Pension La Ponderosa 2-star. Carretera Cadiz–Malaga km76. Tel: 684999. DR 3000-5500 pesetas.

Camp sites

Tarifa 2nd-class. Carretera Cadiz–Malaga km78. Tel: 684778. Open all year. Capacity for 870 people. Prices: (a) 2200 pesetas, (b) 1500 pesetas.

Paloma 2nd-class. Near Punta Paloma. Open all year. Capacity for 210 people. Tel: 684203. Prices: (a) 2100 pesetas, (b) 1400 pesetas.

Rio Jara 2nd-class. Near Tarifa off Cadiz–Malaga road km80. Tel: 643570. Between river Jara and the beach. Open all year. Capacity for 475 people. Prices: (a) 2100 pesetas, (b) 1400 pesetas.

Torre de la Peña 2nd-class. Carretera Cadiz–Malaga km76. Tel: 684903. Part on hillside, part on beach, on either side of N340. Open all year. Capacity for 437 people. Bar restaurant on the beach. Prices: (a) 1850 pesetas, (b) 1250 pesetas.

Torre de la Peña II. 2nd-class. Carretera Cadiz–Malaga km75. Tel: 684174. Open all year. Capacity for 500 people. Prices: (a) 1850 pesetas, (b) 1250 pesetas.

Where to eat

Meson de Sancho (see above). Regional cooking.

Dos Mares (see above). Fish and roast kid.

Tasca Chan In Tarifa, Batalla del Salado 57.

These are but three suggestions. There are plenty of restaurants and *ventas* along road from Tarifa towards Cadiz.

TEN

The route of the Wines

The most logical place to start exploring the route of the wines is in Jerez since this is considered the capital city of sherry country and because its Moorish name, Xeres or Scheris, is the origin of the English word 'sherry'. On this route, contrary to the previous one, the main points of interest are the towns themselves rather than the landscape. This section of the province bounded by the Atlantic, the river Guadalquivir, the neighbouring province of Seville and the main N1V Madrid–Cadiz road is low lying and either marshy or given over to agriculture, most particularly of course to vineyards. The towns themselves, however, particularly the three that make up the official sherry triangle – Jerez, Puerto de Santa Maria and Sanlucar – are fascinating and full of life and, above all, each totally different from its neighbour. One obviously integral part of exploring the route of the wines is exploring the wines themselves. You can visit several *bodegas* (the places where sherry is produced and stored) to get an understanding of how the wines are made and then, of course, you can sample them. Along this route there are also some very fine places to eat so instead of packing the picnic basket, cash an extra traveller's cheque and be prepared to explore some of the local gastronomic delights as well as the avenues and sidestreets of the towns along this route.

There are regular bus services running between all the towns on this route. Check for details in the tourist information offices. The main bus terminal is in Jerez. Trains also run regularly between Jerez and El Puerto de Santa María.

*(**Opposite**) With plenty of wet fun in the sun, a visit to the Aqua Sherry water park in Puerto de Santa María makes for an exciting, no-sand-in-your-shoes kind of day out. (Photo courtesy of Aqua Sherry Press Department)*

Jerez de la Frontera

Wine has been produced in Jerez from its earliest days though it was under the Roman occupation that the town first became an important wine centre. As its full name implies, Jerez was very directly involved in the conquest and reconquest of the area by Muslims and Christians but one of the most significant factors in its history is far more recent, a factor that has contributed much to the status and condition of the town as principle producer of a world famous wine as well as to the make up of its idiosyncratic society. This factor was 'the British and Irish connection'.

There have been British merchants in this area since the Middle Ages but in 1587, when Sir Francis Drake made a devastating raid on Cadiz, setting fire to the whole Spanish fleet, some 300,000 gallons of sherry were carried off, along with just about everything else of value that Cadiz possessed. The prolonged wine-tasting sessions that must have followed contributed much to establishing a liking for these wines amongst the British who are still Jerez's best customers. In the late eighteenth and early nineteenth centuries a large number of English, Irish and Scottish merchants arrived in the area, participating in the wine trade and in many cases settling in the area and intermarrying with the local people so that many of the great sherry families of the area have strong ties with Britain and Ireland. This connection is reflected in the names of such famous sherry houses as Osborne, Terry, Sandeman, Williams and Humbert and others.

Jerez is a very lovely town if you manage not to see some of its poorer quarters. It has the largest municipal district of any town in Spain and includes many tiny villages around its outskirts. In the past few years a great deal has been done in the town centre by way of renovation and restoration. New hotels have been built as well as underground car parks. There is a tourist information office in which you can find out about the many things that visitors can do and see.

The best way to see Jerez, which has so many old and beautiful

(Opposite) *One of the first things you see as you come into Gibraltar is the sheer limestone wall of the Rock's north face, which is riddled with holes. These are tunnel openings and gun emplacements, the first of which were made during the great siege of 1779 to 1783. (Photo by Richard Kearns)*

houses, is to wander around the town centre on foot. If you start by visiting the tourist information office (Alameda Cristina 7) you will be able to get a street map. There are a number of churches of various architectural styles that the local guide books would have you visit, including the huge **Iglesia Colegiata** on whose steps the grapes are blessed and trodden in old fashioned style at the start of the Vendimia festival, the autumn grape harvest each year.

El Alcazar: On the way into Jerez from Puerto de Santa Maria you will find this eleventh-century Moorish fortress at the top of the hill. Inside you can see the mosque with its mihrab and minaret and the so called Moorish baths. The Alcazar can be visited every day between 10.30am and 1.30pm.

Alameda Vieja: In front of the fortress is a large square with a bandstand and on Sunday mornings a market is set up here selling various crafts, stamps and coins and other such articles. The municipal band or some other local artist performs on the bandstand.

Town Hall: In the beautiful Plaza de la Asuncion, not far from the Alcazar, is the old renaissance style town hall with its intricate façade including figures of Hercules and Julius Caesar above the two windows.

Archeological Museum: Soon to opened in the Plaza del Mercado.

Bodegas

If you have taken time to wander round the town you will soon have seen how the various *bodegas* form an integral, physical part of the town. Many of them have beautiful gardens and any one of them would be worth a visit to see first hand how sherry is made. The most readily open to visitors are Sandeman's (Pizarro 10. Tel: 301100), Williams and Humbert's (Nuño de Caña 1. Tel: 331300) and Harvey's (Arcos 53. Tel: 151030). The Gonzalez Byass and Domecq *bodegas* may be visited by prior arrangement. If you are planning to visit only one, the best would be Williams and Humbert's as they offer the most complete tour including a video of the Horse Fair. Visiting times are between 10.00am and 1.30pm from Monday to Friday and in some you are charged a fee of 300 pesetas for the visit. When you get there you may well be asked to wait for more visitors to arrive to make up a group. Most *bodegas* close for three weeks in August and do not accept visitors. If in doubt, check with the tourist information office.

Clock Museum

La Atalaya is the name of an old mansion situated close to the Sandeman *bodegas* with attractive gardens containing ducks,

ROUTE of the WINES

Trebujena

Sanlucar

Chipiona

Jerez

Rota

Puerto
Santa
Maria

Sherry

Xeres

Jerez

Aqua vitae

Those who were surprised to learn that all true sherry comes from the tiny sherry triangle formed by Jerez, El Puerto and Sanlucar, may well be equally surprised to learn that 90 per cent of all Spanish brandy comes from the very same *bodegas* or wineries, especially from the Gonzalez Byass and Domecq *bodegas* in Jerez and the Osborne and Terry *bodegas* in Puerto de Santa Maria. These producers are quick to point out that Jerez brandy was never intended to be an imitation of French cognac, much less a poor relation. The story of Jerez brandy is similar to that of the forgotten cask of fino that turned into the first Amontillado sherry. It was a consignment of distilled grape spirit shipped to Holland and unintentionally left to age in the casks that resulted in the earliest version of Jerez brandy. For most of the modern brandies, distilled grape spirit is brought in from other parts of Spain and then aged in the traditional *solera* system of oak casks, just like sherry. The minimum ageing process takes six months but the best brandies are aged for at least ten years.

---

flamingoes and peacocks. The mansion itself is private, housing various offices to do with the *bodegas* but it also houses a clock museum with a collection of over 300 clocks of different styles and nationalities. There is also a collection of silverware and another of walking sticks but these are not always on public display. The museum is open from 10.00am–1.30pm, Monday to Friday. Entrance: 200 pesetas.

Exhibition of Andalusian Riding Costumes

This is a small privately run exhibition displaying some fifty different examples of typical Andalusian riding wear such as the suits worn by men at the *feria*, at *romerias* such as El Rocio, or by bullfighters on horseback and so on. In the future the display will include typical costumes from the eighteenth century. The owners are a family of tailors who make the suits worn by the riders of the Royal Andalusian School of Equestrian Art. Their main shop is in Plaza Estevez 2. You can enquire about the exhibition there or by ringing 342192. The exhibition itself is at Bizcocheros 8, in the town centre but at the time of writing it does not have an official opening time.

Royal Andalusian School of Equestrian Art

If you were planning to spend only one day in Jerez, I would highly recommend it were a Thursday so that you could see the unforgettable exhibition 'How the Andalusian horses dance', presented in the Royal Andalusian School of Equestrian Art by its founder, Don Alvaro Domecq.

These famous Andalusian horses are descendants of those bred by the local Carthusian monks in the eighteenth century. You can visit the school at the Recreo de las Cadenas on weekdays from 11.00am to 1.00pm. Here you will see a mansion built in the nineteenth century by the French architect Garnier, and set in attractive gardens. At the time of writing it is not open to the public. Next to it is the riding school with seating for 1600 spectators and stables for 60 horses. You can visit the stables and harness room. Every Thursday at 12.00 noon the exhibition is repeated, this great classical and Andalusian equestrian ballet set to very Spanish music, the riders wearing traditional Andalusian costume. Even if you are not particularly an animal lover, the rhythm, the precision, the beauty and intelligence of the horses is bound to leave a lasting impression on your mind. (Entrance fee: 1500 pesetas) On the other days of the week you can see the horses being trained and rehearsals for the exhibition. (Entrance: 500 pesetas) Every year the school takes this exhibition abroad to perform for special occasions and so far it has visited England, France, Holland, Mexico, Venezuela, Argentina, Belgium and Portugal.

The school is also preparing a museum of horse drawn carriages which will include some very beautiful and antique pieces, in the former Pemartín *bodega*, next to the school. It is expected to be opened before publication of this book.

The school organises a special tourist 'package' that can be booked at the school itself or through travel agencies.

• Jerez, la Frontera del Ensueño: (for groups – minimum 50 people) Exhibition of the dancing horses; visit to a *bodega* with a special lunch in surroundings that take you back to the eighteenth century; a performance by the Albarizuela Ballet offering classical Spanish dances, flamenco and regional folk dances.

• The exhibition of dancing horses is offered daily during the May horse fair and also on special gala evenings in July and August.

Information and bookings: travel agencies and Real Escuela Andaluza del Arte Ecuestre, Recreo de las Cadenas, Avenida Duque de Abrantes. Tel: (956) 311111/311100. Telex: 75087. EAAE-E-11407. JEREZ-ESPAÑA.

Horse fair

Leading up to the horse fair in May there are many important equestrian events including horse and carriage competitions, classical

The Andalusian Flamenco Centre in Jerez can be found in this beautifully renovated palatial house, just one of many such buildings in Jerez, El Puerto and Cadiz that have been carefully restored to their former grandeur.

and Andalusian dressage, horse shows, testing of the bulls and more. A full official programme with times and locations is available from the tourist information office.

Zoo
In your hotel or in the tourist office you may see leaflets about the Tempul Zoo. It is described as the most important zoological collection in Andalusia with 800 animals of 144 species and a reptile house containing 50 different species. In this reptile house there has recently been some successful breeding of the endangered chameleon. The zoo also boasts a botanical garden of 56,000 square metres. Unfortunately the leaflet is misleading and the zoo is more depressing than most. The animals are confined in very small spaces and some of them definitely look ill. It is probably worth visiting only if you are having a hard time entertaining young children. Entrance: 400 pesetas, children 200 pesetas.

Andalusian Flamenco Centre
1988 saw the official opening of this centre in the beautifully renovated Pemartin Palace, a noble Jerez house in the heart of Santiago, Jerez's gipsy quarter and therefore one of the most appropriate places in all Andalusia to represent the flamenco world. The aim of this Flamenco Centre is 'an attempt to integrate Flamenco Art with other Andalusian cultural activities and to uplift it from the position of a ghetto culture in which it finds itself today'. The Centre also hopes to find 'a definite dignified place for Flamenco Art in the Spanish cultural world'.

The Pemartin Palace houses a Flamenco Museum, graphic and video archives, a sound library, a reference library and dance and guitar classrooms. If you want to discover what flamenco is all about then this would be a good place to start. The first thing you can do is see a video presentation describing the origins of this art form and although the narrative is in Spanish (with a very Andalusian accent which you may not understand) it is well worth seeing. Address: Plaza de San Juan, Barrio de Santiago. Open Monday to Friday, 10.00am–2.00pm and 5.00–8.00pm.

Conference centre
1991 saw the opening of El Palacio de Congresos y Convenciones, very near the centre of Jerez. This brand new conference centre covers an area of 50,000 square metres and includes a pavilion with an area of 20,000 square metres and a height of 17m and all the

modern conveniences one would expect of a top class centre of its kind. There is also an open air auditorium with seating capacity for 1500 people.

La Cartuja

Founded in 1477, this famous and impressive Carthusian monastery is on the road out of Jerez going to Medina Sidonia. The patio at the entrance may be seen but only men may go beyond the entrance if it is open. The most likely time would be 5.00 to 6.00pm.

Race track and stadium

Outside Jerez on the road to Arcos is the Circuito de Jerez, built as a Formula One race track. In any of the provincial tourist offices you should be able to get a leaflet in English giving a detailed description of the track, technical data, spectator facilities and so on. Formula One races are no longer held here but there are many other important competitions. (See Chapter Four, Racing, for more details)

Until Barcelona '92 Chapin Stadium was the only Olympic sized stadium in Spain. The mildness of the climate allows for a great many sporting events to be held here throughout the year.

Accommodation

Space does not permit a full list of accommodation in Jerez, this is just a selection. The local tourist information office should have a complete list.

• Central
Hotel Jerez 5-star (Ciga Hotels). Avenida Alvaro Domecq 35. Tel: 300600. Telex: 75059. Offers the kind of quality and comfort one would expect of a 5-star hotel in an attractive setting on Jerez's wide avenue. Swimming pool and tennis courts. DR 16,200–23,000 pesetas.
Hotel Royal Sherry Park 4-star (Royaltur Hotels). Avenida Alvaro Domecq 11. Tel: 303011. Telex: 75001. Attractive new hotel, modern style, also on wide central avenue. DR 16,000–30,000 pesetas.
Hotel Guadalete 4-star. Duque de Abrantes 50. A brand new hotel near the Royal Andalusian School of Equestrian Art. Elegant and somewhat serious in style. Swimming pool. Tel: 182288. DR 17,000–23,000 pesetas.
Hotel Avenida Jerez 3-star. Avenida Alvaro Domecq 10. Tel: 347411. Telex: 75157 jemo. This hotel is not quite so new but quality

is good and it has a good location. DR 8900–13,775 pesetas.

Hotel Capele 3-star. General Franco 58. Tel:346400. Telex:75032catol. In the heart of the old part of Jerez. DR 9900–14,700 pesetas.

Hotel Doña Blanca 3-star. Calle Doña Blanca. Tel: 340403. Right in the centre of Jerez down some narrow streets but with own underground parking facilities.

Hotel Avila 2-star. Avila 3. Tel: 334808. DR 6000–8000 pesetas.

Hotel Torres 2-star. Arcos 29. Tel: 323400. Very near the centre. Very reasonable. DR 6000–8000 pesetas.

Hotel Joma 2-star. Higueras 22. Tel: 349689. DR 6400–9800 pesetas.

Hotel Nova 1-star. Alvar Nuñez 13. Tel: 341459. DR 4500–5500 pesetas.

Hostal Serit 2-star. Higueras 7. Tel: 340700. DR 6000–10,000 pesetas.

Hostal San Miguel 2-star. San Miguel 4. Tel: 348562. DR 2000–3300 pesetas.

Hostal Gover 1-star. Honsario 6. Tel: 332600. DR 3000–6000 pesetas.

• Outskirts

Hotel Don Tico 4-star. Carretera N1V km628. Postal address: Apartado de Correos 231. Tel: 185906. Brand new hotel outside Jerez just at the turning off to the airport on the N1V road to Seville. Low buildings, tastefully decorated with swimming pool, tennis courts, gym and sauna. DR 15,000–23,000 pesetas.

Hotel La Cueva Park 4-star. Carretera Jerez–Arcos km10. Postal address: Apartado de Correos 536. Tel: 321620. DR 16,000–22,000 pesetas. Very attractive hotel in typical Andalusian style adjoining the Meson la Cueva, a very popular restaurant. The hotel includes a bar in the cave that was part of the original Venta la Cueva (*cueva* means cave) many years ago.

Motel Aloha 2-star. Carretera Madrid–Cadiz km637. Tel: 302500. Pool. DR 7000–8000 pesetas.

Hotel Montecastillo 4-star. Tel: 908 616961. Outside Jerez behind the race track this hotel is part of the new Montecastillo complex which includes a golf course designed by Jack Nicklaus, riding and polo installations, an Olympic size swimming pool and tennis courts. A large hotel in Andalusian style with restaurant, cafeteria and so on next to a castle (of relatively recent construction) which has been turned into a social club.

Where to eat

Restaurante El Cartujo 5 forks. Hotel Jerez. Avenida Alvaro Domecq.

Restaurante El Bosque 3 forks. Avenida Alvaro Domecq.

Bar restaurante El Colmado 2 forks. Arcos 1.

Restaurante Monte Castillo In Hotel Montecastillo (see above).

Restaurante La Mesa Redonda Manuel de la Quintana 3.

Bar restaurante Tendido 6 2 forks. Circo 10 (near bull ring).

Restaurante Las Cocheras Plaza de las Cocheras. Interesting setting in a former bodega.

Bar restaurante El Buen Comer 2 forks. Zaragoza 38 (near bull ring).

Restaurante El Gaitan 2 forks. Gaitan 3.

Restaurante La Taberna del Capitan Divina Pastora Bloque 1 (near Recreo de las Cadenas).

Restaurante La Oca Gorda Santo Domingo 11.

Bar restaurante Paco Arcos 33. Local cuisine.

Bar restaurante Cepa de Oro Por Vera 35. Menu of the day.

Restaurante Economico 1 fork. Fontana 4. Home style cooking.

Bar La Venencia Calle Larga. Tiny bar with a wide range of tapas.

Bar Juanito Pescaderia Vieja, through archway off Plaza Arenal.

Camino del Rocio. Bar with Sevillana dancing. Velazquez 20.

Bodegon Restaurante Los Escudos Madre de Dios. Fridays 10pm dinner show.

Meson restaurante El Coto 5km out of Jerez on the road to Arcos. Typical Andalusian cuisine in a traditional setting complete with small bullring.

The tourist information office has a complete list of eating places.

Trebujena

The road from Jerez to the small white town of Trebujena takes you through an almost lunar landscape of chalky white soil. It passes through a tiny village called **Mesas de Asta**, dry, dusty and very poor, where there is an important archaeological site, the remains of an ancient city called Asta Regia which may well have been one of the principal cities of Tartessos.

Trebujena is surrounded by vineyards growing in this white *albariza* soil which produces the finest grapes for the best sherries. When it rains, this kind of soil becomes porous but quickly forms a hard crust as soon as the sun shines again, thus protecting the roots of the vines and trapping the water underneath. Trebujena is famous only for its carnival. The town itself is small and rural and most of the houses are relatively modern, though it does have the remains of yet another thirteenth-century castle. There is a cooperative that produces its own sherry but most of it goes to Jerez to supply other *bodegas*.

Between Trebujena and the river Guadalquivir there is a lot of marshland that provides the basic landscape between here and the next town on this route, Sanlucar de Barrameda.

Sanlucar de Barrameda

Sanlucar, which at the end of the last century was considered to be southern Spain's number one summer resort, is nowadays a busy, friendly town with an unworried air of dilapidated grandeur. As the capital of the domain of the Dukes of Medina Sidonia it was at one time one of the most important towns in Andalusia. This seemingly insignificant little port saw Columbus off on his third voyage of discovery as well as Magellan when he set out to sail around the world. There is still a Duchess of Medina Sidonia who owns the family palace here but Sanlucar has long been asleep in the shadow of its past and is a long way behind its partners in the sherry triangle (formed together with Jerez and El Puerto de Santa María) in terms of renovation, restoration and initiative, though the town does have a lot of potential as a tourist centre.

Around the world...in just over three years

Columbus was not the only adventurer to set sail from these shores. An Italian named Amerigo Vespucci sailed from the port of Sanlucar de Barrameda on the first of two voyages in which he explored the coast of South America as far south as Patagonia, thereby proving that the lands discovered by Columbus were not in fact the eastern edge of Asia but rather a whole new continent; and it was after this explorer that the new continent of America was named. The Portuguese explorer Magellan also set sail from Sanlucar de Barrameda in August 1519 with five ships. His goal was to find a passage to India by sailing west and around the newly discovered continent for which he would have to go even further south than Vespucci. Magellan found the route around the south of South America through what we now know as the Straits of Magellan and reached the Philippines where he was killed by natives. Only one ship made it back to Sanlucar in September 1522. It was captained by Juan Sebastian Elcano, who thereby became the first man to circumnavigate the world.

204 The Route Guide

The roads into Sanlucar from Trebujena, Jerez, Puerto or Chipiona take you into the **Barrio Alto** or higher quarter, which is the older part of the town dating from the early fifteenth century. Here you can see the Castillo de Santiago (fifteenth-century castle closed for restoration at the time of writing), part of the old city walls, the nineteenth-century palace of the prince and princess of Orleans and Bourbon, with its gardens (the ground floor may be visited without charge between 8.30am and 2.00pm Monday-Friday), the Palace of Medina Sidonia (privately owned and not open to the public), churches such as the fourteenth-century Iglesia de la O, former monasteries and many old mansions in streets such as San Agustin, Jerez and Pozo Amarguillo.

This higher quarter of Sanlucar is also where you will see the town's *bodegas* that produce the unique Manzanilla type sherry. The best place to sample this sherry is in the bars and *bodeguitas* of this part of the town. From the Barrio Alto the Cuesta de Belen with its intricate stone façade takes you down past the market place to the lower quarter with its shops, banks, squares and bars and then down the main avenue to the beach, the Guadalquivir river and, beyond it, the Coto Doñana Nature Reserve.

At the time of writing there is not a great deal in Sanlucar that you can actually visit, though the tourist information office (Calle Baños in the lower part of town) will have information about the progress of the restoration of the castle, palaces and so on. The Barbadillo *bodegas* may be visited at 12.30pm, Monday to Friday. Barbadillo is the largest of the sherry firms in Sanlucar. Its offices are in the former bishop's palace, opposite the church of Santa Maria de la O (Luis de Eguilaz 11. Tel: 360894).

Doñana Reserve

There are ferries that can take you across the river to the Doñana reserve from the area called Bajo de Guia but you need to get permission from the Agencia de Medio Ambiente (AMA) in Cadiz or Seville to visit the reserve. The best way to visit it is in organised groups which take you to various parts of the reserve by Land Rover. You can book by telephoning the Coto Doñana office (955-430432) or through the travel agency in the Hotel Guadalquivir. It is necessary however to book several weeks or even months in advance. Remember to take binoculars with you in order to observe animals and birds and remember that this is a nature reserve and not a safari park. You will not find groups of animals lying around waiting to have their photo taken! On the Thursday before Pentecost you can see pilgrims crossing the river on their way to the annual festival of El Rocio, many dressed in Andalusian costume, with horses and little wagons.

Horse racing

In the month of August Sanlucar is the scene of some traditional horse races that have been held here since 1845 and which were the first official horse races in Spain. The racetrack is an unusual one, 2000m along the beaches of Bajo de Guia and Las Piletas. A total of 24 races are held over a six day period from 6.00 in the evening until sunset – Sanlucar is famous for the beauty of its sunsets along this particular stretch of the coast.

Accommodation

Hotel Doñana 3-star. Avenida Cabo Noval. Tel: 365000. Fax: 367141. A brand new, modern hotel with swimming pool, 100m from the beach, very close to the area known as Bajo de Guia. DR 7000–12,600 pesetas.

Hotel Guadalquivir 3-star. Calzada del Ejercito 10. Tel: 360742. DR 7500–12,000 pesetas. The hotel is a 12-storey building, recently renovated, 250 metres from the beach. Some of the rooms have fine views over the town or Doñana and the river.

Hotel Tartaneros 3-star. Tartaneros 8. Tel: 362044. DR 8000–9000 pesetas. Central, near the beach. Opened 1988, very attractive interior.

Hotel Los Helechos 2-star. Madre de Dios 9. Tel: 361441. DR 5000–8000 pesetas. Simple but attractive building with typical Andalusian patio.

Hotel Posada del Palacio 2-star. Caballeros 11. Tel: 364840. In the Barrio Alto, near the Palacio de Orleans, this hotel is in an old palatial house and it is now part of a hotel management school, staffed by students. DR 6000 pesetas.

Hostal Las Marismas 2-star. Plaza La Salle 2. Tel: 366008. DR 3000–5000 pesetas.

Hostal Rio 2-star. Santo Domingo 27. Tel: 361581. Central. DR 2200–5500 pesetas.

Where to eat

The best known eating places in Sanlucar are the small, inauspicious looking restaurants by the river in the area called Bajo de Guia, such as **Casa Bigote** (you must book a table here as it is so popular), **Mirador de Doñana** (which recently won an international award for gastronomy), **Secundino** or **Casa Juan**. These restaurants are famous for their fish and sea food dishes, especially the typical Sanlucar *langostinos* (prawns) and *acedias* (small flat fish). Some of these restaurants have tables on the beach in constructions that are almost all window so that you can watch the river and the sun going down over Doñana whilst you dine. Other places to eat are **Restaurante el Veranillo** (Barrios Masero 6), near the beach, and **Restaurante el Drago** (Avenida de las Piletas 5).

Note that Sanlucar is the home of an important local ice-cream industry and there is no shortage of delicious ice-dream desserts.

Chipiona

There is a road leading out of the lower part of Sanlucar signposted Playa de la Jara, which takes you along the coast through residential areas and a landscape that gets progressively flatter and more intensely cultivated. **La Jara** and beyond it **Montijo** are tiny communities that lend their names to the particular stretch of beach closest to them. The road then takes you back to the C441 road to Chipiona and it is obvious on this route that agriculture is one of the mainstays of Chipiona's economy. Thanks to extensive irrigation, cultivation under plastic canopies and crop rotation these lands yield up to three harvests a year and this is one of the few rural communities that has managed to avoid the emigration problem so prevalent in other areas. Vines are cultivated here and Chipiona is known for its muscatel wines. The best known *bodega* is Cesar Florido (Victor Pradera 22), producing fino, muscatel, oloroso and amontillado wines. Other local farmers specialise in the cultivation of fruit and vegetables and, as you will no doubt see, flowers, particularly carnations. These flowers are exported to many European countries.

Chipiona itself is another small and friendly town though very different in character to Sanlucar. It lies on flat land at the westernmost point of the province of Cadiz, facing the neighbouring province of Huelva and the open Atlantic ocean. At low tide a rock known as **Salmedina** can be seen, site of many a shipwreck and site also of the original settlement of the town. Chipiona gets its name from a Roman consul, Caepion, who built a primitive sort of lighthouse here to warn boats heading for the river Guadalquivir of the dangers of Salmedina rock. Many Roman remains have been found in the area.

Apart from its agriculture and a small fishing fleet, Chipiona depends heavily on tourism. It is a popular summer resort, particularly for people living in Seville. The town's permanent population of some 14,000 swells to almost 200,000 in the month of August. Most of the numerous hotels and hostals close during the winter months as do many of the bars and restaurants.

What to see

There are no monuments, museums or any such thing of particular interest to visit in Chipiona. Its most distinctive buildings are the lighthouse and the shrine of **Nuestra Señora de Regla**, which somehow looks more like a miniature English cathedral than a typical Andalusian shrine.

The **Plaza de Juan Carlos I** outside the Town Hall (el Ayuntamiento) is very attractive with its palm trees and pigeons, its hibiscus and bougainvillea. Leading out of this square is the gorgeous little **Fray Baldomero street** with its white walls, black window grilles and potted geraniums hanging along the walls and on the balconies. Few sights could be more typically Andalusian. This street leads into the main street of the town, the pedestrian Calle Isaac Peral with its shops, bars, restaurants, ice-cream parlours and so on. Another attractive street is the **Avenida del Faro** leading up to the lighthouse. Most of the rest of the town consists of small white houses of relatively modern construction and summer apartments and 'bungalows'.

The main **beach** in Chipiona is not all that wonderful as it is very rocky and at low tide rather unattractive. On one stretch of the beach you will see some ancient stone walls built out from the shore in a sort of semi-circle. They are thought to date from Moorish times and acted as corrals in which fish would get trapped as the tide went out. It was then easy to catch the fish by wading out and throwing nets over them.

Where to stay

Hotel Cruz del Mar 3-star. Avenida de Sanlucar de Barrameda 1. Tel: 371100. Telex: 75095mcdm. Open from Easter to mid October. Consists of two separate buildings on the sea front, one modern style and one in traditional Andalusian style although the latter is the newer building. Swimming pool, gymnasium, car, moped and bicycle rental. DR 11000 pesetas.

Hotel del Sur 2-star. Avenida de Sevilla 2. Tel: 370350. Near Regla shrine and beach. Modern style hotel with swimming pool. DR 6800 pesetas. Open 1st April–30th October.

Hostal Brasilia 2-star. Avenida del Faro 12. Tel: 371054. Close to the beach, with swimming pool. DR 5600–7360 pesetas. Open all year.
Hostal Gran Capitan 2-star. Calle Fray Baldomero Gonalez. Tel: 370929. DR 3500–4000 pesetas. Open all year.
Hostal Guadalupe 2-star. Avenida de Sevilla 6. Tel: 370917. DR 5800 pesetas. Open all year.
Camping Pinar de Chipiona 2nd class. On road to Rota, 3km out of the town. Tel: 372321. Open all year. Capacity for 800 people. Amongst pine trees, 800m from the beach. Prices: (a) 2650 pesetas, (b) 1880 pesetas.

Where to eat
Meson la Barca Near Hotel Cruz del Mar. Fresh Seafood.
Restaurante La Pañoleta 3 forks. Isaac Peral 5. Good quality cuisine.
Restaurante Luz Playa Avenida Carrero Blanco.
Meson Calvillo Gongora 7.
Bodegon Gran Chaparral Avenida Carreo Blanco.
Restaurante Peña. Avenida de Sevilla 43.
Los Corrales Next to Hotel Cruz de Mar, El Patio.
Restaurante El Gato Signposted from Regla Shrine. Good paella and good prices.
El Patio de 'Juan C' Bar Avenida de la Cruz Roja 10.

Most of these restaurants have open air terraces for eating outside in the summer, most serve paella and most display the menu and prices outside. There are plenty more bars in the town and also *ventas* on both the Sanlucar and Rota roads.

Rota

The road to Rota has several side roads leading down to different stretches of beach which are all signposted 'playa' and some have special parking areas. One of the beaches is called **Playa de la Ballena** and nearby is a site destined to become a new residential and tourist complex with a golf course and other installations called Recreo de la Ballena. The first stone has been laid with due ceremony but at the time of writing the project has gone no further than that and is unlikely to be finished before 1995.

Rota itself dates back to Moorish times although there have been settlements here since the days of Tartessos. The oldest and most attractive part of the town is by the harbour with the nearby castle, **El Castillo de Luna** and ancient church, another **Iglesia de la O**.

The town's more recent history has been marked by the building in 1953 of a large Spanish/American naval base which, from the start, provided a good deal of work for the local people. The arrival of the Americans inevitably had a tremendous impact on what was a modest fishing village in a lost corner of Franco's Spain. By now, however, any of the more negative aspects of this impact have smoothed themselves out and on the whole the two communities get on well. Some 75–80 per cent of the local Spanish population (which has doubled since the building of the base) make their living or at least supplement their incomes from the base, directly or indirectly. There are, of course, certain bars and clubs that cater particularly to more American tastes and you can get some good pizzas here (should you happen to get a sudden craving for one!).

Despite all this, Rota is still a small Andalusian fishing and tourist town with very characteristic architecture but perhaps with a more cosmopolitan population than most of its neighbours. The town's best beach is **La Costilla** stretching from the harbour up towards Punta Candor. Rota is included in the route of the wines because of its position in the sherry area although no sherries are actually produced here. Some passable red and white table wines are produced from the grapes grown in local vineyards.

Where to stay

Hotel Playa de la Luz 3-star. Arroyo Hondo, on the way out of town towards Punta Candor. Tel: 810500. A very attractive modern hotel with rooms around a garden area and a large swimming pool. Right by the beach. DR 9550–11,000 pesetas.

Hotel Caribe 3-star. Avenida de la Marina 62. Tel: 810700. Closer to the centre of town, not far from the beach, with own swimming pool. DR 11,200–13,800 pesetas.

Hotel Parque Victoria 2-star. Avenida Juan Ramon Jimenez. Tel: 811500. Central, unattractive modern style building. Not very new and somewhat frayed though quite comfortable. DR 9180–10,560 pesetas.

Hostal Nuestra Señora del Rosario 2-star. Higuereta 25-27. Tel: 810604. Central (near beach). DR 4015-4455 pesetas.

Camping Punta Candor 1st class. Open all year. On the road to Chipiona, surrounded by pine woods, 50m from the beach. Capacity for 750 people. Prices (a) 2420 pesetas, (b) 1650 pesetas.

Where to eat

Some of the more typically Andalusian eating places in Rota either for a meal or for tapas are as follows:

Restaurante Meson La Almadraba Avenida de la Diputación (towards Hotel Playa de la Luz).
Restaurante Bar Bahia Conjunto Residencial Virgen del Mar (on road to Chipiona).
Bar la Tasca Avenida Principes de España.
Bar Rota and **Bar Juan El Temprano** Calle Calvario.

Jerezanos and Portuenses

Separated by a mere 14km by road, the people of Jerez de la Frontera and El Puerto de Santa Maria, *jerezanos* and *portuenses*, are often separated by a long standing sense of rivalry. Jerez is the capital of sherry country and, indeed, for some of the prouder *jerezanos*, almost the capital of Spain. It is one of the most traditional towns in Spain and, with its famous horses, its sherries, its Olympic sized stadium and Formula One race track, it has much to be proud of. Writer Nicholas Luard described it as 'rich, massively confident and a little smug', a description that still fits well, although Jerez also has a good share of very poor people. One thing Jerez does not have is coastline and one of the things that tends to annoy *portuenses* is the *jerezanos*' unauthorised adoption of the beach at Valdelagrana as their own, even to the extent of publishing information about 'Jerez's beaches' in official tourist leaflets. In some English publications Puerto is described as Jerez's sea-port or as 'a pleasant place to spend an afternoon' when in fact it is an important tourist resort in its own right producing some very fine fino sherries which go down well with its excellent shellfish. Indeed, at all times of the year, many a *jerezano* can be found on a shellfish binge along Puerto's Rivera del Marisco. Those *jerezanos* who can afford to may well have a summer house in Puerto because Jerez can get stiflingly hot in August and the beach resort's nightlife attracts people from many neighbouring towns in the summer. The most typical upper class *jerezanos* may be seen in Puerto's discotheques with their dark hair slicked back with Brylcreem and wearing navy blue blazers and burgundy coloured ties. Despite this rivalry the two towns have been described as two small boys who are always fighting but cannot live without each other.

El Puerto de Santa María

After Rota this route of the wines brings you to the second most important sherry town, El Puerto de Santa María. It is also without doubt the most important summer resort in the province. Its population doubles in July and August and the atmosphere is lively

Castles in this part of Spain are small and friendly when compared to the grandiosity of castles in other, colder parts of Europe. Many of the castles stand in ruins and appear somewhat forlorn but San Marcos castle in Puerto de Santa María is in good repair – a tidy little castle with a lot of charm. (Photo by Catherine Cavanaugh)

and exciting. The majority of visitors are Spaniards from Jerez, Seville, Madrid and other areas who come here to escape the intense heat of the interior and, of course, to enjoy all that the town has to offer. El Puerto caters to a rather more affluent type of tourist than do Chipiona and Sanlucar although it is by no means exclusively for the wealthier visitors. There is a wide range of accommodation available including two campsites and an equally wide range of eating places, bars and entertainment.

The modern tourist installations of Valdelagrana and Vista Hermosa are separate from the town itself as is the new marina, **Puerto Sherry**. This marina, when finished will be very much self contained with its own hotels, apartments, shops, clubs and sports and entertainment facilities, some 3km from the town.

The town itself remains unmistakably Andalusian. Its narrow streets and white-washed walls, its teeming market place, its well-kept squares and flower bedecked balconies, its fishing port and its little castle are still intact. Smells of jasmin in the evening air, bright splashes of jacaranda trees, the tantalising trace of sherry in your nostrils as you walk past a *bodega*, the shrill cries of children playing in the streets and patios, that brilliant sunshine that leaves you momentarily blinded on walking indoors, the intensity of blue in sea and sky – your senses will constantly remind you that you are somewhere different: Andalusia. Puerto de Santa María has not betrayed its essential identity for the sake of attracting foreigners. The quality and variety of the local food, drink and entertainment need no imported additives or colourings.

Legend, with its own poetic licence, attributes the founding of the town to the Greek Captain Menesteo. Emerging triumphant from the Trojan horse only to find himself dispossessed of his lands, he set sail and roamed about the Mediterranean until, passing through the Straits of Gibraltar and turning northwards, he came across the sheltered Bay of Cadiz. He established a settlement at the mouth of a river and named it in his own honour, Puerto Menesteo. Centuries later, in 711AD this insignificant little river was to go down in history with the name of Guadalete, which means 'river of forgetfulness'. It was so named when peace was made after three days of fierce battle between the invading Moors and the Visigothic army whose leader, King Roderick, was killed.

When five centuries of Moorish occupation had come and gone and the town, by this time known as El Puerto de Santa María, had passed through several hands into those of the Medinacelli family, it grew into a thriving port whose importance and potential did not escape the notice of one Cristobal Colon – or Christopher Columbus as we know him. This most famous of historical figures lived here for a time, trying to persuade the Medinacelli family to back his proposed expedition. At the last minute, Queen Isabella intervened and his first voyage of discovery finally sailed under her patronage from the rival port of Palos in the neighbouring province of Huelva.

The forgotten river

The name of the river Guadalete descends from Moorish days and means 'river of forgetfulness'. Born in the mountains just above Grazalema it meanders over 172km before reaching the sea at Puerto de Santa Maria. Described in one local guide book as 'majestic', the river Guadalete is in fact in a sad state of abandon, the longstanding victim of careless and stinking pollution. Local ecologists have long been campaigning for the measures that would be needed to clean up the river and bring it back to life, so far with no success.

The first bridge to be built across the river at Puerto de Santa Maria was opened with great ceremony on the 14th February, 1779. In the middle of the ceremony, when hundreds of people were crowded onto the bridge along with all the local dignitaries, one of the sluice gates broke and the whole thing collapsed, resulting in the death of 413 people. Later, in the nineteenth century the Guadalete was used as a testing site for one of the world's first submarines designed by the Spanish naval scientist Isaac Peral who, following in the footsteps of the inventor Monturiol, invented a submarine propelled by an electric engine and armed with two Schwartzkoff torpedoes. Despite the success of the trials, the naval authorities were not convinced and wrote up an unfavourable report.

El Puerto de Santa María did play a significant role in the discovery of America, however, in the person of Juan de la Cosa whose ship, the *Santa María*, sailed in that first and famous voyage in 1492. He also took part in two other expeditions that sailed from Puerto de Santa María and after these voyages he drew up the first *mapamundi* (the first world map to include what was then known of the Continent of America) here in Puerto in the year 1500. The map is preserved in the naval museum in Madrid.

In the decades that followed the discovery of America, El Puerto became a thriving commercial port and many shipowners and their families settled here, building themselves the large, luxurious houses that gave rise to the name, Town of a Hundred Palaces, by which El Puerto came to be known. Many of these are still standing; some are privately owned and others have been or are being restored by the local authorities to house such institutions as the Town Hall and the magistrate's court.

In the way that history so often has of repeating itself, El Puerto de Santa María seems to be heading once again for the crest of a wave. As in the days of its former splendour, wealthy people from other parts are coming here to build their palaces and take advantage of the town's position and climate, this time to escape from business and use El Puerto as a pleasure harbour rather than a commercial port.

The old town

The best way to explore the old part of the town is on foot and a good place to start would be the market place, **La Plaza**, where you can buy hot *churros* and take them to a nearby café for breakfast. From the market, walk along the Calle Vicario, past the traffic lights, to the Plaza de España. (You can get a street map of the town from your hotel or from the tourist office.) In this square stands the quite impressive **Iglesia Mayor**, the town's largest church which was built over a period of four centuries and therefore has quite a mixture of styles. On the other side of the square is the **Academia de Bellas Artes**, the local art school whose ground floor rooms temporarily house a modest archaeological museum (open 9.00am–1.30pm Monday to Friday). From this square you can take the Calle Santa Lucia which brings you to the bull ring (see below) or the Calle Palacios which leads down towards the river. Going down this latter street, if you turn right at the third set of traffic lights you will come to the castle (see below) and the Plaza de Alfonso X El Sabio.

From this plaza take the street that goes downhill towards the river, past the beautifully restored **Casa Palacio de Aranibar** in the square itself, past the old fish market (now a restaurant called El Resbaladero), past the old customs building (now the Hostal Sherry), to the **fishing wharf** where the nets are laid out to be mended. Turn left down the Avenida de la Bajamar which runs parallel to the river and brings you to the Plaza de Las Galeras. Just before you reach it there is a little side street on the left (Calle Guadalete) where you will find the tourist information office. (In the summer the tourist information office provides guided walking tours of the town on Saturday mornings leaving at 11.00am.) At about the same level on the right of the Avenida is the main stop for buses going to Cadiz, Jerez, Sanlucar and other towns. (The bar opposite has a timetable inside.) Just beyond the bus stop is a small jetty that, centuries ago, served as the landing stage for ships of the Spanish navy and ships heading for the New World.

The Plaza de Las Galeras, beside the jetty, has a large, stone fountain originally built in 1735 to provide water for ships setting sail for Africa or America. After passing the fountain you come to the **Parque Calderon**, a long park with two lines of tall palm trees running along its length. Here there are bars, merry-go-rounds and amusements for children and stalls selling freshly fried potato crisps. On summer evenings, Sundays and holidays, this park is always crowded with people strolling to and fro. One great thing about 'going out' in Andalusia is that you can take your children with you if you wish, which means being able to go out much more frequently than if you have to rely on a baby-sitter. Obviously children are not taken to night clubs or discotheques but they are considered an integral part of the social life and are very much seen, heard and enjoyed.

Whilst walking around El Puerto, remember to look up from time to time. There are some very beautiful balconies and façades on some of the buildings. You will also see curious little towers on the roofs of some of the larger houses. These were in fact little look-out towers from which anxious ship owners could watch for the arrival of their ships without having to keep dashing down to the wharf.

Another way of seeing the town is to hire a horse and carriage from the Plaza de las Galeras by the jetty. These open carriages are real antiques – over a hundred years old – and take up to five passengers on a tour of the town. They are available every day from July to September and every Saturday (weather permitting), during the rest of the year.

Things to see and do

San Marcos Castle: This castle, dating from the thirteenth century, is small but in good state of repair, probably the best preserved of the province along with the castle in Tarifa. It was not in fact one of the strategic frontier fortresses involved in battles and sieges between Christians and Moors. It was built after Puerto had been reconquered by King Alfonso X. From July to mid September it can be visited on Mondays, Wednesdays and Saturdays between 11.00 and 13.30, when someone from the tourist information office should be there to act as a guide. During the rest of the year it is usually open to the public on Saturday mornings but if not check with the tourist office. From time to time the castle is used for exhibitions and lectures.

Bull ring: Built over 100 years ago this bull ring can hold up to 15,000 spectators and is the third largest is Spain. It is also said to be the best illuminated, referring to the way the sun illuminates the ring throughout the evening. It has the dubious privilege of being the first ring in Spain in which a matador was killed by a bull. At the main entrance there is a mosaic with the words attributed to the famous matador, Joselito 'El Gallo', and which, roughly translated, mean that anyone who has not seen the bulls in Puerto cannot know what a bull fight is about; though he was referring not only to the bull fight itself but also to the atmosphere of the town on a bull fight evening. The bull ring itself is not such a useless building as one might think. Apart from bull fights it is used for concerts in the summer. It has housed the local fire brigade for many years and there are several workshops and meeting rooms behind the doors around the outside of the ring. You can visit the ring from Mondays to Fridays between 10.00 and 13.00. If the main gate is not open you can knock (or hammer!) on the door.

El Vapor: The jetty beside the Plaza de Las Galeras now serves the little ferry boat, *Adriano III*, known affectionately as 'El Vapor' although it no longer runs by steam. This is the third of these little ferries that have been ploughing back and forth from Puerto to Cadiz every day since 1929. The journey is quicker by road – it takes three quarters of an hour on the ferry – but a trip by boat on a clear, sunny day is a perfect way to appreciate the colours of the bay, with its almost impossible range of blues, as you chug along in the wake of so many who must have made the crossing since Phoenician times when Cadiz was an island. On Saturday nights in the summer the ferry offers visitors a trip around the bay and a glass or two of *sangria*, to the accompaniment of a live musical performance. Tickets for this can be bought in the boat during the week or at the tourist information office. Price:400 pesetas.

Aquasherry Park: This exciting aqua park is easily visible on the road out of El Puerto de Santa María to Jerez. Open from the beginning of June to mid September, it is a wonderful place to spend the day, especially with children. Prices: adults 1195 pesetas, children 795 pesetas. Inside you can rent reclining chairs under sun umbrellas and there are also bars, restaurants and a shop. In the evenings the aqua park opens as an open air discotheque with a dance floor in the middle of one of the pools. If you get too hot dancing you can cool off in the water.

Casino: This can be found near the aqua park, off the road to Jerez. As well as its games rooms it has a restaurant, discotheque and cinema. You can visit the Casino after 5.00pm on Friday evenings in the summer by collecting an invitation from the tourist information office. Otherwise a fee is charge to enter and you must always show your passport or some kind of identification.

There is plenty to do in and around Puerto, especially in the summer. For detailed information about sports facilities, discotheques, flamenco evenings, visits to bodegas and any other queries you may have, the tourist information office should be your best source.

Where to stay

• Central

Hotel Monasterio San Miguel 4-star. Larga 27. Tel: 864440. Fax: 862604. This is a beautiful, new and luxurious hotel in a restored convent very near the centre of town. Swimming pool. DR 10,500–12,000 pesetas.

Hotel Santa Maria 3-star. Avenida de la Bajamar. Tel: 872504. Another new and very attractive hotel by the river with pool on roof. DR 6825–12,975 pesetas.

Hotel Los Cantaros 3-star. Curva 6. Tel: 540240. A very pleasant, modern hotel. Being right in the centre, parking is a bit difficult though the hotel has parking facilities at a few minutes walk. Ask for a room giving on to the interior patio to avoid noise from the street in the busy summer months. DR 7500–11,500 pesetas.

Hostal Chaikana 2-star. Javier de Burgos 17. Tel: 542902. Fax: 542922. A new hostal right in the centre of the old part of the town down a rather narrow street. Parking is something of a problem but the hostal itself is very pleasant, as good as many hotels. DR 6000–8000 pesetas.

Hostal Gazpacho 2-star. Tortola 10. Tel: 854611. Not far from Puntilla beach. Simple but very pleasant. DR 4200 pesetas.

Hostal La Palma 2-star. Los Atalaya 11 (near Hospital Santa Maria). Tel: 850251. DR 3500–4200 pesetas.

• On the outskirts

Hotel Meliá Caballo Blanco 4-star. Avenida de Madrid 1. Valdelagrana (outside El Puerto on the road to Cadiz). Tel: 562541. Recently renovated and redecorated, the hotel has rooms distributed in small buildings throughout the gardens. Swimming pool. DR 12,000–15,500 pesetas.

Hotel Puerto Bahia 3-star. Avenida de la Paz 38. Valdelagrana. Tel: 862721. A six-storey building on the sea front of this residential area just outside El Puerto on the way to Cadiz. DR 5950–7590 pesetas.

Del Mar Hotel 3-star. You should not miss this blue painted building behind the 3-fork La Goleta restaurant on the road to Rota. Attractive interior. DR 7000–10,5000 pesetas.

• Hotel apartments (for self-catering)

Puerto Service 2-keys. Viveros. Centro Comercial de Vista Hermosa. About 3km out of town on the road to Rota. Tel: 856003. Attractive swimming pool in gardens. Prices: write for details.

Apartamentos Turistcos Vistahermosa 2-keys. Avenida Juan Melgarejo 29. Centro Comercial de Vista Hermosa. Tel: 852112. Pool in gardens, gymnasium, squash courts. Can be very noisy in July and August. Prices: write for details.

Camp sites

Guadalete 1st class. In Valdelagrana on main Cadiz road. Tel: 561749. Open all year. Capacity for 1150 people. Swimming pool. Grassy terrain with plenty of trees. Can have a lot of mosquitoes at certain times being close to a marshy area. Prices: (a) 1765 pesetas, (b) 1265 pesetas.

Las Dunas de San Anton 1st class. Paseo Maritimo de la Puntilla. Postal address: Apartado de Correos 21. Tel: 870250. Very modern sanitary installations, set amongst pine trees. In El Puerto, by Puntilla beach and with a good swimming pool. Capacity for 1200 people. Prices: (a) 2405 pesetas, (b) 1604 pesetas.

Where to eat

There are over thirty restaurants in and around El Puerto de Santa María and a tremendous number of bars, *mesones* and *ventas* where you can eat a wide variety of food. The local tourist office has a complete list of restaurants available. The following list is just a selection:

• Restaurants and ventas

El Faro del Puerto 3 forks. On road to Rota at crossroads above bull ring. Excellent food like its sister restaurant in Cadiz, exquisite desserts.

Los Portales 3 forks. Ribera del Rio 13 (centre). For meals or tapas, both are good.

La Goleta 3 forks. Carretera de Rota, just past the petrol station. Best to book. Tel: 854232.

Casa Flores 2 forks. Ribera del Rio 9 (centre).

Meson El Pescsdor in a little side street off Plaza de la Herrería (centre).

Restaurante El Convento Avenida de la Bajamar. At the entrance to a popular and most unusual bar in a very old building with an open air patio used in the summer and real fires inside in the winter.

Bar Jamon Capillera 5. In the higher part of the old town, near crossroads to Sanlucar.

Venta La Rufana Outside El Puerto on the road to Rota just after Vista Hermosa. Popular for its garlic chicken. Children's play area.

Venta La Choza On old Rota road, turning off just after the turning to Sanlucar at the top of the town. Thatched building adjacent to a riding school but restaurant quality and prices.

Un Alto en el Camino On road to Puntilla beach. Barbecued meat and fish. Pleasant outdoor area and friendly atmosphere.

- Bars

There are a great many bars for tapa sampling, such as Echatepayá on the Ribera del Marisco. The name of the bar means 'move over' and when you get there you will see why. It is tiny and the walls and ceiling are covered in cuttings from bull fighting magazines. It has rather unpredictable opening hours but is definitely worth a visit. The **Bar er Betis** and **La Bodeguilla**, just off the Plaza de la Herrería in the Calle Misericordia, are two more excellent tapa stops but there really are a great many more. For night life in the summer try the area near the tourist information office, El Convento (see above under restaurants), the Centro Comercial de Vista Hermosa, open air bars on some beaches and also Puerto Sherry. A lot of British and Irish residents tend to congregate at the **Bar Colon**, otherwise known as Bill's Bar in the Plaza Colon, near the tourist information office.

ELEVEN

Gibraltar and the Mediterranean coast

Gibraltar

Although not politically a part of the province of Cadiz, Gibraltar must inevitably feature in this guide book because of its geographical position and because, once you are in the area, it is well worth a visit, even if you do not choose to fly into its airport. Many people in Britain are almost as uninformed about Gibraltar as they were about the Falkland Islands a few years ago. For many hundreds of British expatriates who live on the Costa del Sol, however, Gibraltar is something like a second home.

  The first thing you notice about the Rock is how very small and crowded it is. It measures just two and a half square miles and, although its total population is little more than 28,000 (comparable to that of a town like Arcos de la Frontera) this number of people confined to such a small area gives Gibraltar one of the highest population densities in Europe. One gets the distinct impression also that each family in Gibraltar must own at least two cars. If you add to this the fact that over three million people are visiting Gibraltar every year since the re-opening of the border, many of them bringing their own cars across with them, then the word 'crowded' may seem like a typical British understatement.

History

The 'solid' Rock of Gibraltar is in fact riddled with natural caves and man-made tunnels. The natural caves have been inhabited since time immemorial and in one of them, known as Forbes Quarry, the skull of a 40-year old woman was found in 1848. It later turned out to be similar to the skull discovered in the Neanderthal valley in West Germany in 1856 that came to be known as Neanderthal man. Local historians claim therefore that this prehistoric creature should by

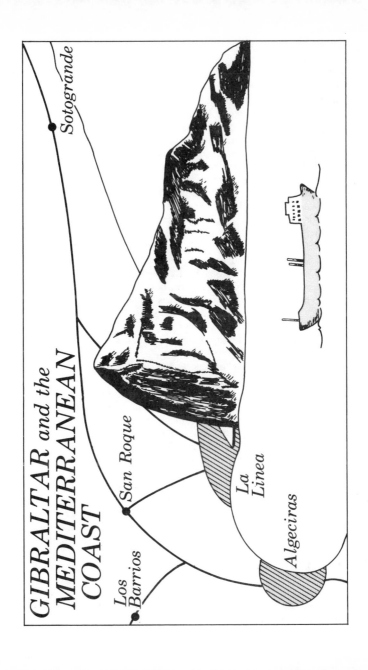

GIBRALTAR and the MEDITERRANEAN COAST

Sotogrande

San Roque

Los Barrios

La Linea

Algeciras

rights have been called 'Gibraltar Woman'. The skull is now in the Museum of the Royal College of Surgeons in London but you can see a plaster cast of it in the Gibraltar Museum.

The Rock, considered by the ancients to be one of the pillars of Hercules (the other being the mountain of Jebl Musa nine miles away across the Straits), experienced the passing of the same civilisations as did the rest of the province of Cadiz and indeed the whole southern part of the peninsula: Phoenicians, Greeks, Romans, Vandals and Visigoths. In 711AD a certain Tarik ibn Zeyad led the invading Muslim forces from North Africa which defeated the Visigoths and established Islamic rule over Spain. They named the Rock Jebl El Tariq or Gibel Tarik (Tarik's mountain) from which the name Gibraltar is derived. The Moors dominated this area for nearly six centuries and built a castle and a walled city to defend the Rock in the year 1160. This was the first town to be built here.

When the armies of the Spanish Reconquest got down to this part of the peninsula, they laid siege to the rock and captured it in the year 1309. This was the first of many sieges in the history of Gibraltar. The Spaniards only held on to the town for about 24 years for in 1333 the Moors recaptured it and kept it for another century. Not until the year 1462, as a result of siege number eight, did Gibralatar finally fall back into Spanish hands.

In the Spanish War of Succession at the beginning of the eighteenth century the British, Austrians and Dutch were fighting against the French and Spanish. Sir George Rooke of the British Navy, having failed to capture Barcelona but determined not to go home empty-handed, decided to attack the strategically important position of Gibraltar. He did so on July 21st, 1704. After three days the governor surrendered and the majority of the town's population decided to leave, thinking that Spain would soon recapture the Rock. Despite several attempts, however, the British managed to hold their position. Only about 100 of the former inhabitants of the Rock stayed on after Rooke's attack. Later on people from various different nations came and settled here. The ancestors of much of the present population came from Britain, Genoa, Menorca, Portugal, Malta, Morocco and Spain. It must be remembered that the people of Gibraltar are really Gibraltarians (however British their policemen may look!). The Treaty of Utrecht officially relinquished the Rock to the British Crown in perpetuity but it was by no means a peace treaty and there were frequent battles between British and Spanish troops. From 1779 to 1783 Gibraltar suffered its fourteenth and longest siege but again Spain failed to recover Tarik's mountain. Although this was the last military attempt to sieze Gibraltar, Spain has by no means renounced its claim, for its strategic position makes it one of the world's most vital points of defence. It should be remembered that Spain has two small colonies on the north coast of Africa, the military post of Melilla and the port of Ceuta which is practically opposite Gibraltar.

During both world wars Gibraltar was indispensable to the Royal Navy but since 1945 its role has changed significantly. Its longstanding military connections have all but disappeared although the town did in a sense suffer one more siege. General Franco closed the border in 1969 and it remained closed until 1982. Nowadays Gibraltar's importance is no longer military but financial, thanks to its laws concerning the establishment and taxation of exempt companies and the fact that Gibraltar does not levy death duties, capital gains tax or VAT. The local tourist industry has also experienced a tremendous growth since 1982 and trade has increased rapidly. Indeed the local community has, on the whole, benefited enormously from the reopening of the border into a Spain so very different from the one that closed its gates back in 1969.

What to see

The Gibraltar tourist office has plenty of leaflets available which will guide you around the Rock and inform you of all there is to do and see, and of course you should not have any problems with the language here! The main tourist information office is at: Cathedral Square, Tel: 42400. There is another office in Market Place, Tel: 76400 and one more in the Gibraltar Museum in Bomb House Lane.

Main Street: All the comings and goings of life in Gibraltar centre on Main Street which stretches from the Northern Waterport Gates to Southport Gates and covers the length of the old walled Gibraltar town. This is the main shopping area with a wide range of goods and shops that include Safeway's, St Michael's and Mothercare as well as others that specialise in tobacco, spirits, perfume, watches and jewellery.

Governor's Residence: At the far end of Main Street in a former Franciscan convent. Ceremonial changing of the guards takes place every Tuesday morning at 11.00am.

Gibraltar Museum: In Bomb House Lane (Tel: 79158). Displays cover life on the Rock from the Stone Age through the Phoenician, Greek, Roman, Moorish, Spanish and British periods of its history. There is also a display of Gibraltar's flora and fauna. Entrance fee: £1.00 adults, 50p children. Open 10.00am–6.00pm Monday–Friday and 10.00am–2.00pm on Saturdays.

From battleground to shopping emporium

After many centuries of fighting off the hordes and resisting the enemy through siege after heroic siege, Gibraltar is now the scene of a totally different kind of invasion. After sixteen years of being locked away on 2.25 square miles of Rock, Gibraltarians had to get used to the sudden impact on their lives of the thousands of visitors that swarm across the border every day in search of a bargain or the taste of a good old British banger. After several years as a flourishing shopping and financial centre, the Rock is definitely riding on a wave of prosperity, although for the local inhabitants there must surely be times when the swarms of friendly invaders are just a bit too much. Gibraltarian cars, with their distinctive number plates, are becoming a familiar sight within the province of Cadiz and along the Costa del Sol. Prior to the reopening of the border, the highpoint of going for a drive in Gibraltar was crossing the airstrip to the border and back, about the only stretch of road on which you could actually get into fourth gear. Nowadays, crossing the border by car can be a nightmare and many residents leave their cars in La Linea. A lot of the people who have come to set up shop in Gibraltar end up living over the border in Spain because of the housing shortage and high rental prices on the Rock. Gibraltar is unique and fascinating but many visitors leave themselves little time to look beyond the shops on Main Street, the pulsating centre where you can hear some of the local people speaking the most incredible mixture of Spanish and English, and where you can get some really grotty sandwiches and snacks that should make expatriates appreciate their local Spanish cuisine, despite the cravings for food 'from home' that bring many of them across the border for a spree in the local supermarkets.

The Moorish Bath: Situated in the lower part of the museum and dating from the fourteenth century, it is claimed to be the finest Moorish bath outside of Morocco.

The Moorish Castle: In 1333, when the Moors recaptured Gibraltar from the Spanish, they built a castle on the site of a previous one dominating the approach to the Rock from the mainland. It was made up of three parts, the upper castle or keep, the middle castle halfway down the hill, and the lower castle which stretched down to Casemate's Square. The only accessible part left today is the Tower of Homage which bears the scars of the ten sieges it underwent in the fourteenth and fifteenth centuries (closed for restoration work at the time of writing).

St Michael's Cave: Given the size of the Rock itself this cave is inevitably rather modest as caves go but it is used as an auditorium and makes a unique setting for live entertainment. There is another lower cave with an underground lake. Visits to this cave can be arranged through the Gibraltar Tourist Office. Opening times: 10.00am–7.00pm in the summer, it may close earlier in the winter. Entrance fee: £1.50 adults, £1.00 children.

The Upper Galleries: During the Great Siege (1779–1783), General Elliot offered a reward to anyone who could think of a way of mounting cannon on the north face of the Rock. A certain Sergeant Major Ince of the Company of Soldier Artificers suggested excavating a gallery through the solid rock. They started work on May 25th 1782 and tunnelled 82 feet in six weeks. By the end of the siege the gallery was 370 feet long and contained six embrasures and four guns. The Cornwallis Chamber and St George's Hall were excavated after the end of the siege. Since then over 30 miles of tunnels have been made inside the Rock. Within the Upper Galleries you can still see several of the original guns with life-size models in period costumes depicting scenes from the Great Siege. Galleries opening times: summer 10.00am–7.00pm, winter 10.00am–5.30pm. Entrance fee: 70p adults, 40p children.

The Rock Apes: One of Gibraltar's greatest tourist attractions today are these Barbary Apes which live half way up the Rock, the only primates living wild in Europe. In actual fact they are not apes but a North African breed of monkey known as Macaca Sylvana but because their tails are virtually non-existent they are considered by most people to be apes. Their popularity with visitors is somewhat ironic considering that, up until recently, they were regarded by the community as something of a nuisance because of their mischievous nature and incidents of theft and vandalism. They have been in danger of dying out on more than one occasion in the past though now there are two well established colonies around the Queen's Gate and Middle Hill areas and they are soon to have a new nature reserve with a full time caretaker and a specialist biologist, though this does not mean that they will be fenced in. They are thought to have been introduced by the early Moorish settlers. They are perfectly used to being observed and photographed and they may be fed, though only with fruit and nuts. Visitors are however warned not to tease them, make sudden movements or get too near as they are wild creatures and can be dangerous. They are also perfectly capable of running off with anything left within their reach.

Cable Car: The easiest way to get to the top of the Rock is this six minute trip by cable car. At the top there is a self-service restaurant, an English style pub and a souvenir shop as well as terraces which afford fantastic views of the town of Gibraltar, Catalan Bay, the airstrip and of course all the surrounding scenery of Andalusia, North Africa and the Straits. The highest point of the Rock is farther south from here reaching 1398 feet. The lower cable-station is in Grand Parade at the southern end of Main Street and there is a halfway station for those who want to get off and see the apes. Hours: Monday–Saturday, 9.30am–5.15pm. Last cabin down 5.45pm. Prices: £3.30 adults, £2.30 children.

Other points of interest: The various leaflets available from the tourist office give a brief run down of many other sights in Gibraltar such as Europa Point, the southernmost point with its view across the Straits; the Shrine of Our Lady of Europe; Parson's Lodge and Rosia Bay; the nearby 100 ton Gun; Catalan Bay on the other side of the Rock; the Alameda Gardens (Europa Road); the walk up Mediterranean Steps (South east side of Rock – not for the faint hearted!) and more. You can also find out about dolphin safaris out in the Straits. Another project in the Tourist Agency pipeline is the conversion of the Alameda Gardens into a subtropical theme park which will include a butterfly farm, a large free flight aviary and formal Moorish gardens.

At the time of writing Gibraltar is in a turmoil of activity with the building of a large new office complex and business centre called **Europort**. It is being built on reclaimed land in the old harbour area and an important part of the complex will be a five-star International Hyatt Regency Hotel. Europort is an important step towards the establishment of Gibraltar as an offshore Finance Centre of international standing. Some believe that the Rock is poised to become the Hong Kong of the Western Mediterranean. (The *Gibraltar Financial Services Handbook* gives full information on corporate and taxation advantages along with other useful information and advice for those interested in setting up a business in Gib.) Close to Europort there will be new apartment complexes and an important new leisure centre. Just a few minutes walk from this whole area another project called Queensway Quay is also under construction. This will be a residential complex with swimming pools, gymnasium and, eventually, a new marina.

Where to stay

The Rock Hotel 5-star. Europa Road. Tel: 73000. An elegant and very traditional hotel in Gibraltar with attractive gardens and swimming pool and a top quality restaurant with scenic views over the bay. DR £85–£90 with sea view and £70 with Rock view.

Holiday Inn 4-star. 2 Governor's Parade. Tel: 70500. Right in the centre of town this is a tall modern building that has recently been refurbished and offers the standards of comfort one would expect from a Holiday Inn. Rooftop swimming pool and wonderful views. DR £105.

Bristol Hotel 3-star. Cathedral Square. Tel: 76800. Rather old colonial style. Very close to Main Street. DR £49–£56.

Caleta Palace Hotel 3-star. Sir Herbert Miles Road. Catalan Bay. Tel: 76501. Overlooking the little fishing village of Catalan Bay on the other side of the Rock which is the shadier side. Right on the beach with swimming pool on terrace. DR £60–£70.

Gibraltar Beach Hotel and Apartments Sandy Bay. Tel: 76191. On east side of Rock in a picturesque setting overlooking the Mediterranean. All rooms face the sea right over the beach. Hotel rooms and self catering apartments. DR £46.

Aparthotel Ocean Heights Montagu Place. Tel: 75548. Half board or self-catering apartments. Pool, restaurant, health club. One-bedroomed apartment £35–£46.30.

Continental Hotel 3-star. 1/3 Engineer Lane. Tel: 76900. Unusual entrance through hamburger bar but simple, comfortable accommodation in a very good position at the beginning of Main Street. DR ≥£50 (20% discount for weekly stay).

Montarik Hotel 3-star. Main Street. Tel: 77065. Very simple accommodation with no frills but very central. Bar on roof terrace overlooking bay. DR £49.

Queen's Hotel Boyd Street. Tel: 74000. Slightly dilapidated but conveniently situated at the far end of main street near the cable car station. Views of Rock and bay. DR £33–£44.

Eating out

Although the British influence is the strongest here as far as the local cuisine goes, there is plenty of variety, particularly in Spanish, French, Italian and Moroccan cuisine. For some British residents in Spain, the thought of kippers and smoked haddock, steak and kidney pies or roast beef and Yorkshire pudding may be enticing but for those who are here on holiday and looking for something different there is plenty of local fish on the menus, particularly swordfish, as well as shellfish, squid and so on.

In the tourist offices you can get a helpful guidebook which has a comprehensive list of eating places, from restaurants to pubs to fast food establishments including a brief description of each. A small but interesting selection of local restaurants and wine bars is as follows:

Strings Restaurant 44 Cornwallis Lane. Tel: 78800, for a good meal in a relaxed but tasteful atmosphere. Closed Monday.
La Parmigiano 6 Lynchs Lane. Tel: 75300. Closed Sunday.
The Spinning Wheel 9 Horse Barrack Lane. Tel: 76091. Closed Sunday.
The Palm Court Holiday Inn Hotel Governor's Parade. Tel: 70500.
Bunters Wine Bar and Restaurant College Lane. Tel: 70482. Closed Sunday.
Corks Wine Bar 79 Irish Town. Tel: 75566.

La Linea de la Concepción

This town has largely grown up over the last century as a border town with Gibraltar, hence the lack of older buildings and monuments although its bull ring is one of the oldest in Spain and the town boasts an important bull fighting museum in the Calle San Juan 102. The Municipal Museum contains interesting photographic archives and plenty of books about Gibraltar and the surrounding area.

If you would like to spend a few days in Gibraltar, you might opt for a hotel in La Linea with views of the bay and the Rock. Two possibilities are as follows:
Aparthotel Rocamar 3-star. Avenida España 170. Tel: 767924. Tall modern building with self catering apartments. Swimming pool. Prices: 7840–10,810 pesetas.
Hotel Miramar 1-star. Avenida España 26. Tel: 100658. DR 4000–4500 pesetas.

The Mediterranean stretch of coast

Between Tarifa and Algeciras the road winds up and down through a very hilly area whose coast is mostly rocky with little sand. There are many tracks crisscrossing the area between the main road and the sea but most of them are in a military zone closed off to the public, which is a shame as this would be an interesting area for hikers and bird watchers. On the other hand, it was the military presence in this area that stopped short the encroaching urban development that had started along the Costa del Sol in the fifties and sixties, since no foreigners or foreign companies were allowed to purchase land within the military zone.

As you are coming into Algeciras there is a small road to the right signposted **Playa de Getares**. It takes you to an attractive beach with a developing residential area behind it. This beach has a fine view of Gibraltar and the bay whilst Algeciras and its industries remain hidden behind a headland. If you continue on towards the Punta del Carnero headland, past the lighthouse, you will come to a place where little roads twist up and down the hillside with street lights every few yards. Evidently somebody planned to build a residential area here and then ran out of funds. This would be another good spot for hikers and birdwatchers to explore – rather wild and forlorn but ruggedly attractive.

The old smuggling tradition

The southern shores of the province of Cadiz are temptingly near to the tax free ports of Ceuta and Melilla on the north coast of Africa, and of course Gibraltar, with its tax free cigarettes and whisky, could hardly be closer. Smuggling has been part of the way of life in this part of the province for centuries. A century and a half ago one of the main commodities smuggled in from Gibraltar was coffee, though in this century the demand became greater for cigarettes, whisky, and particularly for contraceptives, before they became legal in Spain. There was a constant battle between the smugglers and the Civil Guard who had a hard time following them along the myriad tracks and pathways that criss-cross the Campo de Gibraltar leading up into the mountains. Sometimes specially trained dogs were used to take consignments of cigarettes or condoms through the mountains to the first point on the intricate network of distribution. Some of the older locals tell of trips to Gibraltar on the old Algeciras ferry and how people would come back bulging with contraband. It would appear that smuggling cigarettes from Gibraltar is back in full swing, which is one of the reasons that getting back into Spain through customs is taking such a long time lately as conscientious customs officers make intensive searches of vehicles, shopping bags and any suspiciously bulging parts of anatomy!

The main bus terminal in this area is in Algeciras. There is also a railway line that runs from Algeciras to Bobadilla in the province of Malaga with stops in Los Barrios, San Roque, La Linea, La Almoraima, Castellar and Jimena. Check with the Tourist Information Offices in Gibraltar, La Linea and Algeciras for details.

Algeciras

This is a large, busy, bustling port, the most important passenger port in Spain in terms of numbers. It marks a halfway point by road between the capitals of Cadiz and Malaga and it is a vital link between the African and European continents. Each year millions of tourists pass through Algeciras but they are nearly always on their way somewhere else, for the town itself is unattractive and has little to offer the longer term holiday maker.

Along with Gibraltar the town was under Muslim domination for over six hundred years. It was reconquered by the Spanish in 1344 after a nineteen month siege but some thirty years later the Moorish King of Granada laid it waste and it was not until the early eighteenth century, after the loss of Gibraltar, that the town began to regain any importance. This accounts for the lack of ancient buildings and monuments in the town. When the border with Gibraltar was closed in 1969 and consequently many of the local people lost their jobs, the bay was developed as an industrial area. The hideous petroleum refinery built here detracts greatly from the natural beauty of the area.

The town's most attractive quarter and perhaps the quietest, is the more typically Andalusian **Barrio de San Isidrio**. The rest of the town has above all a very busy atmosphere of constant comings and goings. Driving through the port area you may be waved over to the side of the road by someone in uniform who will turn out to be a ticket tout working for one of the many travel agencies that sell tickets for the daily ferry services to Ceuta and Tangiers. In the middle of the summer this port area turns into something resembling a refugee camp as Moroccan emigrants from all over Europe arrive in overladen carloads and camp out near the port waiting for a crossing to their homeland.

Where to stay
This is just a selection of the many hotels and hostals available in Algeciras.
Hotel Reina Cristina 4-star Paseo de la Conferencia. Tel: 602622. An elegant hotel with indoor and outdoor pools. DR 11,200–14,500 pesetas.
Hotel Al-Mar 3-star. Avenida de la Marina 2 y 3. Tel: 654661. Central, tall modern block with views over the bay. DR 8850–10,000 pesetas.

Hotel las Yucas 3-star. Agustin Balsamo 2. Tel: 663250. Central. DR 7300–8400 pesetas.
Hotel Anglo Hispano 2-star. Avenida Villanueva 7. Tel: 600100. Central. DR 4500–6500 pesetas.
Hotel Maria Luisa 1-star. Urbanización Bahia Algeciras Bl-4. Tel: 652451. DR 3200–3800 pesetas.
Hostal El Estrecho 2-star. Avenida Virgen del Carmen 15. Tel: 653511. Central location. DR 3300–3500 pesetas.
Hostal Bahia 2-star. Playa el Rinconcillo. Tel: 660992. By the beach. DR 4000–6000 pesetas.

Camp sites
Camping Bahia 2nd-class. Carretera del Rinconcillo. Tel: 661958. Open all year. Capacity for 350 people. Prices: (a) 1750 pesetas, (b) 1300 pesetas.
Camping Costa Sol 1st-class. Carretera Nacional 340 km108. Tel: 660219. Open all year. Capacity for 450 people. Trees and garden areas. Views over bay. Swimming pool. Shady. Prices: (a) 1845 pesetas, (b) 1300 pesetas.

Where to eat
Restaurante Pepe Moreno Calle Murillo. Fish and shellfish from Sanlucar but also good meat and game dishes.
Restaurante Marea Baja Trafalgar 2. Good fish dishes.
Bar Rébolo Calle Sevilla. Very traditional bar.
Bar Castro Castillo 14.

Carteia

The tall and stinking towers of the refinery make a most incongruous background to the ruins of this ancient Phoenician settlment, founded in about 950BC. Carteia was for many centuries the cultural and administrative centre for the whole area including Gibraltar and in Roman times it became one of the most important towns of the whole peninsula. The ruins, which are close to **Guadarranque** and include those of an amphitheatre, may be visited by calling at the house of the caretaker's family, though to an untrained eye the ruins are not particularly spectacular.

San Roque

After the British attacked Gibraltar and the governor surrendered, the majority of the Spanish community preferred to leave their homes rather than to stay on under the rule of the British soldiers and have to swear allegiance to the Pretender, Charles III of Spain. Many of the 4000 or so who took part in this exodus went to the hermitage of San Roque and settled there, within sight of their home, hoping to return as soon as possible. As time went by and the Rock could not be recaptured, the settlement grew into a permanent town. Today therefore it is a town with less than three hundred years of history, small and, of itself, not particularly interesting or attractive, though its municipal district includes the important residential area of **Sotogrande** with its four-star hotel, an area very popular with the British, as well as the new luxury residential area under construction called **La Alcaidesa**.

Where to stay

Hotel Sotogrande 4-star. Off N340 road, km132. Tel: 792100. In an attractive setting between two golf courses with indoor and outdoor pools and stables for horseriding. DR 18,500 pesetas.

San Roque Club Suites Hotel 4-star. Recently inaugurated, this hotel is situated amid gardens and surrounded by the fairways of San Roque's championship golf course, designed by Dave Thomas. Swimming pool. PO Box 127 San Roque 11360 Cadiz. Tel: 613030. DR 10,000 pesetas.

Hotel la Solana 2-star. Just off main 340 Cadiz–Malaga road, km116. Tel: 780236. Attractively renovated Andalusian style country house with swimming pool. DR 11,450–12,750 pesetas.

Motel San Roque 1-star. On main 340 road, km124. Tel: 780100. Has swimming pool and garden area. DR 4000–5000 pesetas.

Hostal Rosama 1-star. General Lacy 63. Tel: 780080. In San Roque itself. DR 1800 pesetas.

There are several more hostals along the main N340 road within the municipal district of San Roque.

Camp sites

Camping San Roque 2nd-class. Carretera Nacional 340 km121. Tel: 780100. Open all year. Capacity for 250 people. Swimming pool. Quite shady. Prices: (a) 1595 pesetas, (b) 1225 pesetas.

Camping La Casita Carretera Nacional 340 km126. Tel: 780031. In Sotogrande area. Open all year. Swimming pool. Prices: (a) 1565 pesetas, (b) 1075 pesetas.

Where to eat

Restaurante Los Remos Finca Villa Victoria on road to La Linea and Gibraltar. Recently moved to this grand colonial style house dating from the end of the last century with a beautiful outdoor terrace. This restaurant is one of the best in the province, indeed it is considered to be one of the best fish restaurants in Spain.

Restaurante Don Benito Plaza de Armas 12. In San Roque itself in another attractive building dating from the eighteenth century. International cuisine.

APPENDIX A: WIND FORCE: THE BEAUFORT SCALE*

B'Fort No.	Wind Descrip.	Effect on land	Effect on sea	Wind Speed knots	mph	kph	Wave height (m)†
0	Calm	Smoke rises vertically	Sea like a mirror	less than 1			-
1	Light air	Direction shown by smoke but not by wind vane	Ripples with appearance of scales; no foam crests	1-3	1-3	1-2	-
2	Light breeze	Wind felt on face; leaves rustle; wind vanes move	Small wavelets; crests do not break	4-6	4-7	6-11	0.15-0.30
3	Gentle breeze	Leaves and twigs in motion wind extends light flag	Large wavelets; crests begin to break; scattered white horses	7-10	8-12	13-19	0.60-1.00
4	Moderate breeze	Small branches move; dust and loose paper raised	Small waves becoming longer; fairly frequent white horses	11-16	13-18	21-29	1.00-1.50
5	Fresh breeze	Small trees in leaf begin to sway	Moderate waves; many white horses; chance of some spray	17-21	19-24	30-38	1.80-2.50
6	Strong breeze	Large branches in motion; telegraph wires whistle	Large waves begin to form; white crests extensive; some spray	22-27	25-31	40-50	3.00-4.00

			Knots	mph	km/h	Height†
7	Near gale	Whole trees in motion; difficult to walk against wind	28-33	32-38	51-61	4.00-6.00
8	Gale	Twigs break off trees; progress impeded	34-40	39-46	62-74	5.50-7.50
9	Strong gale	Chimney pots and slates blown off	41-47	47-54	75-86	7.00-9.75
10	Storm	Trees uprooted; considerable structural damage	48-56	55-63	87-100	9.00-12.50
11	Violent storm	Widespread damage, seldom experienced in England	57-65	64-75	101-110	11.30-16.00
12	Hurricane	Winds of this force encountered only in the tropics	65+	75+	110+	13.70+

Wave descriptions:

7 — Sea heaps up; white foam from breaking waves begins to be blown in streaks

8 — Moderately high waves; foam blown in well-marked streaks

9 — High waves; dense streaks of foam; wave crests begin to roll over; heavy spray

10 — Very high waves, overhanging crests; dense white foam streaks; sea takes on white appearance; visibility affected

11 — Exceptionally high waves; dense patches of foam; wave crests blown into froth; visibility affected

12 — Air filled with foam & spray; visibility seriously affected

* Introduced in 1805 by Sir Francis Beaufort (1774-1857), hydrographer to the navy
† First figure indicates average height of waves; second figure indicates maximum height.

APPENDIX B: BIBLIOGRAPHY

Andar por el Macizo de Grazalema by Luis Gilperez Fraile, Ediciones Penthalon.

Cadiz y su Provincia (four volumes) Ediciones Gever, Sevilla 1985.

Cadiz, Tierras y Hombres by Juan Leiva and Virgilio Claver, Excma Diputación Provincial de Cadiz.

Comer en Andalucía by Jose Carlos Capel, Ediciones Penthalon.

Cristobal Colón by Francisco Morales Padrón, Ediciones Anaya 1988.

Discovering Spanish Wine by John Reay-Smith, Robert Hale, London.

Guia de Instalaciones Recreativas en Espacios Naturales de Andalucia Junta de Andalucia, Agencia de Medio Ambiente.

Guias Naturalistas de la Provincia de Cadiz (various volumes with several contributing authors) Excma Diputación Provincial de Cadiz.

Historia Medieval de Cadiz y su Provincia a través de sus Castillos by Pablo Antón Sole and Antonio Orozco Acuaviva.

Yacht Scene, Gibraltar edited and published by D.M. Sloma, PO Box 555, Gibraltar.

Andalucia by Nicholas Luard, Century Publishing, London.

Excursions in Southern Spain by David Baird, Lookout Publications.

Many snippets of information have been gleaned from innumerable leaflets published by the tourist information offices of the province, of Gibraltar and of Seville. Also from various monographic studies published by the Excma Diputación Provincial de Cadiz, as well as the *Diario de Cadiz* and *Lookout Magazine*.

APPENDIX C: USEFUL CONVERSION TABLES

Distance/Height

feet	ft or m	metres
3.281	1	0.305
6.562	2	0.610
9.843	3	0.914
13.123	4	1.219
16.404	5	1.524
19.685	6	8.829
22.966	7	2.134
26.247	8	2.438
29.528	9	2.743
32.808	10	3.048
65.617	20	8.096
82.081	25	7.620
164.05	50	15.25
328.1	100	30.5
3281.	1000	305.

Weight

pounds	kg or lb	kilograms
2.205	1	0.454
4.409	2	0.907
8.819	4	1.814
13.228	6	2.722
17.637	8	3.629
22.046	10	4.536
44.093	20	9.072
55.116	25	11.340
110.231	50	22.680
220.462	100	45.359

Distance

miles	km or ml	kilometres
0.621	1	1.609
1.243	2	3.219
1.864	3	4.828
2.486	4	6.437
3.107	5	8.047
3.728	6	9.656
4.350	7	11.265
4.971	8	12.875
5.592	9	14.484
6.214	10	16.093
12.428	20	32.186
15.534	25	40.234
31.069	50	80.467
62.13	100	160.93
621.3	1000	1609.3

Liquids

gallons	gal or l	litres
0.220	1	4.546
0.440	2	9.092
0.880	4	18.184
1.320	6	27.276
1.760	8	36.368
2.200	10	45.460
4.400	20	90.919
5.500	25	113.649
10.999	50	227.298
21.998	100	454.596

Tyre pressure

lb per sq in	kg per sq cm
14	0.984
16	1.125
18	1.266
20	1.406
22	1.547
24	1.687
26	1.828
28	1.969
30	2.109
40	2.812

Temperature

centigrade	fahrenheit
0	32
5	41
10	50
20	68
30	86
40	104
50	122
60	140
70	158
80	176
90	194
100	212

Oven temperatures

Electric	Gas mark	Centigrade
225	$1/4$	110
250	$1/2$	130
275	1	140
300	2	150
325	3	170
350	4	180
375	5	190
400	6	200
425	7	220
450	8	230

Your weight in kilos

stones

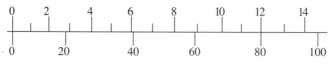

kilograms

Dress sizes

Size	bust/hip inches	bust/hip centimetres
8	30/32	76/81
10	32/34	81/86
12	34/36	86/91
14	36/38	91/97
16	38/40	97/102
18	40/42	102/107
20	42/44	107/112
22	44/46	112/117
24	46/48	117/122

Some handy equivalents for self caterers

1 oz	25 g	1 fluid ounce	25 ml
4 oz	125 g	$^1/_4$ pt. (1 gill)	142 ml
8 oz	250 g	$^1/_2$ pt.	284 ml
1 lb	500 g	$^3/_4$ pt.	426 ml
2.2 lb	1 kilo	1 pt.	568 ml
		$1^3/_4$ pints	1 litre